Lives of Confucius

Civilization's Greatest Sage Through the Ages

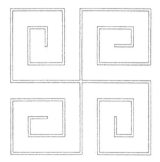

Lives *of* Confucius

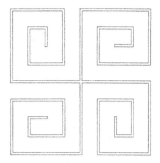

Michael Nylan and Thomas Wilson

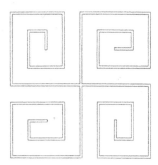

Doubleday

New York   London   Toronto   Sydney   Auckland

DD

DOUBLEDAY

Published in the United States by Doubleday Religion, an imprint of the
Crown Publishing Group, a division of Random House, Inc., New York.
www.crownpublishing.com

DOUBLEDAY and the DD colophon are registered trademarks of
Random House, Inc.

Library of Congress Cataloging-in-Publication Data
Nylan, Michael.
Lives of Confucius : Civilization's Greatest Sage Through the Ages / Michael
Nylan and Thomas Wilson. — 1st ed.
p. cm.
Includes bibliographical references and index.
(alk. paper)
1. Confucius. 2. Confucianism. I. Wilson, Thomas. II. Title.
B128.C8N95 2010
181'.112—dc22
2009036770

ISBN 978-0-385-51069-1

Printed in the United States of America

Design by Lauren Dong

10 9 8 7 6 5 4 3 2 1

First Edition

For James P. Geiss (†) and Hart and Joe Graves

Michael

For my teachers,

Peter Bennett, Herman Mast, and Edward Ch'ien,

who showed me the path,

Thomas

Contents

Acknowledgments

I would like to thank Robert Joseph Litz, Naomi Noble Richard, and Willis Barnstone—three superb writers—for their helpful comments on this manuscript.

—MICHAEL

I have benefitted greatly from the comments of my students and colleagues at Hamilton College, Michael Nylan, and Naomi Noble Richard. I am grateful to Jeni and Richard Hung for their help in Qufu.

—THOMAS

1

Kongzi, in Sima Qian's Shiji and the Analects

THE DISCIPLE HADN'T SPOKEN WITH THE MASTER FOR ALMOST a decade. The last time they'd seen one another, Kongzi[1] (Confucius) was sending Zigong 子貢 south to serve as minister at the Chu court.

In the early fifth century BCE, the Central States were a chaos of civil and interstate wars. Of the more than one hundred states and city-states that once had submitted to the scion of the Zhou as overlord, a mere forty had survived—each virtually independent and all at war or on the brink of war with their neighbors. Over the course of the previous two and a half centuries, thirty-six rulers had been assassinated and fifty-two domains brutally conquered. Alliances were formed only to be broken; renegotiated only to be violated. The courts of each state had become playgrounds for would-be traitors. As the fortunes of powerful households waxed or waned, factions moved quickly to betray actual and suspected enemies. To an aspiring statesman like Kongzi, such turbulent conditions represented both an opportunity and a nightmare.

The disciple Zigong, now in his prime, had distinguished himself as a diplomat for some ten years; the master had not. In his wanderings from state to state in search of employment, the master was frequently reduced to begging for food and shelter. Several times the master and his dwindling entourage had confronted serious danger; once he'd even been clapped in jail.

It was early spring when Zigong made the long trek from Chu in the south to Kongzi's home in Lu 魯, the state to which the master had returned after all the years on the road. The seventy-three-year-old man who finally hobbled to the door was leaning heavily on a cane. At first glance he bore little resemblance to the tall, commanding figure of Zigong's memory. If ever there was an occasion for an affectionate reunion, this was it. But instead of a warm greeting, the master scolded his disciple for having waited so long to come. Then, "the master sighed."

Sima Qian, the greatest historian China has ever known and the first to write a formal biography of Kongzi around 100 BCE, resisted the impulse to explain that sigh. Sima simply invites us to interpret it. But as what? Regret at having spoken so sharply to a beloved disciple? Sorrow over his own failed career? Disappointment that at his advanced age he had no one to entrust with the management of his household? A profound acknowledgment of mortality? All of these? Whatever the sigh's meaning, with his next breath Kongzi began to chant a few lines from one of his beloved *Odes*. As befitted a man of such erudition, the master had chosen the passage well. It richly evoked all the many emotions that crowded in:

> *Ah! Mount Tai is crumbling!*
> *The pillar is falling!*
> *The sage is passing!*

The song reduced the old man to tears.

After all, Zilu 子路, another disciple from the inner circle, had recently died, and that death could not have been far from the thoughts of either the old master or the middle-aged Zigong. Equally important, Kongzi lamented the moral chaos of their world, a world of wars that was dominated by greed, a world painfully in need of moral guidance. And then there was the master's own poor fate. Not one ruler in all the states of the Central Plain even paid lip service to his values, let alone implemented his policy proposals. Acutely aware of his failures, bowed by a lifetime of frustrated ambitions, Kongzi the eloquent had been reduced to stifled silence.

Curiously, until these closing passages of Sima Qian's biography of Kongzi, when we see Kongzi near death, Sima's hero appears to be a self-absorbed, unlikable, and crabbed personality. Sima's portrait is carefully fashioned to suggest both the reasons for Kongzi's near-continual failures in politics during his lifetime, and also his final apotheosis. As Sima Qian's story has it, until he was in his mid-sixties, Kongzi was a sanctimonious and arrogant know-it-all, an adviser apt to hector rulers whom he sought to instruct and to condescend to contemporaries who came to study with him. He had to struggle to conceal his resentment against those who succeeded where he had not. Understandably, few of those in power wanted to employ him, and often those who did regretted it. Even faithful disciples occasionally bridled under his autocratic manner. Though he may have been more learned and wise than others, the master's presumption of superiority rankled. Only late in life, with his ambitions dashed, did Kongzi finally become the kind of man Sima Qian could portray as a sage: a man whose eagerness to learn exceeded his eagerness to teach.

In order to achieve the maximum impact from the narrative that he, the Imperial Archivist, had composed, Sima Qian, the greatest storyteller ever to write in Chinese, chose to relate a flat tale of Kongzi's youth and middle age, wagering that the biography's dramatic conclusion would incite more empathy for his subject if the beginning and middle of the account seemed utterly unremarkable. When completing the *Records* in which the biography of Kongzi appears, Sima Qian did not need to tell readers that Kongzi had been pronounced the "uncrowned [or shadow] king" of the ruling Han dynasty, then in power for slightly over a century.

Kongzi was portrayed by many as the patron saint whose precepts ostensibly ordered the empire. Temples had been erected in Kongzi's honor and sacrifices offered, so that the master had become popularly a demigod with an unblemished reputation for integrity, embodying the ideals of supreme civilization. Some even thought him a manifestation of the astral Black God, briefly come down to earth to establish a new ideal dispensation through the Han house. The old texts and oral traditions associated with his teachings had been elevated to secure canonical status. As an exemplary teacher, Kongzi became, in writing and public speeches, an acknowledged authority to be reckoned with by all politicians, thinkers, and persuaders, regardless of their ethical orientations. As everyone knew, the four centuries after Kongzi's death in 479 BCE witnessed his gradual coronation along with the construction of an extensive genealogy fabricated by interested members of the Kong family. What Sima Qian hoped to convey were the reasons behind the mingled devotion and antipathy that Kongzi's name continued to inspire four centuries after his death.

In Kongzi's chanting of the ode to Zigong, therefore, there lurk sparks of anger and resentment signaling the master's fear of obscurity. Sima Qian then has Kongzi tell Zigong of a dream he had—a premonition that his corpse would be placed on a bier between two pillars in the main hall of Kongzi's house, in the precise ritual location in which the ancient Shang had placed their dead a millennium before. The details of the dream, at first hearing needlessly pedantic, ultimately serve to make Kongzi's argument: this master who had spent a lifetime praising the model of the Duke of Zhou, brother to the Zhou founder, traced his own descent from the very Shang people who had been conquered by Zhou; the culture of refinement was fated to be transmitted through the weak and humbled, or *Ru* 儒.[2] A man for whom the time was supremely out of joint, Kongzi, in bearing witness to his own mortality, had situated himself within an ancestral line reaching deep into the archaic past. He could hardly have predicted his unparalleled influence over future history.

Seven days after Zigong's arrival, Kongzi died. It was April in the sixteenth year of the reign of Duke Ai of Lu, 479 BCE by our calendar. The duke's eulogy bemoaned the immeasurable loss to his kingdom that the sage's death represented: the head of state could no longer avail himself of the master's wise counsel. Zigong, deeply offended by the duke's hypocrisy, retorted tartly that the duke had never once offered the living Kongzi a position of real authority. So even in the first days after the master's death, ambitious princes were scrambling to appropriate his name to shore up their own reputations. Accordingly, Sima Qian, in the closing lines of the biography, records his implicit condemnation of those who have neglected the teachings of his hero.

North of the city, near the river, Kongzi's disciples gathered for the burial. (Over the centuries Kongzi would be credited with huge numbers of disciples, but this first biography mentions a mere seven or eight loyal followers in fairly constant attendance upon the sage, most

of whom seem to have been roughly the same age as the master.) Most
of the disciples stayed in Lu for the customary three years of mourning, though Zigong tended the grave for a full six years. Soon a hundred families or so from Lu moved to the vicinity of the master's
tomb, and over several generations the small settlement called Kong
Village grew into a sizable town. A temple erected in honor of the
master housed a collection of Kongzi's personal belongings—his caps,
gowns, musical instruments, and (supposedly) his library. On the temple grounds an academy was built, where devotees met informally to
discuss their choices and commitments. Festivals and archery contests
regularly commemorated the sage's life and teachings. Kongzi's followers served as his descendants in spirit.

Genealogy was important in Sima Qian's world, for honors paid to
one man became the basis of the family fortunes. To inherit an illustrious ancestor was to be blessed with a patrimony through which land,
high rank, and wealth could be obtained. Some cynics spoke of the
Kong "family business." In Sima Qian's account, however, Kongzi's
real descendants were not the members of the Kong family, his blood
relatives who continued to live in Lu, battening on his good name. His
true descendants were his disciples and their ethical followers who
maintained the cult to Kongzi and circulated story cycles about the
master. [Jesus in the gospel of Matthew bitterly observes that one is
never a master in one's own house, but only in the field with those
who believe.] They, the noble in spirit, ultimately created a great "ancestor" as an icon in their own image, so that Kongzi, a man born in
relatively humble circumstances, would ultimately enjoy greater
renown than any other figure in the history of China. Sima Qian seems
to find in the manifest failures of Kongzi an inspiration for all who fail
to receive the fame they deserve. Sima Qian's own tragic story is certainly germane here: castrated for his quiet but courageous defense of
a general out of favor at court, Sima Qian in his humiliation could
hardly help but identify with the master. Hence, Sima Qian's decision
to finish his *Shiji* biography of Kongzi on a personal note, citing another passage from the *Odes*:

> *High is the mountain I look up to*
> *And bright his example for emulation!*

Though I cannot reach the heights
My heart leaps up to it.[3]

In early adulthood, Kongzi made the long journey from Lu (present-day Shandong) to the Zhou capital on the Yellow River (near present-day Luoyang)—just about the distance from Tucson to San Francisco—in order to study the rites. Reversing the course taken by Kongzi, Sima Qian traveled from the Han capital to Kong Village in Lu in order to gather materials for his biography of Kongzi. He visited the temple, where he gazed upon—perhaps even fingered—the precious robes and caps supposedly worn by the master. He consulted the local classicists who claimed Kongzi as their inspiration while immersing themselves in the study of the rites and political history. There, in the very place of Kongzi's birth and death, Sima Qian would have tried to imagine how the master looked and acted, since meditating upon a subject was the proper prelude to both the offering of sacrifices and the writing of history. In recounting his pilgrimage to Kong Village, Sima Qian has readers recall an earlier passage in his biography in which Kongzi conjures up, through the disciplined study of music, the image of the Duke of Zhou as composer of several odes reflecting the finest moral principles.

Sima Qian concludes his biography with the following observation: "Throughout history, there have been emperors, kings, and great men whose awesome reputations perished with them. Yet Kongzi, the man clad in a common gown, became the acknowledged master of generations of advisers, the ultimate authority in the execution and interpretation of all six polite arts, the reputed author or editor of parts or all of the Five Classics." The unsettling possibility existed that if Kongzi had in fact won high rank at any of the many courts in the Central States, he might well have been forgotten. By his despairing turn from politics to writing history, Kongzi ensured that he would become at once the author, subject, and object of history. Most memorably, he defined a new kind of heroism—of spirit rather than body—and a new kind of power based on unswerving commitments to ethical decency, which charismatic power by design offset, if not replaced, brute force. So Kongzi rescued from oblivion, both by his writings and by his own example, such unlikely exemplars as Bo Yi and Shu Qi, two recluses who had died unattended on Shouyang Mountain. Perhaps justice was obtained after all, not manifested in a single lifetime but after a long interval.

Though Kongzi aimed to be a statesman, in the end he, like Sima Qian, won fame as an archivist-historian. Perhaps that is why Sima Qian adopted the same formulae of subtle "praise and blame" that Kongzi purportedly applied so judiciously in his compilation of the *Spring and Autumn Annals*. Both men claimed comparable moral authority to act as unerring arbiters of history. In drawing bold parallels between his double, Kongzi, and himself, Sima Qian sought to restore his own family's reputation. He would dignify his abysmal failures at the court of Han Wudi (r. 141–87 BCE) by linking them with the lasting accomplishments accorded the fabled Kongzi. But only in the last passages of the biography, sketching the master's last days, his funeral, and his posthumous fame, does Sima Qian give an inkling that he regards his protagonist as "the High Mountain I look up to." In weaker moments, as Sima Qian struggled to endure the inevitable slights occasioned by his mutilated state, he apparently took comfort in the farfetched notion that one day he, too, would have temples built in his honor (as indeed happened in later centuries). After all, Kongzi was known for wresting triumph from ignominy. To secure his reputation, Sima Qian need only, like Kongzi, write a history to serve as an intelligent and persuasive guide to matters great and small.

EXAMINING THIS FIRST BIOGRAPHY of Kongzi, composed by Sima Qian about 100 BCE, we see a subtle clear structure. At birth, Kongzi had no high status or important family connections aside from distant ties to a ruling house extinguished about five centuries earlier. Despite poverty and probable illegitimacy, auspicious signs might indicate that he was destined for greatness. However, it was Kongzi's self-discipline and determination to prove his mettle that really did the trick. As a child, Kongzi was an avid student of history, ritual, music, and poetry. In the process of cultivating himself, he developed an overweening ambition to *rectify* social roles and relations along with the self-righteousness that often goes with ambition. No wonder time after time Kongzi was in trouble. Perhaps he brought some or all of it on himself.

But late in middle age, after a long string of reversals and disappointments, we note a change in the Kongzi of Sima Qian's conception. As a young man, Kongzi had been sharp, impatient, and often dismissive of others. He never listened. As an older man, he shed the mantle of omniscient master to become again a humble student, compensating with intense effort in areas for which he had no natural aptitude. We see this change first in the devotion Kongzi brings in his later years to the study of music—a study all the more impressive because his abilities as a musician were clearly limited. Evidently the cultivation of true humanity depends more on true dedication than on inherited gifts. Where once he led his students with confidence, Kongzi now consults his disciples on the proper course of action, regarding them as peers and companions along life's journey. Most strikingly, he develops a sense of humor, especially about himself. All this happens, according to Sima Qian, *after* he has been forced to abandon his laudable career goals, when by necessity he must be content to spend his days in service to the unseen Way, reading, studying, and perfecting himself in the arts of sociality.

Sima Qian's terse account of the sage's life takes up fewer than forty-five pages in translation. Nowadays, almost any scholarly book about Kongzi—and there are thousands—would boast at least that many pages of endnotes. Yet Sima Qian's portrayal of Kongzi holds a special place in Chinese literature—and not only because it is the earliest extant attempt to pull together known facts about Kongzi's life within a single narrative. As chief archivist at the Han court, Sima Qian had access to a huge collection of anecdotes about Kongzi—a collection that *may* have included the *Analects* or *Selected Sayings* ascribed to Kongzi, which seems to have been compiled just around the time Sima Qian was writing. Sima Qian also knew the *Zuo zhuan*, a romance often employed as commentary on Kongzi's *Annals*—or at least he knew some of the sources that inspired the *Zuo*.[4] And finally he had access to the *Mencius*, a text ascribed to a self-proclaimed champion of Kongzi who lived a full century after the master. Sima

Qian had moreover visited the old capital areas of Xia, Shang, Zhou, and Lu, to see the sights and inquire of the elders what they had heard. Sima Qian was free to select his materials as he chose, given that his masterwork was a labor of love and filial devotion undertaken for his father and not intended as an official history designed to exalt his superiors. Often Sima Qian borrows stories that either parallel or draw upon the *Analects*—we don't know which—but his versions of many of these stories highlight the foibles of the master. In Sima Qian's version, too, the master's conversations with his disciples often take the form of pithy postmortems on the sage's absurdly futile encounters with power-hungry schemers. Occasionally the passages depict this so-called sage as petty or out of touch with reality. Not surprisingly, Kongzi is ignored or scorned, mistaken for a notorious bandit, or run out of town. Why do his disciples put up with him? we think. He's simply awful.

As in all of his "Hereditary Houses" chapters,[5] Sima Qian begins his portrait of Kongzi with a genealogy, telling us that Kongzi is distant kin to a lateral branch of a once-distinguished family driven out of the small and powerful Central States domain of Song—a striking contrast to the usual statements made in late imperial China, in which Kongzi figures as the illustrious scion of kings. Sima Qian names the only three known ancestors (no lengthy list of noble forebears here): Kongzi's great-grandfather (Kong Fangshu), the first in the family to move from Song to Lu; his grandfather (Boxia); and his father (Shuliang He), who held the relatively minor post of prefect in a small town near the capital of Lu, in Qufu.

In 551 BCE, the twenty-second year of Duke Xiang of Lu, Kongzi came into the world, a product of a union—apparently illicit—between the elderly prefect and a young girl from the Yan clan. Kongzi was conceived "in the wilds" [i.e., in the suburbs of the city, outside the city walls, rather than in the honorable marriage bed of the Kong ancestral home]. Born with a "hill-shaped" deformity on his forehead (we might say "shovel-shaped"), the newborn was named Zhongni ("Middle-son Hillock") and given the style name of Qiu ("Mound"). Shortly thereafter, the prefect died. If Sima Qian is to be believed, the child Zhongni didn't even know his father's name, though the local prefect should have been well known in the vicinity. Oddly enough, Zhongni's mother refused to reveal his father's name or where his father was buried. We do not know whether the boy Kongzi was upset by his mother's recalcitrance, but Sima Qian's narrative shows the boy Zhongni entertaining himself by performing elaborate make-believe rites and sacrificial offerings. Obviously this foreshadows Kongzi's future prominence as ritual master, but it also allows us a glimpse into his mental formation. So lonely was the child that he sought communion with his unknown ancestral dead; so bereft of ordinary social relations that he fashioned himself as chief officiant in a series of rites.

Some time after his mother's untimely death, an elderly woman in the village finally decided to reveal to Kongzi his father's name. Eager for some shred of legitimacy, Kongzi went to considerable expense to have his mother buried alongside his father, Shuliang He, at Mount Fang. Once he had performed these rites, he could claim to be the son of a gentleman; and as such, he was a *shi*, a "knight," a member of that estate granted the right to bear arms in service to the ruler. Equipped with a new family name, a reputable enough lineage, and both the knowledge and the will to perform the all-important mourning ceremonies, Kongzi with his newfound status expected to meet opportunities hitherto denied him. But, in Sima's account, no sooner did the youth Kongzi move onto the public stage than he was brutally snubbed.

Kongzi came to a banquet for all local gentlemen hosted by the Ji clan, one of the three powerful families ruling Lu, only to be turned away by Yang Hu, the steward of the Ji clan, the man who virtually ran the state of Lu from 505 to 501 BCE. "Tiger" Yang doubted whether Kongzi could claim rank sufficiently high to qualify for admittance to the party. Note the pattern set by this anecdote: the cynical representative of an illegitimate power excludes the very man of integrity who will one day figure as the final source of all legitimacy. (Yang Hu pops up several times in Sima's narrative as a would-be adventurer determined to usurp power under the weak Duke Zhao, and once because Tiger Yang's enemies—in an irony of ironies—mistake the sage for Yang, since both men were unusually tall speakers of Lu dialect.)

Next, Sima Qian relates a highly improbable tale—one whose improbabilities would have been patent to anyone familiar with the history of Lu. Meng Xizi, a high official in Lu, on his deathbed, advises his son and heir to go study with a young man of seventeen named Kong Qiu (i.e., Kongzi). Meng Xizi says that Kongzi, as a descendant of sages, probably will someday attain sagehood himself. Meng Xizi's son dutifully assents to his father's dying wish and, accompanied by another local man, Nangong Jingshu, goes off to study the rites with Kongzi. But the traditional dates for the birth of Kongzi and Meng Xizi's son—not to mention the date of Meng Xizi's death—make Kongzi a mature thirty-four years old at the time of Meng Xizi's death, not a teenager of seventeen.[6] Of course, an experienced teacher was a much more likely tutor for the heir to a minister than was an unknown and untested teenager. But the transposition of Meng Xizi's deathbed scene in time accomplishes two things for Sima Qian: it provides a sharp contrast with Tiger Yang's inability to discern Kongzi's inherent nobility, and, in doing so, reminds readers that not all the tales told about the sage are accurate. The narrative juxtaposition between brutal rejection and warm approbation provides immediate satisfaction: scorn for the shortsighted, praise for the discerning. Petty fools who spurn the humble will soon get their comeuppances!

In his first appointment, Kongzi worked in the granary of the powerful Ji clan, where he inventoried the millet and wheat collected by tax agents. His next assignment, only marginally better, was to supervise the animals grazing the Ji clan pastures. The sheep and cows reportedly flourished—a nice indication that Kongzi, like Jesus of Nazareth, would take upon himself a pastoral role. Then, for reasons never fully explained, Kongzi left Lu for Qi.

The first great period of Kongzi's wanderings had begun. Unfortunately, no sooner did Kongzi arrive in neighboring Qi than he was expelled. Song and Wei treated him no better, and he had trouble crossing the border between Chen and Cai. Fourteen years of such setbacks occurred before Kongzi turned back toward Lu. In Lu, at least, Kongzi still had contacts, one of whom was Nangong Jingshu. It was this same Nangong who had first secured permission from the Duke of Lu for himself and Kongzi to travel to the Zhou capital, where they studied the ancient rites and ceremonies. The duke graciously condescended, upon that occasion, to lend two horses and the services of a page for the travelers. It may be significant that it is not Kongzi himself who is granted the extraordinary favor. As we shall see, those in Kongzi's circle were employed far more often than was the master.

Naturally, while visiting the sights in the Zhou capital, the two men from Lu met with the "old master" 老子 in charge of the archives. (Since Han times, at least, this old master has been identified as Laozi, the putative author of the *Daode jing*.) On parting, Laozi offered Kongzi a piece of advice: articulate and opinionated advisers like Kongzi always pose a danger to themselves since they can't refrain from pointing out the flaws of others. The price of plain speaking could be mutilation or death. Kongzi paid no heed to the old master, and, as Sima's narrative unfolds, Kongzi's life seems to illustrate the perils of ignoring Laozi's solemn admonition.

Upon his return to Lu, Kongzi was able to attract more students, presumably because he had acquired specialized knowledge of the rites during his sojourn at the Zhou court. Kongzi was thirty or so. If we can believe the *Analects*, Kongzi proudly declared, "At thirty, I took my stand." For the first time, in any case, Kongzi stepped onto the political stage, ready to advise any local ruler.

The leaders of the state of Lu, which was cruelly hemmed in by stronger rivals, knew that an alliance with any one great power would invite the wrath of the rest. If ever the Duke of Lu needed sage counsel, this was the time. But when Duke Jing of Qi, accompanied by his minister Yan Ying, came to Lu on a state visit, we see Kongzi employing his mastery of historical precedents in self-serving ways. Upon meeting Duke Jing in court, Kongzi immediately brings up events of the previous century in the distant state of Qin, when the assumption by the Qin ruler of a hegemon's role as the head of a confederation of states rested upon his wise promotion of the very ablest man to the highest office in the land. Kongzi means by his speech to do more than just flatter Duke Jing, who longs to become hegemon in his own era. He is transparently angling for the duke's favor, asking Duke Jing to allow him to replace Yan Ying as chief minister at the rival court of

Qi. In making such a pitch, he gained nothing except the lasting en-
mity of Yan Ying, the most celebrated minister of his day.

Shortly thereafter, Lu descended into turmoil. In the wake of a
quarrel over a cockfight, Lu's three major clans rebelled, and Duke
Zhao of Lu beat a hasty retreat to Qi, with Kongzi not far behind.
While in Qi, Kongzi once again sought employment as court adviser
to Duke Jing.

At first, Duke Jing didn't seem to notice him at all. Not until Kongzi
threw himself wholeheartedly into a study of the ancient music cele-
brating legitimate succession, concentrating so deeply that "for three
months he did not know the taste of meat," did he finally attract Duke
Jing's attention. In audience with the duke, Kongzi was repeatedly
questioned about good rule. He replied with the principle, now inanely
termed the "Rectification of Names," that one who bore the title of
king would do well to learn to behave like a king, and ministers like
ministers, fathers like fathers, and sons like sons. Initially the duke liked
what he heard. He could readily grasp the basic concept, and he ap-
proved Kongzi's other riffs on the virtues of frugality. After all, if he reduced the state expenses, he might well have more money left for his
army. In any case, the duke was sufficiently impressed to give Kongzi a
small area to administer. Then Yan Ying, sensing a potential threat to
his own position, complained at length to the duke that advisers like
Kongzi make unreliable bureaucrats. Coming from out of state, their
true loyalties may lie elsewhere. They have a taste for expensive antiquarian objects and practices. They are eager for handouts. And because they insist on elaborate rituals, especially funerals, their policies
actually undermine frugality rather than support it. They would have
their rulers drain the resources of families and bankrupt the state,
heedless of the long-term consequences of such activities. Far better to
employ the state's coffers in the old ways, and thereby strengthen its
armies.

Yan Ying condemned Kongzi as an elitist. (It was hardly the last
time that Kongzi's opponents would declare that they alone had the
welfare of the common people at heart.) The duke promptly withdrew his support from Kongzi and never again consulted him on matters of public policy. Kongzi's prospects had been adroitly sabotaged

by a wilier adviser than he. Realizing that there was nothing more he could accomplish in Qi, Kongzi reluctantly headed home again.

Now forty-two, Kongzi still had no secure position, nor any king-maker's ear. His prospects in Lu were dim, for Lu's three ministerial clans, the Ji, Meng, and Shushun, continued their mutual intrigues for supreme control of the state. His opinions were solicited only on ar-cane matters: the origin and identity of a strange hermaphroditic crea-ture, of a large dinosaur bone, and, much later, of a strangely marked arrow (see below). Kongzi's answers, which proved correct in each case, tended to underscore his vast knowledge of obscure facts. He came off as a smug purveyor of trivia, increasingly oblivious and ir-relevant to the larger political struggles tearing his region apart. Meanwhile, Yang Hu, the steward who, decades earlier, had excluded Kongzi from a gentlemen's banquet, became more openly ruthless, ar-resting his rivals and worse. Kongzi had no choice but to withdraw temporarily from public life, returning to his work on poetry, music, history, and rites transmitted in oral or written form, and improving his most marketable skills. And still, they say, the number of his disci-ples increased, some coming from far.

Eight years pass before Sima Qian picks up his story again, just as Kongzi turns fifty. A noble in league with Yang Hu rebelled against Duke Zhao of Lu, and when their rebellion failed, the two escaped to nearby Qi. When the noble asked Kongzi to come see him, Kongzi's eager reaction was entirely inappropriate. He was ready to go at a mo-ment's notice to work for a traitor on behalf of his old nemesis, Yang Hu. Apparently, Kongzi had been preparing himself for a ministerial post for so long that he had forgotten *why* he wanted to serve his country. Originally he had planned to *rectify* politics in the state of Lu as the first step toward restoring just rule by Lu's overlord, the reigning house of Zhou. A just man forfeited his reputation by serving traitors, and so in order to justify his willingness to consort with just this sort of men, Kongzi likened his efforts to those of the legendary founders of the great Zhou house, Kings Wen and Wu—two heroes who led a suc-cessful rebellion against their liege lord and then went on to expand their small domain in the far northwest across the whole of the Yellow River valley. Kongzi's most outspoken disciple, Zilu, chastised him for such delusions of grandeur, and in the end Kongzi could come up with no further rationalization for serving the rebels. He reluctantly declined the offer and stayed in Lu, a decision that proved advantageous.

For soon the new Duke Ding of Lu appointed Kongzi steward for the walled city of Zhongdu. Within a year, according to Sima Qian, Kongzi had transformed Zhongdu into a model city. In recognition of his talents, the duke promoted Kongzi to the office of overseer of public works and judge. Kongzi seized the chance to move onto the bigger stage of interstate diplomacy when Duke Ding made Kongzi a member of his party during a peace conference with Duke Jing of the rival state of Qi—the same Duke Jing whom Kongzi had begged for a job nearly a decade earlier. Kongzi demonstrated the indisputable value of erudition when he cited ancient precedents to persuade Duke Ding to bring a military escort to the treaty-signing. Kongzi then proceeded to supervise the rituals. No sooner had the initial rites been concluded than a Qi officer rushed forward with a suggestion that musicians and dancers should perform. Duke Ding raised no objections. But Qi had brought no ordinary musical troupe to the border. They had brought skilled martial artists who swung their staffs and banners to the drum music, leaping and twirling their weapons. Alert to the impending danger, Kongzi intervened—with exquisite politesse. The solemnity of the peace conference, he suggested, would be diminished by acrobatic displays. When the troupe (probably by design) moved nonetheless to continue their act, Kongzi intensified his objections, politely but so firmly that the Duke of Qi had no choice but to acquiesce. Undeterred, another officer asked that at least the Qi palace musicians be allowed to play. Kongzi countered that request by ordering the swift execution of all the performers involved, including actors, singers, and dwarves. In Sima Qian's version of the story (only one of many), the Duke of Qi was mortified because his more civilized counterpart from Lu had caused him to lose face before his peers and underlings. To erase the ignominy, the Duke of Qi promised, in an unexpected show of generosity, to return some lands that Qi had once stolen from Lu. In this instance, Qi may have had the power, but Lu, thanks to Kongzi, had the brains.

Perhaps Sima Qian didn't need to remind readers that the Qi party had intended to kidnap or assassinate the Duke of Lu. After all, the

Zuo already depicted Kongzi in the most favorable light possible: as a superb strategist using his ritual expertise, military authority, and rhetorical skills to avert a catastrophe for Lu. In the *Zuo* story, the dramatic troupe was cut down because it was trained to kill. The question is, why did Sima Qian leave such dramatic incidents out of the story he crafted? The Kongzi of the *Zuo* is a brilliant tactician of exquisite courtesy yet brutal effectiveness, an early Zhou Enlai. By contrast, the Kongzi of Sima Qian's *Shiji* is harsh at best. He denounces the dancers as barbarians, and his swift call to execute the dwarves from Qi is cruel and cunning, even if it is warranted by the circumstances. Most likely, Sima Qian was shaping a portrait of Kongzi that would focus on his slow and somewhat improbable development as a sage. A life in progress. If the Imperial Archivist had wanted to emphasize the potential for growth in Kongzi as everyman, the potential that Kongzi represented for even the least of human beings, it would be counterproductive to reveal Kongzi in middle age as a fully perfected human being.

Fresh from this diplomatic triumph, Kongzi had nonetheless to witness yet another indignity inflicted upon the ruling house of his home state: the three powerful clans in Lu began to construct walled fortifications around their home bases. In no uncertain tones, Kongzi told the duke that in a well-ordered state, no subject should be allowed to maintain a private army or to fortify his territories. The duke assigned Zilu, one of Kongzi's followers, to the dangerous task of razing the three strongholds. The Ji clan complied with Zilu's orders, but the Meng family refused the order to remove its towers and parapets. The duke then laid siege to the city where the Meng clan made their base, despite the city's strategic location in a crucial buffer zone between Lu and its powerful neighbor Qi. Although the siege utterly failed, the duke—quite inexplicably—promoted Kongzi to the post of *sikou*, a post often rendered as "Minister of Justice" but more likely to be local "justice of the peace."

At the age of fifty-six, Kongzi had finally achieved the highest office he could reasonably expect to attain, given his lack of aristocratic connections. One of his first official acts was to have Yang Hu's brother, Shaozheng Mao, then holding a high position at court, executed for treason. And it was not long before Lu began to thrive as the lives of its subjects improved. The Lu meat merchants, for example, no longer cheated their customers at market; traffic on the streets became orderly; and lost objects were duly returned to their owners. Visitors from other states were deeply impressed by this evidence of Lu's increasing prosperity and good order. "When clients from the four corners came to the Lu capital, they no longer sought officials to bribe or to seek redress for crimes committed in Lu. They merely gave in the goods they had brought as tribute and went home." Under Kongzi's good influence, the local authorities no longer tried to fine travelers on trumped-up charges.

But an orderly and strong Lu was a threat to neighboring Qi. Lu might well restore itself to the exalted place it had enjoyed during the early years of the Zhou empire, some five hundred years previously. Such a prospect badly frightened Qi, its neighbor and the main power in the region. To forestall that resurrection of Lu prestige and power, Qi worked to undermine Kongzi's influence at the Lu court. A simple expedient was found. Qi sent to Duke Ding of Lu eighty of its prettiest dancing girls and more than a hundred of Qi's finest horses. The duke, not to mention other high-ranking members of his court, quickly became so besotted with nonstop sex and hunting that they neglected their official duties. The duke was even too distracted to participate in the most important annual sacrifice, the one dedicated to Heaven—an honor granted to Lu alone among the Central States, by virtue of its glorious descent from the illustrious Duke of Zhou. This neglect of duty was especially galling to Kongzi. Disgusted by his superiors' abandonment to dalliance, Kongzi sneered, "I have yet to see anyone pay as much attention to virtue as they do to sex." He then went into voluntary exile, heading west to the state of Wei, where the brother-in-law of his disciple Zilu enjoyed a measure of influence.

This poignant failure—Lu coming so near to fully implementing Kongzi's ideals and yet retreating from the verge of success—raises as many questions about Kongzi's ministerial abilities as it does about Lu's reigning duke. Kongzi blamed the speedy collapse of his reforms on the hapless dancing girls sent to entice the Duke of Lu. Yet this unfortunate episode would surely have brought to the minds of Kongzi's contemporaries a celebrated counterexample: the outstanding Zichan of Zheng, who was able, in a much shorter time (three months, not three years), to turn around the customs of his state and to make all such enthusiastic supporters of his sound policies that even rival states and their agents were powerless to assault the integrity of Zheng's borders. The seed of doubt was planted. Did Kongzi not yet understand how to wield the "gift of speechmaking" in the art of persuasion? Had Kongzi, an occasional partisan of the Meng clan, moved too quickly against the other factions? Or, even more fundamentally, had he ignored his own injunction to be "mindful of the limitations of others" (*shu* 恕)[7]—a mindfulness that he eventually termed the "one thread" running through his mature teachings?

In any case, the Duke of Wei, hearing of Kongzi's arrival in his realm, offered to match Kongzi's old salary in Lu if he would agree to stay on as his adviser. Kongzi accepted the offer, but before long someone at the Wei court slandered Kongzi. Rather than lose face by directly expelling Kongzi, the duke sent an armed officer unannounced to storm the gates of Kongzi's residence. Kongzi got the message and left Wei in a hurry.

Heading farther west, Kongzi arrived in the state of Chen. There, as he passed through the city of Kuang, he was mistaken for the notorious Yang Hu, brother of the miscreant whom Kongzi had recently executed. The locals surrounded his carriage and hauled him off to jail. Five days later a few of Kongzi's entourage who had lagged behind managed to locate their master in prison. For the first time in Sima Qian's narrative, Kongzi calls directly upon Heaven to save him: "If Heaven intended such culture as His to perish, those living after King Wen would never have come in contact with it, as I have done." Luckily for both Kongzi and Heaven's Way, the case of mistaken identity was eventually resolved and Kongzi released.

Kongzi then spent a month in nearby Pu before returning to Wei. As soon as she heard of his return to Wei, Lady Nanzi ("the daughter of the south") invited him to a palace audience. Torn between the ambition to realize his political program and his fear lest he be seen as a lackey, Kongzi decided there was no polite way to decline her invitation. Scandalized by his agreeing to meet with Nanzi in her private apartments, Kongzi's disciples were only slightly mollified by Kongzi's assurances to them that both parties, male and female, had conducted themselves with the utmost propriety. Then, a month later, Kongzi was invited to join the Duke of Wei and his lady on an outing. As their entourage passed through the streets of the capital, Kongzi, riding in the carriage behind Nanzi, noted how the crowds turned out in full force to see this beautiful woman who was the subject of so much salacious gossip. No crowds would ever have turned out to see a man of virtue. Suspecting that he'd been used by the wily consort as cover for her many affairs, Kongzi promptly left Wei for Cao.

In Cao, Kongzi ran into more trouble when Huan Tui, Minister of War in nearby Song, decided that Kongzi had better be assassinated so as to prevent the master's charismatic presence from strengthening Cao. Kongzi had taken to practicing the rites with his disciples under a big tree. While Kongzi was thus engaged with his students, Huan ordered his henchmen to uproot the tree. Badly shaken, the disciples tried to get Kongzi to hurry through the ceremonies, but Kongzi, outwardly calm, responded only, "Since it is Heaven that produced the virtues in me, what can someone like Huan Tui do?" Even so, the master vanished with his group before Huan Tui's men could come back to finish the job.

Somehow, in their hasty flight to Zheng, Kongzi got separated from his disciples. "Have you seen our master?" The locals described a man they had seen standing alone at the East Gate of the city: While he had something of the air of the sages of old about him, he also reminded them of a forlorn dog worn out and addled by neglect "in a house of mourning."[8] Modestly declining the comparison with the sage-kings, Kongzi roared with laughter at the townsfolk's depiction of him as a dog unwanted and underfoot. "That is just what I really am!"

Zheng's ruler was the next to fail to appreciate Kongzi, so Kongzi and his band continued their wanderings in the war-ravaged Central States, finally landing back in Chen just before it was invaded by Wu, Chen's powerful neighbor to the southeast. Thereafter, in short order, many cities of Chen fell to the barbarian armies. During one particular siege, a hawk pierced by an arrow landed in a courtyard of one of

Chen's last remaining strongholds. Asked to interpret this omen, Kongzi gave another spectacular display of erudition and reasoning power. The hawk must have come, he said, from someplace far away or have come with someone having ties to a distant land. Indeed, the arrow was like that of the distant Shushen people in length and type of wood used for the shaft, as well as in the style of flint arrowhead. Kongzi recalled that long ago the legendary King Wu of Zhou, having handily defeated the Shang and established the Zhou, had received just this sort of arrow as tribute from the Shushen. Kongzi predicted that they would find similar arrows in Chen's own arsenal, since King Wu gave the arrows to his beloved daughter upon her marriage to the first Duke of Chen. Sure enough, a group of similar arrows turned up in Chen treasure houses, underscoring Kongzi's belief that the descendants of Chen's royal house must never forget their indebtedness to the royal house of Zhou and its old allies. That this type of arrow would pierce this particular species of hawk must be a Heaven-sent reminder of Chen's shared history with Zhou.

Even as Chen was swept up in a war between Wu, Jin, and Chu, Kongzi managed to stay on there for three more years. Finally Kongzi thought he might as well go home. He announced to his disciples that he feared his younger students in Lu needed tending. They were "wild, reckless, and eager for advancement." As foreigners passing through Pu, Kongzi and his party were then surrounded by hostile combatants. One of those in Kongzi's party had under his command armed guards riding in five chariots. He was raring to bludgeon his way out. Intimidated by the guards, Kongzi's would-be attackers relented; they offered to let Kongzi go, so long as he promised not to return to the enemy state of Wei. Kongzi duly swore a solemn oath to that effect, but as soon as he was freed, Kongzi headed straight for Wei. The disciple Zigong was outraged at the Master's breach of good faith, but when Zigong called Kongzi on it, Kongzi replied mildly that the gods do not consider oaths made under duress to be binding.

Hearing the news of Kongzi's approach from foreign parts and anxious to ascertain the news about the current military situation, the Duke of Wei raced to the borderlands to meet him. The duke then proceeded to grill Kongzi on the subject of whether Pu could be safely attacked at this time. Kongzi replied that the men of Pu were willing to die for their state, and even their women were prepared to protect the banks of the West River at all costs. Consequently, the Duke of Wei abandoned the idea of moving against Pu. But if Kongzi was hoping that the aging duke would offer him an office in return for this information, he was sadly mistaken. Kongzi complained to his disciples that if he could assume power for just one month, he could put the Wei state in order, and if given three years he could realize his vision of just rule. But with no prospects for advancement in Wei, Kongzi had to consider his options.

Just at that point, a rebel named Bi Xi sent a messenger to Kongzi asking for his help in launching an attack on the leading ministerial families of Lu. Once again, Kongzi was about to accept the summons over his disciple's objection: "Haven't I heard you say that a gentleman doesn't enter the realm of someone who fails to do what is good?" Kongzi eventually relented, but the decision not to join the rebels was far from easy. "Surely I am not to become some bitter gourd that is to be hung up on the wall but never eaten?" he remarked caustically.

Unemployed and underappreciated, Kongzi found himself with nowhere to go and nothing to do. Having failed to become an adviser, he decided to become a student of music, though at first he wasn't very good at that either. In practicing on chiming stones, he struck the chimes with all his might, but still only a single passerby heard him playing. Then he took up the lute under the direction of the Music Master Xiangzi. He made little or no progress for ten days: "I've learned the tune but not the harmonics." The music master told him to continue with his practicing. After ten more days Kongzi had grasped the harmonic scheme but not the mood of the piece. The music master sent him back to practice some more. After some fifty days spent in solid practice, Kongzi came to "understand the composer." In performing the piece, he had so internalized its distinctive features that he had become a simulacrum of his beloved King Wen, the predynastic founder of Zhou. At last he achieved distinction in music.

Still, there were to be many more days of wandering for Kongzi before he turned home to Lu for the last time. Wei, Chen, Cai, and She and back again—all these places passed before Kongzi's eyes in a blur. Gradually, however, Kongzi came to understand himself. To his disciple Zilu, he gave this intimate self-assessment: "A man who never wearies of studying the Way and who never tires of teaching others, a man whose excitement and pleasure over such things is so great that he forgets to eat and even to worry—or even to realize that old age is almost upon him."[9] His critics—and they were legion—mocked his "pointless" attempts to change the world, but still Kongzi persisted, aware that it might lead to nothing. Believing not only in his own humanity but in the potential for great dignity and worth in all human beings, he noted sadly, "One cannot, after all, join birds and beasts."

Shortly before his final return to Lu to die, Kongzi thought of consulting his disciples. What could he be doing wrong? "Is it that our Way is wrong? How is it that we find ourselves in this mess?" Zilu answered with characteristic forthrightness: "Perhaps we are not humane enough, and so others do not trust us. Perhaps we are not wise enough, and so others do not employ us." Kongzi recalled two famous exemplars of the past who had starved to death, despite their fundamental decency. "How do you explain the fate of Bo Yi and Shu Qi?" he asked, implying that as often as not no good deed goes unpunished. Zigong, a second disciple, suggested that Kongzi water down his message to make it more palatable to the average person of ordinary talents and capacity for virtue. Kongzi countered with the observation that no matter how skilled a farmer is, the crop depends on Heaven—meaning, on factors outside his control. Yan Hui, the Master's most beloved student, had the last word, however: "Why trouble yourself that they do not accept you? That we have cultivated this Way for so long yet it goes unused shames only those in possession of the states." (This moving passage appears only in the *Shiji* biography, not in the *Analects*.)

After this honest exchange, Kongzi sends his disciple Zigong off to Chu, where he is a spectacular success. The disciple Ran You leaves to lead the troops of the Ji clan against Qi. And to those who seek Kongzi's advice, Kongzi now replies, "I know nothing." He sets about arranging rites and music. He seldom talks anymore about profit or fate or abstract notions of goodness. Among the people of his home village, he is notably modest. And when Kongzi invites people to sing, if they sing well, he asks them to repeat the song so he can join in.

This is the Kongzi we glimpse in the *Analects*—the Kongzi who not only recognizes what is right, but who has come to delight in it, a Kongzi who accepts his fate and forgets himself. The opening passage of the *Analects* provides a list of the three pleasures that the good person may expect to command (pleasure in learning what is good and then doing it; pleasure in friends; and pleasure in life itself, despite life's vicissitudes). Threading through it is the message that the Way is not merely to be preferred, but to become a source of enduring delight, insofar as it ensures that each and every person will practice and receive courtesy in turn. Thereby all will come to see that they deserve respect as "important guests" during their time on earth. The sublime Way, which so many have found difficult to interpret, consists in the simple precept, "With the aged, one should comfort them, with friends, be trustworthy to them, and with the young, cherish them." "Is perfect goodness so very far away? If we really wanted it, we should find that it was at our very side!"

As the perfect embodiment of heartfelt sociality, Kongzi in the *Analects* was easy in his conscience. He knew perfectly well what the competing states should do to institute a golden age. Their rulers should first see to it that all people perform their assigned social roles, as leaders and followers, parents and children. Members of the governing elite should also accept that the goal of good government is to confer benefits upon the people without asking for returns. Rather than reserving all prerogatives for themselves, they should provide every opportunity for others to get ahead, since this is precisely what they would wish for themselves. Thankfully, "taking one's own feelings as a guide" always suffices when deciding how to act in official and private matters.

Kongzi outlined a coherent program designed to effect good rule in as short a time as possible. Those in charge of a large state must "attend strictly to business, punctually observe their promises, be frugal, show affection for those below them, and be sparing of the ways they employ their laborers." This program, apparently too radical for any administration to implement, then or now, stipulated that the government have at its command "sufficient stores of food, sufficient stockpiles of weapons, and the confidence of the common people." When asked which of the three should take priority, the master said "food and the confidence of the people." Apparently, weapons were to be used only as a last resort, in wars of defense. The opposition of Kongzi to wars of aggression could hardly be more obvious in the *Analects*. When asked about troop formations, Kongzi cut off all further discussion by his curt reply: "I know something about sacrificial vessels. But I never studied military affairs." "If it is really possible to govern countries by ritual and graciousness, there is no more to be said," he insisted.

Particular institutions could vary with place and time. The main thing was for the leaders of the state to keep faith with the common people, ascertaining how best to free them to earn their livelihoods and "ease their lots," because it is only the economically secure who are likely to engage in the polite arts that Kongzi saw as the jewel of human existence. Hence Kongzi's dictum that the ruler should first enrich his populace and only then instruct them. "To lead into battle an uninstructed people is simply to betray them!" "Putting men to death without ever having taught them the Right, that is savagery!" And Kongzi heaped scorn upon those who preferred an empty reputation to a real concern with the plight of the poor. Once when Yuan Shu was appointed governor, he was offered a salary of nine hundred measures of grain, which he proudly declined. Kongzi upbraided him: "Could you not have found people among your neighbors or in your village who would be glad to have had the grain?"

Before leaving the Kongzi of 100 BCE, perhaps a word on Kongzi's attitude to women is in order. Never has so much ink been spilled on a single topic to so little purpose. In the whole of the early traditions about Kongzi, women are mentioned only twice—both times in connection with the notoriously loose Lady Nanzi. First, Kongzi remarked, almost certainly after his interview with that conniving minx, "Women and servants are very hard to deal with. If you are friendly with them, they take advantage, and if you keep your distance, they resent it." Kongzi's critics have taken this to mean that he despised all women, even if the single comment seems to represent a late tradition appended to the earliest books of the *Analects*. It is more telling that critics charged Kongzi's early followers and associates with treating women too well! Still, we have no hard evidence to ascertain Kongzi's attitudes toward women, aside from the courteous treatment he is said to have given his mother and a daughter. It is obvious why women do not appear often either in the *Analects* or in Sima Qian's biography of Kongzi: the compiler of the first text focuses on the interactions Kongzi had during his travels with his disciples and with the Central States rulers, while the author of the second text (a castrated male, as it happens) takes Kongzi as his model for official and unofficial relations in court circles. Women did not figure largely in court settings, for whatever political influence they exerted was mainly informal. In any case, the Kongzi of the early stories lived in aristocratic societies— quite unlike our own—where hereditary status nearly always trumped gender in importance. Judging by the standards of the time—the only criterion that good historians care to apply to the past—Kongzi was no wild-eyed misogynist or ascetic railing against females. Perhaps the worst that the earliest figure of Kongzi can be charged with was a failure to notice women outside their ritual roles, domestic duties, and aristocratic prestige, despite his originality and daring in characterizing many sorts of human relations. An assessment by Zixia, Kongzi's disciple, seems relevant, however: Kongzi's ideal, when "seen from afar seems to be severe, but when seen close up, is found to be mild." And "The Master's manner was affable yet firm; commanding but not harsh; polite and easy," according to the *Analects*.

CONCLUSION

In the two thousand years since Sima Qian's biography, society has made Kongzi by turns into a fortune-cookie phrasemaker, a brilliant moral philosopher, a fusty antiquarian, a divine sage, an old man with a scraggly white beard fussing over some detail of ritual, or a down-to-earth thinker with an honest assessment of the human propensity to falter. Some commentators have chosen to emphasize Kongzi's moral philosophy; others have stressed his political theory; some have focused on his activities as scholar or historian; and still others have recounted his arduous journey along the path of cultivation.[10] The image of Kongzi, like that of those other radicals, Socrates, Jesus, Plato, Laozi, Moses, Muhammad, and the Buddha, has been adapted—and sadly tamed—to fit the perceived needs of every succeeding age. Searching for the "authentic" Kongzi in history, we find no single convincing portrait, for the essence of Kongzi's life and teachings was just as hotly contested in 100 BCE, in the courtly circles that produced Sima Qian's version and the *Analects*, as it is in China today.

Gu Jiegang, the greatest historian of twentieth-century China, was right to demand that we consider "one Kongzi at a time." For that reason, this book will present six additional portraits of Kongzi that have proven compelling to successive generations: those of Kongzi as the butt of criticism; the exalted Kongzi of Han; the Kong Family Man; the Supreme Sage of True Way Learning; the Kongzi of late imperial cults; and the confusion of politicized Kongzis bandied about today. The ultimate question may be "Was there a Kongzi?" As with the Buddha and Laozi, one can say with certitude, "There were many." But we will not go far wrong, perhaps, if we consider Ezra Pound's thirteenth Canto:

> *Kung walked*
> *by the dynastic temple*
> *and into the cedar grove,*
> *and then out by the lower river.*

Sima Qian's biography of Kongzi ends with a stirring eulogy:

The Imperial Archivist said, 'There is this in an Ode:

> *A tall mountain, one looks up to it*
> *A broad road, one travels forth on it.*'

When I read the writings of Master Kong, I longed to see what kind of person he really was. So I went to Lu and took a close look at his temple, hall, chariot, robes, and ritual vessels, as well as the many students practicing the rites at the appropriate times at his grave. I tarried there awhile, awestruck. The world has known many rulers and worthy officials who were famous in their own time, but nothing once they died. Kongzi was a lowly commoner, but after more than twenty generations he is still revered by all those who are cultivated. From the emperor and kings on down, everyone in the Central States, when speaking of the six polite arts, takes the Master as the standard of perfection. He is rightly called the Ultimate Sage.

The end of the story is somewhat darker, however, according to witnesses three centuries earlier than Sima Qian. Mencius, a follower of Kongzi-the-local-hero who hailed from a small principality within an hour's walking distance of Qufu, gave this testimony about what happened after Kongzi died:

> When the three-year mourning period had elapsed, his disciples packed their bags and prepared to go home. They went in and bowed to Zigong [his disciple, who had decided to prolong his own mourning for the Master for three more years]. . . . One later day, Zixia, Zizhang, and Ziyu [three of the most famous disciples of Kongzi] wanted to serve You Rou as they had served Kongzi because of a physical resemblance. They even tried to force Zengzi to join them, but he refused, saying, "That will not do. Washed by the Yellow River and the Han, bleached by the autumn sun, so immaculate was he that his blazing whiteness could not be surpassed!"

Marvelous teacher though he had been, his own disciples were ready to abandon the memory of Kongzi-as-master and serve another soon after his death.

The next chapter tells us how Kongzi was catapulted from the status of mere teacher to that of Ultimate Sage and perfect spokesperson for the Middle Way. To learn that story, one must read on.

SUGGESTED READINGS

Three translations of the *Analects* are recommended: *The Analects of Confucius*, translated by Arthur Waley (London: G. Allen Unwin,

1938); *Analects of Confucius,* translated by Simon Leys (New York: W. W. Norton, 1997); *The Analects of Confucius,* translated by Roger Ames and Henry Rosemont Jr. (New York: Ballantine Books, 1998).

On Sima Qian, see Stephen W. Durrant, *The Cloudy Mirror: Tension and Conflict in the Writings of Sima Qian* (Albany, NY: SUNY Press, 1995).

On the early history of Kongzi's clan, see Robert Eno, "The Background of the Kong Family of Lu and the Origins of Ruism," *Early China* 28 (2003): 1–41.

For general background on the Warring States period in relation to classicism, see Geoffrey Lloyd and Nathan Sivin, *The Way and the Word: Science and Medicine in Early China and Greece* (New Haven: Yale University Press, 2002).

Michael Nylan, *Five "Confucian" Classics* (New Haven: Yale University Press, 2001).

Nicholas Zufferey, *To the Origins of Confucianism: The Ru in Pre-Qin Times and During the Han Dynasty* (Bern: Peter Lang, 2003), Part I.

For another view of Confucius in the Zuozhuan, see Ann-ping Chin, *The Authentic Confucius: A Life of Thought and Politics* (New York: Scribner, 2007).

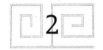

Kongzi and His Critics

Ever since man came into this world, there has never been one greater than Confucius.

— MENCIUS 2A/2

WITHOUT HIS CRITICS, CONFUCIUS WOULD BE NOTHING. Like a portrait bust sculpted by subtraction, the face of Kongzi emerging in the Han and pre-Han sources is defined by the swift strikes aimed at the Master by his many detractors. These same enemies capture and caricature his likeness. Since nasty critiques and backhanded compliments forced continual reassessments of Kongzi's Middle Way, they also throw into relief the sheer monumentality of this otherwise somewhat shadowy figure. Inevitably the figure of Confucius looms larger in the mind's eye because the Confucius of the late Warring States and Han traditions seems miraculously to have anticipated, and countered, every serious objection to his teachings, including the remarkable degree of self-sacrifice and imagination required to undertake the all-important tasks of cultivation of character and elegant self-presentation. So fifty years ago Arthur Waley wrote that the incredible success of Kongzi's message was "that it contrived to endow compromise [i.e., the Middle Way] with an emotional glamour." The careful crafting of that message by Kongzi's early adherents entailed a series of useful compromises made in the name of the Master.

Reading the critics of Kongzi is vital for another reason: it is easy to forget that in the centuries leading to the unification of "all-under-heaven" in 221 BCE, it was never clear that Kongzi would eventually be hailed as unique and the most important figure in Chinese history. We can trace our enduring sense of Kongzi as Ultimate Sage to the Han dynasty (206 BCE–220 CE) events and institutions (see chapter 3). However, in the centuries after Kongzi's death, the teachings of several rival thinkers held equal or greater appeal for members of the governing elite in the Central States region. In particular the teachings of Mozi and Yang Zhu exerted far greater influence upon the courts and courtiers of the fourth and third centuries BCE than did Kongzi's ideas.[1] While Confucius remained a figure to contend with in Lu tradition, he was also the butt of jokes, lighthearted and cruel, in stories that circulated outside Lu. Such stories made him into a lazy dreamer, a shrill pedant, and a laughable failure. Only the elegant defenses of the Master's teachings by Mencius (a century after his death) and by Xunzi (a century after Mencius) rescued the Sage from oblivion, or so the Han dynasty sources say. For Mencius and Xunzi, Kongzi was a local hero. Mencius was from Zou, a morning's walk from Qufu, Kongzi's hometown, and Xunzi held the post of libationer in nearby Lanling. But neither Mencius nor Xunzi was a direct disciple of Kongzi, so both thinkers had to translate and adapt his teachings to make them relevant to the vivid questions of their own days. Thanks to Mencius and Xunzi, the figure of Kongzi became more "glossy and appealing." They accomplished this portrait by cleverly equating a commitment to self-cultivation in the moderate Confucian Way with the arduous course of training that nobles underwent in preparation for battle.

Thinkers of the fourth and third centuries BCE now hold the collective name "the Hundred Masters." Like Kongzi, most of these masters were freelance advisers, learned men who sought the patronage of rulers and ministers and looked to attract disciples over the course of their careers. With the possible exception of Zhuangzi (a pen name adopted by possibly more than one figure), these masters were highly skilled consultants in the business of selling their painfully acquired historical knowledge of precedents to the highest bidders. To distinguish themselves from competitors, the masters often wrote acerbic satires of one another and other well-known figures, including Kongzi. Indeed, to show off their own policy proposals, to get in veiled criticisms of court and commoners, they contrasted their notions (see later in this chapter) with those of Kongzi. In doing so they reveal Kongzi's many faces as teacher, adviser, thinker, and private person. After all, as Kongzi's stature grew after his death (thanks to several highly placed disciples eager to promote his reputation, which would also embellish their own standing), no policymaker could entirely avoid engaging with the legendary Kongzi. Nor did they want to.

Like quarreling biographers, each master tended to locate a different message or flaw in the Confucian Way. They borrowed freely from him and generally reshaped his image to suit their own needs. Some defended what they saw as the compelling vision behind Kongzi's teachings against less demanding interpretations of his Way. Others lampooned the Sage, portraying him as a self-important, self-promoting fussy antiquarian, as a dangerous distraction from real reform, or as a man utterly irrelevant to the task of governing. Even as they attacked or praised and cadged material from Confucius, the real targets of their critiques were his disciples and disciples of disciples, with whom they competed for official favor at the courts. Given the centuries of attention to Kongzi's teachings, it is not surprising that early critics attacked the points where they found the Sage's character and teachings most vulnerable: his insistence on the primacy of the family over the state, on the critical need to preserve one's integrity, even to die for it, and on the value of grand-scale ritual performances.

In reading these ancient masters today, their writings still convey their sense of urgency, their determination to bring order out of chaos; morality out of rape, pillage, and treachery; and civility out of brutality. The times were perilous, not only for the states and their rulers but also for the rulers' advisers. From the eighth century to the end of the fifth century—dubbed the "Spring and Autumn" (Chunqiu) era after Kongzi's own chronicle—it seemed to many that conditions could hardly get worse. But even while Kongzi watched the events of his day, the relatively low-casualty skirmishes and gentlemanly jousting that had once characterized warfare in the North China Plain began to yield to massive military campaigns employing tens of thousands and even hundreds of thousands of foot soldiers. Before long, some hundred and twenty states were reduced to a mere forty, but those neat figures mask far messier realities, for in such wars the defeated lost their lands, their titles, and often their freedom or their lives. Still, it was the rare ruler who did not hope to expand his territories while fending off incursions by predatory neighbors, coups d'état by powerful families, and local peasant rebellions, and so the two and a half centuries after Kongzi's death in 479 BCE have been aptly called the Warring States period. By then only seven major states contended for supreme power in the Central States, but the battles grew larger in scale and fiercer in destruction, involving up to a million combatants, until the bloody rounds of conquests and annexations finally ended in 221 BCE with the unification of a vast territory (roughly that of present-day China, minus the Autonomous Regions) under the leadership of a single state of Qin, from which China gets its name. The brutality of the Thirty Years' War in Europe provides an apt comparison for this Warring States period, except that the wars in the Central States and surrounding areas raged for more than two centuries longer.

We know little about the day-to-day operations of court and state during the centuries after Kongzi's death, except that each domain was originally ruled by a single family. As the generations proceeded, however, power seldom remained in the hands of the original ruling family. After all, high mortality rates were the norm (with as many as three children out of five dying at birth), and those men and women who were lucky enough to survive to adulthood faced a variety of additional challenges, not least of which were bearing children and fighting wars. Frequent intermarriage among the noble clans, no less than incompetence and lack of interest among the scions of ruling houses, meant that an individual court's policy was frequently directed less by the nominal ruler of the state than by his hereditary ministers. In Confucius's own lifetime, as we have seen, the dukes of Lu seldom made a move without first "consulting" the heads of three such families, especially the Ji clan. Thus the few accounts that we have from the period show great statesmen and rulers determining policy and conducting diplomacy in ways that enabled the realms, however small, to hold their own or even gain territory amid the larger general conflicts.

If life was perilous for rulers, it presented as many challenges to itinerant advisers-for-hire—along with tremendous opportunities for the ambitious. Han Feizi, shortly before unification in 221 BCE, discusses the grave difficulties of persuasion. He cites the necessity to pander to the ruler's interests to gain a hearing, but not to pander too much, lest one incite the suspicions of his ministers. With all this, wartime conditions tended to make for an unprecedented degree of social mobility, up and down, and the adviser whose advice worked reliably would, in most cases, be favored above his highborn counterpart who contributed little to decision making. Meanwhile, the birth and background of the warrior mattered less than his ability to win battles. Advisers and generals were ultimately concerned with praxis— what particular set of habits would most directly lead the person and the state to the desired goals. Within the state, the central question was, What particular acts will bring the greatest order to the greatest number in society in the quickest possible time with the fewest unintended consequences? Even the most "metaphysical" of the Hundred Masters, in their investigations into human nature, delved into such questions in order to provide a sound basis for the actions they recommended. What we now subsume under that pale abstraction of "ethical concerns" once drove efforts to survive and prosper in ages when life was nasty, brutish, and short.

One reason why the writings of the Warring States masters survive to this day is that they wrote in a memorable style and raised questions of enduring importance: (1) What are human beings like and what motivates them to act? (2) What roles do rituals, traditions, models from antiquity, or laws play in effecting or maintaining order? (3) If rulers and statesmen play a critical role in the health of the body politic, what kind of man is worthy to lead? (4) What do the young need to learn from their elders if they are to play productive roles in the community and transmit the norms of civilized societies? (5) How is wealth to be redistributed so as to achieve the most just and stable order? And (6) in the general tumult occasioned by wars of all against all, what policies offer the best chances for achieving dominance or, at the very least, survival?

Kongzi had addressed only some of these questions. His teachings were premised on three linked propositions: humans are social beings; constructive social relations provide a moral basis for political order;

and political stability and economic justice are absolute preconditions for teaching most people how to behave in socially constructive ways. Every early account we have of Kongzi portrays him as a teacher who advocated ritual and humaneness, rather than punishment and self-aggrandizement, as the only path to the sort of personal and social cultivation that commands admiration, that being the most direct and plausible route to conventional success. But Kongzi, we are also told, refused to speak at length about certain topics, including fate, the spirit realm, and, perhaps most tellingly, human nature itself. About human nature the *Analects* has Kongzi remarking only that humans tend to be very much alike at birth, but the training they receive, first under their parents and teachers and then on their own, makes their habits diverge widely over time.

By the Warring States period, however, every master deemed it necessary to tackle the tricky question of defining human nature, even if they could only devote part of their energies to that task. Since they were all urging particular courses of action upon rulers and ministers, they had to couch their arguments in what they thought was humanly possible for rulers and also for subjects. After all, the set of choices collectively made by individuals as parents, farmers, and soldiers would finally determine the state's rise or fall. Mothers and fathers could raise their children to be loyal and productive contributors to the community or be utterly self-serving; farmers could plan well or ignore the seasonal changes and fail; soldiers could meet the enemy bravely on the battlefield, or they could turn and run. In the Warring States these simple observations propelled the Hundred Masters to begin with human nature when inquiring how to produce a more peaceful and productive world. Most assumed that peace would only come when North China was unified under a single banner, but which state would ultimately prevail and what kind of state it would be depended upon human qualities and capacities.

TWO OBVIOUS BROADSIDES leveled against Kongzi were attributed to a certain Jie Yu, a contemporary who had chosen to live as a recluse in the southern state of Chu. In one encounter with Kongzi, Jie Yu warned him that trying to teach others was risky and likely to end in misfortune. If Confucius continued to preach when the times were out of joint and the rulers dismissed his talents, he was hardly to be admired for his intelligence. Such persistence as he displayed to the very day he died did not mark him as a man of indomitable will, but rather as an old, stubborn, deluded fool. Here is the story of that encounter:

> When Confucius went to Chu, the eccentric Jie Yu wandered by his gate, and called out, "Phoenix! Phoenix! How has virtue failed! The future you cannot wait for. The past you can no longer pursue. When the world has the Way, the sage succeeds. When the world is without the Way, the sage looks to survival. In times like the present, we do well to escape punishments. Good fortune is light as a feather, but nobody knows how to pick it up. Misfortune is heavy as earth, but nobody knows how to stay out of its way. Leave off! Leave off—this teaching virtue to men! It's dangerous, quite dangerous! Fool! You're a fool. Don't try to prevent me from making my own way. I walk a crooked path. . . . Because cinnamon can be eaten, it gets cut down; because lacquer can be used, its tree gets hacked apart. All men know the use of the useful, but nobody sees the inherent utility of being useless."

In a second tale, the same Jie Yu reiterates his condemnation, suggesting that men like Confucius are peddling bogus virtue. They seek to influence others, never having learned to govern themselves. Jie Yu characterized Kongzi's attempts to advise one ruler after another in the following words:

> This is bogus virtue! To try to govern the world like this is like trying to walk the ocean, drill through a river, or make a mosquito shoulder a mountain. When the sage governs, does he govern what is the *outside*? He makes sure of himself first, and then he acts. He makes absolutely certain that things can do what they are supposed to do. That's it; there is nothing more than this. The bird flies high in the sky where it can escape harm from arrows. The field mouse burrows deep under the hill so it won't have to worry

about men digging and smoking it out. Have you got less sense than these two sorts of creatures?

Jie Yu's caricature of Kongzi as a self-righteous windbag fails to discern his true character, which comes through the *Analects* as "an impulsive, emotional, and informal man, a man with wit and humor, a man capable of subtle irony with an acute sensibility."

In this chapter we examine five other critics of Confucius, all deemed masters by their many followers, in roughly chronological order: Mozi (tradit. 470–390 BCE), Yang Zhu (370–319 BCE), Han Feizi (280–233 BCE), Zhuangzi (third century? BCE), and Wang Chong (27–92 CE). Only for Wang Chong do we have somewhat firm dates. Aside from Wang Chong, it is doubtful whether any of the foregoing masters actually set down in writing the traditions later ascribed to them. The writings associated with their names were probably compiled after unification in 221 BCE, some even as late as 26 BCE, near the end of Western Han. Only Mozi among the critics dared to launch a full-scale, head-on attack upon Kongzi himself. Mozi-the-reformer held a position within the Confucian tradition analogous to that of Martin Luther within Catholicism, in that he wanted to reform the Master's teachings from inside the tradition, lessening the pomp and circumstance and focusing more on essentials. The earlier masters, who were contemporary with Kongzi when the legendary Master was just beginning to be taken seriously by those outside Lu, often attacked Kongzi through proxy figures, the straw men called Ru, self-proclaimed specialists in classical learning and the arts. By such ruses, the masters obviated the risk of offending Kongzi's admirers when pitching new programs. The later masters, perhaps not surprisingly, were inclined to view the legendary Kongzi as a kindred spirit whose genius they shared. Given the innumerable dangers that beset the bold advancement of new policy proposals, other persuaders found it more politic to characterize the Ru as well-meaning advisers not quite up to grasping the total picture. By labeling rival plans partial, deficient, and incomplete, they implied that newer views would be more inclusive, exhaustive, and effective.

All advisers, however—not just the professional classicists who saw themselves as Kongzi's latter-day followers—identified Kongzi as a professional "ancestor," a founder of the line of freelance specialists who possessed an enviable mastery of the arts and literature, of history and precedents, of ritual and music, or of administration and military strategy. To the true classicist, knowledge of the lives of the great men of history illustrated not only the codes of conduct worthy of emulation but also the larger patterns operating in the known world. One looked to appropriate gestures, dress, and speech to make an awesome display so that one's own performance and that of one's ruler might be all the more impressive. A command of court precedents was another prerequisite for the good adviser. And because Kongzi had edited the *Annals,* subtly weaving historical events together with "praise and blame," those who prided themselves on their insights into "knowing men" invariably considered themselves to be Kongzi's spiritual heirs, whether they were "Confucians" in the strict sense of "ethical followers of the Way of Kongzi" or just astute persuaders who judged history to be the most reliable guide for thinking about present circumstances. Of course, rhetoricians intent upon advertising their fresh views tended to mock predecessors as absurd holdovers from a benighted age, but that did not mean that the glib speakers necessarily wanted to displace Kongzi from his position as an early master.

By trade, all the classicists were rhetoricians and persuaders, and success in their profession depended upon a knowledge of history, for the "common wisdom" peddled by the masters and their disciples claimed to represent a practical understanding of the ways the world worked, buttressed by evidence about what had or had not worked in the past. The best of the classicists added a distinct moral component to their recommendations while urging their rulers to consider the feasibility of new approaches to governance. All were clever, erudite, and ambitious enough to employ a range of rhetorical ploys in their treatments of Confucius.

MOZI 墨子 ON CONFUCIUS

Mozi, or Master Mo, was born either in Lu or in nearby Song, approximately a century after Confucius and shortly before Mencius. Legend has it that he began life as an artisan, most likely a carpenter;

that at some point he was branded (mo 墨) for a crime; and that he had once been a most devoted follower of Kongzi before becoming one of his fiercest critics. Like another carpenter from another time and place, Mozi is famous for teaching "universal love" (*jian'ai*), which Mozi defined as "loving others impartially" and "working to benefit all," rather than only one's own family and friends. Such qualities, in Mozi's view, let humans imitate Heaven, which shines on all equally. According to Mozi, partiality was the root of all evil, and Mozi, like Kongzi, was determined to improve the world. The story has it that when Mozi heard that Chu, the most powerful state of his time, was planning to attack a smaller state, he walked straight through for ten days and ten nights to dissuade Chu's ruler from this act of aggression. Like Kongzi, Mozi also insisted that rulers often did not know their own minds: they claimed they wanted their domains to be rich, their people numerous, and their rule even-handed, but they condemned their commoners, hard-pressed by taxes and labor services, to labor in the fields like draft animals and to die in battlefields far from home. Life for the vast majority was hellish—all the more so when the administrators in their jurisdictions were venal or incompetent. The common people lacked any means to defend themselves against such denials of their fundamental humanity; having no means by which to advance themselves, they could never be of real use to themselves or others. For this reason, said Mozi, the strong must not be allowed to bully the weak.

Mozi's followers boasted of him, "Even if there were no men in the world, Master Mo's sayings would still stand." Many of Mozi's ideas borrowed or built directly upon the ideas of Kongzi, however. Kongzi was no respecter of persons, when issues of social justice were concerned; the *Analects* had him saying, for example, "A gentleman in his dealings . . . has neither enmities nor affections; he only ranges himself beside the Right, wherever he sees it." Kongzi and Mozi placed equal emphasis upon loyalty to superiors and consideration for others; also upon the ruler "honoring the worthy" over inheritors of high rank, suggesting that both sets of teachings were meant to appeal to those in the lower ranks of the hereditary aristocratic class. Citing the same examples of the same sage-kings lauded by Confucius, Mozi insisted that "when the ancient sage-kings administered the realm, they . . . never showed particular favor to their kith and kin, or to those possessing wealth and honor." Kongzi and Mozi were one in excoriating the hawks at court who sought to "lead the uninstructed masses into war."

So how is it that Mozi's teachings, which supposedly "filled the world" in his own time, came soon to be perceived as a fundamental attack on Kongzi and his Way, rather than as a continuation or an extension of it? Mozi was anathema to Kongzi's followers not only because his fame rivaled or even surpassed that of the Lu Master, and because Mozi was, in contrast to Kongzi, a very effective politician. More important, perhaps, Mozi questioned two basic tenets of belief associated with Confucius: the primacy of the family in moral training, and the moral utility of ritual performances on a grand scale. Mozi, dripping with sarcasm, pointed out that the natural family is not "naturally" harmonious. Whereas Kongzi had emphasized the primacy of the family in moral life, believing, first, that it was the parents who transmitted the most precious gift of life to their children and, second, that the family represented the "base" of virtue, the place where the child was trained to respect and love others and communicate those feelings through civilized speech and behavior, Mozi insisted that to privilege the family above all others was, in fact, to be less than fully human (*ren* 仁). In Mozi's eyes the truly good person treated everyone of his acquaintance with equal benevolence; the neighbor's father might as well have been his own.

Consequently, in the eyes of Kongzi's ethical followers, full acceptance of Mozi's teachings entailed "living as if one had no father," or indeed any kith or kin at all! Had not Mozi enjoined the ruler to ignore all family connections when delegating authority to those in his administration? By Mozi's reasoning, any fool could see that it was better to entrust the care of one's own family members to a society whose members had been trained to see beyond their own narrow, selfish interests, for only in such a society could one's parents, in times of crisis, expect to be cared for. That being the case, it was in the highest filial interest of any child to "first make it a point to benefit other people's parents in the same way that he would have others benefit his parents." Individual and family interests were apt to undermine the general good. The great families in particular acted as powerful special-interest groups, preventing equality within their own ranks and within society at large. Such selfishness had already, time and time again, proven to be completely counterproductive, for "within any given family, fathers and sons, older and younger brothers, had grown to hate one another so that the families split up, and meanwhile, out in the world, people resorted to using water, fire, and poison to harm one another."

It was obviously "the duty of benevolent man to try to promote what benefits the world and eliminate whatever injures the world." To counter the divisive influence of family loyalty, Mozi in his own lifetime organized his adherents into troupes whose members—all of them male, we think—lived and worked together under the direction of a handpicked leader like himself, to whom they pledged absolute obedience. At the leader's death, the management of the troupe passed to that member whom the leader judged most capable. Family background or influence was not to be taken into account. In the troupes, so long as a man had ability, he would be promoted, even if he were a farmer, an artisan, or a former convict. The advantages of Mozi's early version of affirmative action were real enough: each troupe could be mobilized at a moment's notice when it was needed for local defense or for production. The troupes also epitomized and engendered a sense of fair play. Moreover, group action was likely to be more effective than individual efforts; the family unit was simply too small, too fragile, too partial, and too parochial to ascertain and then act in the best long-term interests of its members or of society at large. Better that stalwart men of various families band together in a common cause. And if the bands of men were diligent enough, though a fraction of the population, they could transform the entire society, so long as rulers reinforced, by judicious use of punishments and rewards, the lesson that unselfish behavior would benefit society best. People would soon come to prefer the principle of universal love (i.e., working for the benefit of all) to the principle of filial devotion, because "universal love" alone could create a sense of common purpose among people who were not related by blood or marriage:

Well, one who cares for others will inevitably be cared for by them; one who benefits others will inevitably be benefited by them. And one who hates others will inevitably be hated by them; and one who harms others will inevitably be harmed by them. What is difficult about any of this?

"Confronted with such choices, there is no man, woman, or child" who will not prefer to keep company with those whose concern for others is wide-ranging and strong. Thus it is that "one who cares for others will inevitably be cared for by others." Of this Mozi was certain.

Mozi was right. People *did* come to see the practical logic of his teachings, and if Mozi had not struck a second blow at the heart of Confucian teachings, it is doubtful whether Kongzi's followers would ever have gathered sufficient strength to launch a series of counterattacks (the most famous by Mencius). But Mozi went too far, in their view, when he argued that the grand performances of rites and music at court were worse than useless to the good ruler, even as tools by which the ruler established his awesome authority. Mozi began with a simple observation followed by a question, "What the people want most is life; what they hate most is death." Asking what are the basic conditions that humans need in order to survive, let alone flourish, Mozi answered that people need food, clothing, and shelter, but they cannot begin to earn the basic necessities if the state is always taking away the fruits of their labors in high taxes, interrupting their farm work, or sending them off to prosecute foreign wars. Any surplus wealth should be redistributed in such a way as to support the common people in their endeavors, rather than being spent on luxury items. In short, power-holders would have to give up collecting things and territories, so that the amount of food, clothing, houses, defensive weapons, boats, and carts would finally be enough for all.

The greatest good for the greatest number, Mozi argued, would be achieved if the ruler were to redistribute the vast sums expended on court performances among the common people; the sage by definition "eliminates needless expenditures." Once the ruler no longer actively oppressed his subjects, but rather secured their livelihoods, the people would wholeheartedly contribute their best efforts to his service, and the state would come to know that enviable consensus of opinion on ethical and practical issues that the classical literature identified with the golden age of yore. And while the king was doing away with all sorts of counterproductive rites and musical performances, he might as well rid his court of florid rhetoric, for it, too, represented wasted time, even when it did not actively subvert good sense. The phrase-makers, in filling the king's head with visions of glory, only whetted his appetite for absurd wars of aggression. Plain language makes for better politics, Mozi insisted, and facilitates communication between the ruler and his subjects. Thus the followers of Kongzi, in defending the very policies that undermine the health of the body politic, "confused what is habitual with what is proper, and what is customary with what is right." Mozi claimed that his prescriptions—not those of Kongzi—would restore simple dignity to his fellow human beings while following the true mean:

> A coffin three inches thick is good enough to bury rotting bones; three pieces of clothing are sufficient to cover rotting flesh. The hole in the ground should not be deep enough to reach the water table, nor so shallow that the vapors of the rotting flesh escape. A mound sufficiently large to mark the spot where the corpse is buried is all that is needed. Mourners may weep going to and from the burial, but after that, they should devote themselves to making a living.

"The gentlemen of the world today understand small matters, but not large ones," Mozi sniffed.

Kongzi's followers, of course, cried foul when Mozi ridiculed their persons and attacked the very rites and music that represented the foundation of their professional standing. Kongzi, by Mozi's account, had himself sometimes lacked the basic scruples, in that he accepted wine and meat without asking where they came from, being in this no different, really, from traitors and rebels: "He racked his brain and exhausted his wisdom in carrying out such evil deeds." And when Mozi charged that the classicists were lazy to boot, "behaving like beggars, stuffing food away like hamsters, staring like he-goats, and walking around like castrated pigs," it was too much to swallow.

Even in passages where Mozi adopted a milder tone, retreating from his ad hominem attacks, he struck hard at the classicists, as in the following tirade against music:

> When the benevolent man makes plans to benefit the world, he does not consider merely what will please the eye, delight the ear, gratify the mouth, and give ease to the body. If, in order to gratify the senses, he has to deprive the people of the wealth needed for their food and clothing, then the benevolent man will not do so. Therefore, I condemn music not because the sound of the great bells and rolling drums, the zithers and pipes, is not delightful . . . but because if we consider the world's welfare, we find it brings no benefit to the common people. Therefore, I say, "The rulers employ young men and young women, taking them away from their plowing and planting, their spinning, weaving, and producing large quantities of hemp, silk, and other fibers—these their rightful duties! . . ." Therefore I say, "It is wrong to make music!"

Mozi was arguably tone-deaf. In reply, the classicists offered a very different Kongzi from the one supplied by Mozi: their Confucius prized music and rites not only as the chief civilizing instruments available to gentlemen and to commoners alike, but also as a source of comfort to the poor, aged, and infirm. The world would be a drab place indeed, were there no gorgeous silks, superb food, and colorful spectacles to break the monotony of everyday life. Human beings are far more than the sum of their physical needs.[2]

The classicists argued that Mozi's teachings were repulsive not only because they demanded what is unfilial, but also because they asked for the impossible: that humans love strangers as much as their close kin. Worse, Mozi insisted that ghosts and spirits do exist, and that they take an active interest in human lives, bestowing good or ill fortune upon people according to their just deserts, all appearances to the contrary. (Mozi was sure that atheists and agnostics committed more crimes than believers.) Still others objected to Mozi's unthinking elitism, for in one speech he proclaimed,

The common people devote their strength to carrying out their tasks, but they cannot decide for themselves what is right. They have gentlemen to do that for them. The gentlemen devote their strength to carrying out their tasks, but they themselves can't decide what is right. There are ministers and officials to do that for them. The officers work hard to carry out their responsibilities, but they cannot be allowed to decide what is right. There are the three high ministers and the lords to do that for them.

As with so many conservatives, the paternalistic and the pietistic are closely intertwined in Mozi's thinking. Defining Heaven as "pure eminence and pure wisdom," Mozi believed that "there is not so much as the tip of a hair which is not the work of Heaven." Thus it must be Heaven "who establishes kings and lords to reward the worthy and punish the wicked . . . so that the people may have enough food and clothing." God must be in heaven and all is right with the world. Kongzi, by contrast, while deeply immersed in the ritual and religious life of his era, was distinctly averse to pontificating about the roles that fate and supernatural agency play in determining the course of a human life. When someone asked for an explanation of the Ancestral Sacrifice, he is said to have replied, "I do not know. Anyone who knew the explanation could deal with all things under Heaven as easily as I lay this here" (and then he proceeded to lay his finger on the palm of his hand). When asked by a disciple to explain what death would be like, he responded grimly, "You'll know soon enough." He nonetheless maintained throughout an attitude of reverence, insisting that one who "puts himself in the wrong with Heaven has no means of expiation left."

While Mozi's solution for social anarchy is social hierarchy and its coercive punishments, Kongzi insists on the need for cultivating social ties through an enhanced ability to rule oneself. Still, Mozi and Confucius were very much in agreement about the importance of the ruler's example for his subjects: if a ruler sets an example, the common people are sure to follow it. So the question was not what a state could persuade humans to do for the sake of love or money, but rather how the ruler of the state should act, so as to benefit those inhabiting his domain.

Exemplary figures routinely perform single acts that would seem to be much harder than "loving" all things all of the time. But the course of revolution never does run smooth, for after a time ordinary humans feel their spirits flagging. So Kongzi clearly has the last word in this particular debate because he recognizes in the craving for beauty a natural impulse to be encouraged, not suppressed, and because he believes that "loving everybody"—regardless of people's relation to oneself, regardless of their actions—is too foreign to human nature.

YANG ZHU ON CONFUCIUS

Yangzi, a man of Wei, lived in the early Warring States period, after Mozi but before Mengzi. Though Yang Zhu's teachings were among the most influential during the Warring States period, today we know surprisingly little about his thinking—only that Yang articulated a philosophy that struck at the very heart of Confucian and Mohist morality, and that Yang Zhu's ideas were suppressed to some degree by the Qin and Han ruling houses. Yang Zhu's teachings seem to have been relatively simple. As one early text put it, "Yang Zhu valued his person." Here is how one text expands upon that slogan:

> Yang Zhu said, "The myriad creatures may be different in life but the same in dying. In life, they may be morally obtuse or worthy, honorable or base, and so they differ. In death, they all stink, rot, disintegrate, and disappear, and so they are the same. . . . The noble man and the sage die; the wicked and the obtuse die. In life, they may have been Yaos and Shuns [sages]; in death they are rotting bones. Thus they all are just the same. . . . Let us enjoy our life in the present. Why worry about what comes after death?"

Four points in this statement ascribed to Yang are important: (1) death is the end; (2) death is no respecter of persons; (3) the conventional "goods" of this life—fame, wealth, longevity, and high rank, to name the most coveted—confer upon humans no lasting benefit, and so they should not be pursued; and (4) the simple pleasures in this life should therefore be pursued more avidly. In the cruel confidence game employed by ambitious states (then as now) to produce fearless warriors and selfless subjects, death is cast as a gain. In Yang Zhu's view, the world will achieve good order only when everyone finally refuses to sacrifice himself or others for the sake of the supposed common good, because then no one will seek short-term advantages from serving it. Keeping oneself intact so as to protect one's integrity and wholeness, refusing to let one's body be ensnared by abstract ideals and ambitions—these, to the consternation of the Confucians, were the teachings that Yang Zhu advocated. Kongzi's followers (mis)characterized Yang Zhu's teachings as gross egotism, a self-absorption that was bound to undermine an awareness of the profound debts of gratitude owed first to one's family members and second to one's ruler. The most strident of Kongzi's followers condemned Yang's attitude as "bestial" and worse than that of the barbarians!

Had Kongzi lived long enough to know Yang Zhu, his refutation might have been quite different. Kongzi would have objected to Yang Zhu's assertion that the highest good is preserving one's own life, whatever the cost. Kongzi would have refused to accept the gross material finality of Yang Zhu's vision of life and death. Yang Zhu saw humanity as composed of capacities that were easily damaged or weakened, through an excess of desires, through lack of consideration for one's own health, or through physical assaults by others. Since those capacities were what allowed humans to live out their allotted days, damage to them necessarily ended in a shortened life span. As Yang wrote,

> Therefore, the sage's attitude to sounds, sights, and tastes is that when they benefit his nature, he chooses them, and when they harm his nature, he refuses them. This is the Way of keeping one's nature intact.

Especially worrisome was the loss of one's *qi*, the configured energy thought to be the very stuff of life and health. A powerful argument could be made that nothing was more important, even from the moral point of view, than the conservation of bodily *qi*:

We love riches and honor, ease and fame, for which others praise us, on account of our bodies. It is on account of our bodies also that we abhor poverty and base status, danger and shame, for which others despise us. And of our bodies, what is most valuable? Nothing is more valuable than *qi*. When a person gets *qi*, he lives; when he loses it, he dies. His *qi* is not gold or silk, pearls or jade, and it cannot be sought from others. It is not painted cloth or the five cereals, and it cannot be got by purchase. It exists solely in our own bodies. One cannot but be careful. As the *Odes* say, "Intelligent and wise he is / In protecting his physical person."

Thus, in Master Yang's view, "The possibility that events may lead either to poverty or to wealth is what injures a person's character [by making him greedy or fearful]. The possibility that events may lead either to life or death is what injures a person's courage."[3] Yang Zhu was not necessarily immoral; to risk injury to life and limb for the sake of mere things or fleeting sensations would be to forget that we should never disdain the precious gift of life from Heaven. According to Yang Zhu, each of us can experience genuine emotions and feelings, and these probably constitute the best available guides we have to what we need to sustain life. Our desires to possess things and people reflect societal norms, and the greater the number of our possessions, the more likely we are to indulge in worries that harm the body. Then, too, artificial ceremonies, along with other forms of acculturation, can damage us to the degree that they wean us away from the natural self. Acculturation to society's norms can even alter our picture of the world so dramatically that we consider giving up our lives for the sake of honor or altruism. Heaven, as opposed to the state, would never require that sacrifice of us.

Yang Zhu could point to the legend of old Duke Danfu, the founder of the Zhou noble line, when he wanted to cite a suitable precedent for his brand of morality. When nomadic tribes threatened his state, the duke found himself incapable of sending his subjects to war. Reasoning that it hardly mattered whether these sons and brothers were his subjects or another's, he left his state and moved to the foothills of Qishan. So widely admired was he for this unselfish act that his subjects all moved from their former homes to his new lands.

The sage-king Yao of antiquity provided another model for Yang, since Yao had reportedly tried to cede the empire to a man who was not his own son, reasoning that "only the man who cares nothing for the empire deserves to be trusted with the empire." (As it happens, Yang Zhu tells us, Yao's potential heir refused the empire, citing principles remarkably like those of Yang Zhu.)

According to Yang Zhu, anyone who undertakes a careful cost-benefit analysis will soon see that the person who genuinely "acts solely on behalf of his own person" will most likely do the least harm to himself and others, for he will seek to avoid all potentially harmful activities whatsoever. (Adam Smith said much the same, of course.) One needs to estimate the trouble something will cost, anticipate the possible reversals of fortune that may accrue from a particular act, and calculate whether a proposed action will do damage to one's nature. If men and women always took the trouble to make that sort of careful calculation, few would ever look to "improve their lots" in conventional terms.

> Suppose we have a man who is willing to cut off his own head or his hands and feet in exchange for a cap; suppose we have a man who will let himself be executed in exchange for a coat. The world would certainly think him deluded. Why? A cap is a means to adorn the head; a coat, to adorn the person. If the adorned ends up being executed because he was trying to get the means of adornment, he has failed to understand why he acts.

The person willing to do anything for a single possession—whatever its value—is a person who will stop at nothing, so long as the price is right.

The extreme position attributed to Yang Zhu was that Yang would refuse to give up a single hair of his body, even if it would benefit the whole world. By Yang Zhu's logic, plucking one hair from one's body represents the first step on a perilous path: soon one may be offering to slice off a bit of one's skin in return for a piece of gold, or cutting off a limb in order to win a state. There being no natural end to the desires we have, and no natural end, in consequence, to the bargains we may strike, we must never forget the supreme value of the complete life and intact body. For a human life passes by as suddenly as a thoroughbred steed galloping past a chink in the wall. "Whoever cannot . . . find nurture for the years that are predestined—that is not a person who has fathomed the Way."

One riposte in response to Yang Zhu's rhetoric was put, appropriately enough, in the mouth of Kongzi in an early Han collection of stories:

> Duke Ai asked Confucius, "Does the possessor of wisdom live out his predestined life span?" Confucius replied, "Certainly. There are three ways in which a man dies that are not determined by fate, but are of his own choosing. Those whose residence is not taken care of, those who are immoderate in eating and drinking, those who in toil and idleness go to excess—these will all be killed off by sickness. Those who, occupying inferior positions, like to oppose their superiors; those whose desires are insatiable; and those who seek things incessantly—they will all of them be killed by law. Those who with a few oppose the many, who in weakness insult the strong, who in anger do not take stock of their strength—they will all of them be killed in conflicts. Thus there are three ways in which a man dies that are not determined by fate but are due to his own choices. The *Ode* says, 'If a man have no moderation in his behavior, / What can he do but die?' "[4]

This anecdote does not simply suggest that one who understands destiny as well as Kongzi will not be deceived. It implies also that the Confucian Way will not lead the person to wrack and ruin. Instead, as in *Analects* 2/18, Confucius articulates a Way that serves a person well as he or she goes through life:

> The Master said, "Hear much but maintain silence as regards doubtful points. Be cautious also in speaking of the rest. That way you will seldom get into trouble. See much, and ignore what it is dangerous to have seen. Be cautious, too, in acting upon the rest. Then you will seldom want to undo your acts. He who seldom

gets into trouble about what he has said and seldom does anything that he afterward wishes he had not done—such a man will be sure *incidentally* to get his reward.

Kongzi further insisted that the most basic impulse behind morality—a profound sense of the emotional quid pro quo underlying human relations—is needed if one seeks to sustain one's life: "Approach them with dignity, and they will respect you. Carry out filial duty toward your parents and kindness toward your children, and they will be loyal to you. Promote those who are worthy, train those who are incompetent. This is the best form of encouragement by which to induce ordinary people to treat you well." In Kongzi's view, a selfish concern with one's own life may actually *diminish* one's chances of flourishing.

> Behave when away from home as though you were in the presence of an important guest. Deal with the common people as though you were officiating at an important sacrifice. Do not do to others what you would not like to happen to yourself. Then there will be no feelings of opposition to you, whether it is the affairs of a state that you are handling or the affairs of a family.

As Mencius, a self-proclaimed adherent of Kongzi, proclaimed, "The reason for disliking those who hold to one extreme is that they cripple the Way, insofar as one thing is singled out to the neglect of a hundred other considerations." Yang Zhu had forgotten that life, however important to the human good, is not the supreme good itself. Kongzi had said, "In the morning, hear the Way; in the evening, die content." Of humaneness, he had said,

> To prefer goodness is better than only to know it. To delight in it is better than merely to prefer it. . . . One who really cared for goodness would never let any other consideration come first. Has anyone ever managed to do good with his whole might even as long as the space of a single day? I think not! Yet I for my part have never seen anyone give up such an attempt because he had not the *strength to*

go on. It may well have happened, but I myself have never seen it. Never for a moment does a gentleman quit the Way of Goodness. He is never so harried but that he cleaves to this; never so tottering but that he cleaves to this.

HAN FEI ON CONFUCIUS

Master Han Fei (280–233 BCE), alone among the early Masters, was born into the aristocracy. He was, however, but a minor prince hailing from the embattled state of Han, which occupied a mere fraction— and the most mountainous and the least productive fraction, at that— of the vast territories formerly in the possession of the powerful state of Jin. As prince in a state partitioned by its own ministerial families, Han Fei kept a sharp eye out for the dangers occasioned by factional strife at court, and it was doubtless his keen sense of the precariousness of many late Warring States arrangements that made Han Fei such an implacable enemy of the slow, civilizing processes identified with the Confucian Way. But sometime in his career Han Fei had studied under Xunzi, then the most famous proponent of Kongzi's teachings. Xunzi would have trained Han Fei in the classical curriculum of literature, history, music, and ritual. A man of learning himself, Han Fei admired erudition and civility in others, but his admiration stopped at the point where these qualities might distract a ruler from giving his undivided attention to acquiring supreme strategic advantage in all military and economic operations. Therefore, in the writings attributed to him, Han Fei praised cultivation, humaneness, and adherence to the conventional notions of duty as goals worth pursuing in one's private life. But when it came to the public sphere—the conduct of state and the shaping of policy—he held these same virtues in utter contempt. "One must not lose hold of the vital point," as he put it:

Were I to give advice from the point of view of the private person, I would say the best thing is to practice humaneness and duty and to cultivate the polite arts. By practicing humaneness and duty, you will become trusted, and when you have become trusted, you may receive an official appointment. Similarly, by cultivating the arts you may become an eminent teacher, and as such, you will win great honor and renown. These are the highest goals of the private person. But should this happen—well, looking at it from the point of view of the state, someone who has performed no meritorious service for the realm receives an official appointment; and someone who held no government title enjoys great honor and renown. A domain so ruled will face certain disorder, and the ruler certain peril. The interests of the state and the individual conflict with one another, you see. Both cannot prevail at the same time.

With such pronouncements, Han Fei launched a devastating attack on the Master's teachings without ever once mentioning Kongzi's name. By Han Fei's time, some two centuries after the Master's death, Kongzi had already reached legendary status; in the parlance of the time, he had become a sage. That meant that Kongzi, who never attained high office, was more famous than many a ruler; and his Way reckoned to be superior to some proposals made by later persuaders. In a curious way, then, the Kongzi of legend could conceivably constrain the activities of contemporary rulers, preventing them from considering the full range of options before carrying out their plans. More serious still, Kongzi's admirers took it to be an article of faith that the best-ruled states were those administered by good men like themselves emulating Kongzi's example; Kongzi's followers were all too apt to lay claim to the Master's mantle of authority in order to bask in his reflected glory. If the chief "difficulty of persuasion" was "to know the mind of the person one was trying to persuade, so as to be able to fit one's words to it," it was certainly becoming harder for critics to secure a court's favor after baldly denouncing the Master. One hardly knew anymore what position the court might adopt on such matters. Hence one of Han Fei's opening salvos contained a very backhanded compliment to Kongzi:

Kongzi was one of the greatest sages of the world. He perfected his conduct, made clear the Way, and traveled throughout the area within the four seas. Still, in all that area there were only seventy who so rejoiced in his humaneness and admired his righteousness that they were willing to become his disciples. To truly value humaneness is a rare thing; to adhere to duty is hard. Therefore within the vast area of the world only seventy men became his disciples, and only one man—Kongzi himself—was truly kind and righteous.

Kongzi was a very great man, as Han Fei concedes. The problem is, sages do not come along very often. They are honored precisely because they are rare. Therefore the ruler cannot afford to stand idly by, waiting for a sage to appear, before he acts.

There was once a farmer of Song who tilled the land, and in his fields there was a stump. One day a rabbit, racing across the fields, crashed into the stump, broke its neck, and died. The farmer laid aside his plow and took to watching beside the stump, in the hopes of getting another rabbit in the same way. But he got no more rabbits, and instead became the laughingstock of Song.

Han Fei then draws the moral of his story: "Those who think they can take the ways of the ancient kings and use them to govern the people of today all are stump-watchers of a sort!" Having drawn a laugh or two, Han Fei can afford to let the ruler ruminate on the problems of scale: If even Kongzi himself could attract only seventy men, great sage though he was, how in the world is the average ruler, using Confucian teachings, ever to attract enough followers to rule the age? The rapidly centralizing states of Han Fei's time needed to bind millions to their service; otherwise they would not have enough men to till their fields and man their armies. The ruler had better not try to reform the state through the rule of virtue.

Hardly ten men of true integrity and good faith can be found today, and yet there are hundreds of offices in a state. If they must all be filled by men of integrity, then there will never be enough men to go around; and if the offices are left unfilled, then those whose business it is to govern will dwindle as the numbers of the disorderly increase.

The Confucian program cannot be implemented, Han Fei argues, because there are too few ideal men to run the government in that way. Anyone who thinks a state needs to employ sages like Kongzi has set the bar too high. It is enough to rule a country effectively and efficiently; every millennium or so, the conditions may make for an ideal state ideally governed.

> Nowadays, when the classicists counsel a ruler, they do not urge him to wield authority, which is the certain way to success. Instead, they insist that he must practice humaneness and duty before he can become a true king. This is, in effect, to demand that the ruler rise to Kongzi's level, and that all the ordinary people of the time be like Kongzi's disciples. Such a policy is bound to fail.

An easier and more predictable way to run the government must be provided by advisers to the king—and to that subject Han Fei will return. Meanwhile, before delivering the final coup de grace designed to destroy the prestige and authority of Kongzi, Han Fei succinctly illustrates the clear and present dangers of following Kongzi with two entertaining anecdotes. In the first, which follows the *Analects* of Kongzi in the setup but not in its conclusion, we're told that Honest Gong's father stole a sheep. Gong reported the theft. The ruler was gratified that one of his subjects proved to be law-abiding to this degree, but Kongzi disagreed: upon hearing about the case, he commented tartly, "In my country, the upright men are of quite another sort. A father will screen his son, and a son his father, which, incidentally, is one sort of righteous behavior." Han Fei then tells us the denouement: Although Honest Gong's action demonstrated loyalty to the sovereign's law, the presiding magistrate, bowing to local custom, considered Gong such a despicable son that he had him summarily executed. Han Fei concluded, however, that putting filial piety before obligation to the ruler was but the first step on the slippery slope of ignoring or excusing all crimes, with dire consequences to social order. Thus acting on Confucian principles subverts the principles of justice enshrined in the laws.

In a second story that represents an equally pointed critique of

Kongzi, Han Fei tells of an army conscript who fled the battlefield on three separate occasions because he was the sole support of an aged parent. Kongzi allegedly praised the man and recommended him for a promotion. By contrast, Han Fei is appalled by such desertions from the army. It is obvious to him that public duty and private morality cannot be reconciled. "To regard the two as identical would be disastrous—the result of not thinking things through." People are naturally selfish, says Han Fei, so they will naturally seek to advance the interests of themselves and their families, friends, and allies. The public good, meanwhile, requires that one maximize the country's potential for wealth, power, and good order without regard to individual families and persons. Special interests that encroach on state business will jeopardize the lives and the livelihoods of all. No exceptions can be made or exemptions given, or total victory cannot be secured.

Besides, as Han Fei continues in barely concealed triumph, the Sage was no sage at all, given his many serious errors in judgment in selecting his own disciples. Take Tan Tai Ziyu. At first Kongzi thought him a perfect gentleman, so he was welcomed into his band of disciples. Only later did Kongzi realize his mistake. And then there was Zai Yu. By Kongzi's own admission, his disciple Zai Yu was eloquent, but impractical—and also lazy. If today's rulers are no more perspicacious than Kongzi, and today's orators as glib and well spoken as Zai Yu, how are rulers ever to arrive at the judicious verdicts on matters of great import?

To answer his own question, Han Fei resorts to an extended myth about the past that says a good deal about current dilemmas. "In antiquity," he begins, "when men were few and creatures abundant, human beings could not compete with the birds, beasts, insects, and reptiles. Then a sage appeared who fashioned nests of wood to protect the humans from harm. The people were so delighted that they made him ruler of the world, calling him the Home (Nest) Builder." After securing shelter, people wanted a safer supply of food, for in the second stage, humankind hunted and gathered, eating whatever they could find, but the raw food made them sick. Eventually a sage appeared who brought them fire to cook with. Like the Nest-Builder before him, this inventor so delighted the people that they made him ruler of the world. In the third phase, people wanted to quell the floods, and in response a sage appeared who taught them how to dig canals and channels. This inventor in his turn was duly hailed as "savior" of the people, and he, too, became ruler of the world. But, as Han Fei wryly observes, were subsequent rulers to try to win universal acclaim by imitating the earlier sages in building nests, starting fires, or digging ditches, they would become laughingstocks. From which Han Fei draws a stark conclusion: "The sage does not try to practice the ways of antiquity or to abide by a fixed standard. He rather examines the affairs of the age and takes whatever precautions are necessary" to secure what people need most at the time. For the people in Han Fei's time to enjoy ultimate peace and prosperity, their rulers must send them out to conquer and exterminate rival nations.

In his version of human history, Han Fei identifies what he believes to be the constant patterns. First, continuity does not ensure stability, since the world itself is always changing. Second, living conditions only improve with innovations designed to relieve some pervasive problem. Third, the origin of the state derives from the people's desire to submit to any person who manages to alleviate their sufferings. Sage-kings base their policy decisions on what will meet present needs; they never think of their innovations as fixed precedents for the future. Continuing in that vein, Han Fei adds another crucial observation: the further back one goes in history, the smaller the population and the greater the abundance of food, land, and sustenance. In the present era, he believes, the population has simply become too great for the available resources.

> The people of antiquity cared little for material goods, not because they were benevolent, but because they had a surplus of goods. When people quarrel and snatch today, it is not because they are vicious, but because goods have grown scarce.

Things are getting steadily worse, in Han Fei's estimation. Centuries have gone by with no appreciable alleviation of the accumulating human misery by new sages with new creations. As the physical resources necessary to usher in a new golden age are dwindling or nonexistent, people must adopt a zero-sum approach simply to survive in the modern world. Hence the futility of the gentle Confucian Way, which may have served splendidly in times long past:

> Past and present have different customs; new and old adopt different measures. To try to use the ways of a generous and lenient government to rule the people of a critical age is like trying to drive a runaway horse without using reins or whip. This is the misfortune that ignorance invites.

How, then, will the ruler proceed in order to win the hearts and minds of the people whose support is needed for stable rule? Han Fei believes he has the right answer, and it is "laws."[5] The latest in a series of innovations in the Central States—the writing of laws began in China about the eighth century BCE and law codes were first promulgated a mere century before Han Fei—the laws proposed by Han Fei provide a single standard against which all phenomena—people, things, and events—can be measured with such precision that the punishment will always fit the crime (shades of Gilbert and Sullivan!). The laws moreover allow the ruler to maintain his prerogatives, in that he exists above the law. Arguably, it is also the laws that allow people to "do things by themselves"—and not only because the maintenance of public order is a precondition for any private initiative. When good laws are in place, rewards and punishments "follow the deed; each man brings them upon himself." By Han Fei's logic, then, the benefits accruing from good laws are so great that previous rulers who had enacted the laws should have been hailed as the greatest sage-kings of their day. Why, then, do people resent the law and fear the ruler who enforces it? Why not celebrate the lawgivers?

The people have never regarded the lawgiver as their salvation for the simple reason that no ruler has ever yet made the laws the sole arbiter of justice. No ruler has made the laws particularly clear or trusted to their operations. Rulers have been loath to let laws prevail; they are afraid of giving up the reins of power. Then, too, society holds so many contrary and conflicting values (all sporting their own precedents) that the laws have never been applied fairly, by the ruler or his representatives. Exceptions have become the norm, though the widespread perception of arbitrariness of the laws adds to the chaos. Finally, the people always understand very little about wielding power and ruling states, in this being like small children:

> The reason you cannot rely upon the wisdom of the people is that they have the minds of little children. If the child's head is not shaved, its sores will spread; and if its boil is not lanced, it will become sicker than ever. But when the child is having its head shaved or its boil lanced, someone must hold the child while the loving mother performs the operation. Still, it yells and screams incessantly, for it does not understand that the little pain it suffers now will bring great benefit later.

The people only want to be left alone to seek private advantage. They little realize that their competitive impulses, if left unchecked, will jeopardize the health of the whole body politic upon which they depend for their lives and livelihoods. The people never want to serve in the army, and once conscripted, they show no bravery in battle unless rewards for courage and punishments for cowardice are mandated by the law. The ruler must not adopt their shortsightedness as a model for governance.

For all the foregoing reasons, the broad reach of the law should be certain, and the consequences of lawbreaking swift. Han Fei adduces at least four negative reasons why the ruler has no alternative but to adopt impartial law as his latest and best aid in governing: (1) The parent-child relation cannot be appropriately applied to the ruler-subject relation; (2) nothing that threatens the economic progress of the state and its armies by depleting scarce resources can be good; (3) no advice that leaves the ruler "in two minds" can be good, for it leaves the ruler looking weak and hesitant, a ready prey to attacks from within and without; and (4) no advisers can be trusted, since the more eloquent the adviser, the more duplicitous and self-serving he is apt to be. Asked to weigh in on a certain policy measure, eloquent advisers respond with so many precedents and so many caveats that the ruler feels overwhelmed, flustered, and impressed by turns.

"The height of good government," as defined by Han Fei, "is to allow subordinates no means of taking advantage of the ruler." "Never enrich a man to the point where he can afford to turn against you; never ennoble a man to the point where he becomes a threat; never put all your trust in a single man and thereby lose your state," he continues. The ruler must monopolize all the power in the state, if he means to keep any of it. "It is dangerous for the ruler of men to trust others, for he who trust others will be controlled by them." Everyone has an agenda—except Han Fei, apparently. Consider the interviews that Kongzi had with successive rulers in the Central States—no good! And the latter-day, pale imitations of Kongzi are but parasites gorging themselves at the state's expense. Like other vermin (in which category Han Fei also puts speechmakers with divided loyalties; warriors who assemble personal retinues; merchants exploiting the farmers; and artisans producing luxury goods for the privileged), the followers of Kongzi and Mozi roam from place to place, scrounging for patrons foolish enough to supply handouts. With their fancy clothes and rich carriages, they then find ways to gain celebrity and glory "without the hardships of service in the army." They should instead be seen for what they are: useless subjects, "no different from" the wooden or clay funeral figures that are put into graves to serve the dead in the afterlife. The problem is,

> If men who devote themselves to old writings or study the art of persuasive speaking are able to secure the fruits of wealth without the hard work of the farmer, and if they can gain eminence without undergoing the dangers of battle, then who will not in future take up such pursuits? So for every man who works with his hands there will be a hundred devoting themselves to the pursuit of wisdom. If those who pursue "wisdom" are so numerous, the laws will be defeated, and if those who labor with their hands are few, the state will grow poor. Hence the age will become disordered.

Like many who rail against the "useless" expense of the humanities today, Han Fei insists that support of an idle coterie of scholars is a luxury that no state can afford.

To arguments of this sort, Kongzi had responded in the *Analects*. Taunted with the impracticality of rule by virtue, Kongzi retorted, "If it is really possible to govern countries by ritual and yielding, there is no more to be said"—meaning that this way of governing, if it will work (and no one has yet had the audacity of vision to try it out!), would be manifestly superior to rule by brute force and mutilating punishments. Faced with a person who thought it wiser to employ expediency than virtue, Kongzi responded, "Those whose measures are dictated by mere expediency will arouse continual discontent." The ruler should see that if he values self-interest above all else, it will not be long before those of his subjects who are "daring by nature and suffering from poverty" adopt the same code of values—to the detriment of good rule. "Man's very life is honesty, in that without it he will be lucky indeed if he escapes with his life." Kongzi would hardly have been surprised that Han Fei died in prison, charged with treason by the First Emperor of Qin, a ruler who distrusted his promises to sell out his own country of Han.

ZHUANGZI ON CONFUCIUS

Zhuangzi was by far the subtlest of Confucius's critics—his critiques being shot through with admiration and even affection.[6] Nothing is known of Zhuangzi's life, though some said he was a native of Song, the same state where legend puts Confucius's distant ancestors. (During the classical era in China, Song and its people were the frequent butt of jokes, with the "people from Song" acting in the role of proverbial country bumpkins.) More often than not, Zhuangzi speaks through the figure of Confucius, as in this famous interchange recorded in chapter four of the *Zhuangzi*, entitled, "In the World of Men":

> Yan Hui went to Confucius to ask his permission to go to Wei, whose young ruler had already won a name for himself by "acting in a singular manner." "I have heard you say, Master, 'Leave the state that is well ordered and go to the state in chaos! At the doctor's gate are many sick men.' I want to use these words as my standard, in hopes that I can restore his state to health."

Confucius replied, "Oh, you will probably accomplish nothing but getting yourself executed. . . . The Perfect Man of ancient times made sure that he had it in himself before he tried to give it to others. When you're not even sure what you've got in yourself, how do you have time to bother about what some tyrant is doing? . . . Do you know what it is that disturbs virtue, or where wisdom comes from? Virtue is destroyed by fame, and wisdom comes out of disputation. . . . Though your virtue be great and your good faith unassailable . . . you would simply be using other men's bad points to parade your own excellence, if you appeared before a tyrant and forced him to listen to sermons on benevolence and righteousness. You will be known as someone who plagues others, and he who plagues others will be plagued in turn.

"And suppose he *is* the kind of ruler who actually delights in the worthy and despises the unworthy. Why would he need *you* to try to make him any different? You had best keep your advice to yourself! Kings and dukes always lord it over others and fight to win an argument. You will find your eyes growing dazzled, your face pale, your mouth working to invent excuses, and your body language increasingly humble, until you end up supporting him in your mind. . . . Even the sages could not cope with men who are after fame and gain, much less a person like you!"

Yan Hui persists, asking if it would be all right if he went and showed a grave and diligent attitude. "Goodness, how would *that* do any good?" "Well, what if I am inwardly direct, outwardly compliant, and do my work through the examples of antiquity?" Here, of course, Yan Hui wants to know whether he can succeed if he becomes the perfect student of classicism, to which Confucius again replies, "Goodness, how would *that* do any good?" Finally, after a series of such questions, Confucius advises Yan Hui how to behave:

Before a sacrifice, one fasts with the body. Instead, fast with the mind. . . . Listening stops with the ears, the mind stops once it recognizes something. But spirit is empty and waits on all things.

Ardent waiting, watching life unfold in all its myriad wonders, sustaining curiosity about its processes and refusing to be bitter, no matter one's fate—that's not only what Zhuangzi urges upon us, but also what Kongzi emphasized when he spoke of "understanding fate and taking pleasure in Heaven."

In a second justly famous passage, Zhuangzi's arguments again spill out of the mouth of Kongzi:

> In the world, there are two great decrees: one is fate and the other one is duty. That a child should love the parents is fate—no one can erase this from the heart. That a subject must serve his ruler is duty—there is no place a person can go to be without a ruler, no place he can escape to between Heaven and Earth. These are called the great decrees. Therefore, to serve one's parents and be content to follow them—this is the perfection of filial piety. And to serve one's ruler and be content to follow is the height of loyalty. And to serve your own mind so that neither sadness nor joy sways it, to understand what you can do nothing about and to be content with it as with fate—that is the supreme virtue.

Living in a post-Freudian age, we know, of course, that not all children love their parents, and Mozi and Han Fei recognized this, too. Even so, with only minor emendations, the preceding paragraph works brilliantly. All children, even if they cannot love their parents, are at least preoccupied with them. They are fated to be so. And all of us must live in some society or another that constrains our activities in ways appropriate and inappropriate. What is interesting about this passage—and equally true for the Kongzi of the *Analects*—is that Kongzi does not equate filial duty and loyalty with supreme virtue. (It is a canard that Confucian ethics require blind obedience to one's parents.) The promised rewards for virtue, as formulated in the *Zhuangzi*, recall many an *Analects* passage, for example, "If you act in accordance with the prevailing state of affairs and then forget about yourself, what leisure will you have to love life and hate death? Act in this way and you will be all right!" There is great joy to be had from doing what is required and then accepting the way things are.

On good days, as Kongzi notes, we all know that

life, death, preservation, loss, failure, success, poverty, riches, wor-
thiness, unworthiness, slander, fame, hunger, thirst, cold, heat—
these are the alternations of the world, the workings of fate. . . .
Day and night, they change places before us and wisdom cannot
spy out their source. Therefore they should not be enough to destroy your harmony; they should not be allowed to enter the store-
house of spirit. If you can harmonize with them and delight in them,
master them and never be at a loss for joy, if you can do this day and
night without break and make it be spring with everything—that is
what I call being whole in power.

On such a good day, we can imagine Confucius taking off for the
river to bathe with his band of disciples and friends, relishing the
spring weather along with the opportunity for effortless sociality that
it affords. After all, "running around accusing others is not as good as
laughing, and enjoying a good laugh is not as good as going along
with things as they are . . . to enter the mysterious oneness of
Heaven."

On bad days, however, as other, more mocking, chapters of the
Zhuangzi suggest, this sublime vision of wholeness eludes Kongzi.
Kongzi then appears as a worthy enough chap, but one whose powers
of imagination have been clipped by convention and ambition. (Recall in the *Analects* Kongzi's remark that he has none of the seemingly
natural goodness of his disciple Yan Hui.) Seeing clearly, a true sage
"does not shift with things; since he takes it as fated that things will
change, he holds fast to the source"—that source being the profound
insight that all things are one. But sages "wander beyond this realm"
while men like Kongzi, as Kongzi himself knows, wander well within
its boundaries. Kongzi, on bad days, finds it difficult to remember that
fame means nothing and old age is not to be feared. At his worst,
Kongzi lapses into a preoccupation with mere appearances, with the
result that he fails to see the larger picture. Kongzi at least admits to
himself that he is neither a "singular man" nor a fit "companion to
Heaven."

Still, Zhuangzi had only one major complaint to lodge against
Kongzi. He plainly worries that Kongzi's beloved "ritual consists in
being false to one another." Ritual serves the same function as lan-

guage, after all, communicating its meaning through special gestures, clothing, and rhetorical formulae. Zhuangzi asks if it is not possible for people to communicate better through a simpler means available to all. Kongzi and his most famous adherents grant that there is initially something artificial about ritual, but they go on to argue that there is something artificial about all that is best in human society, and these once highly artificial practices soon become "second nature" (as those of us who learn a foreign language, master a technical discipline, or play an instrument know). The forms and potentials of all social relations must be learned, and all human achievements require a sustained focus, a discipline, and a will to elevate the mundane to the remarkable. If "falsification" ("refinement" by another name) is at the heart of all the civilizing processes, even language and gesture itself, then the human task must not be to jettison all instances of falsification, but to consider what sorts of refinement most conduce to a social order in which all humans "achieve their proper place," enjoying a sense of dignity and self-worth.

WANG CHONG ON KONGZI

Critiques of Kongzi continued for long centuries after the supposed apotheosis of the Master in the Han period (the subject of chapter 3). Attacks on Kongzi by the Eastern Han skeptic Wang Chong seem broadly aimed at Wang's contemporaries who tried to claim a special authority when they taught the Classics purportedly authored or edited by Kongzi. Wang's critique of Kongzi boils down to five points: (1) the Classics are just as riddled with error as other books, so they should not be treated as infallible; (2) Kongzi failed to carefully elucidate a great many of his ideas when he conversed with his disciples; (3) Kongzi contradicted himself fairly often, but good teachers try to send consistent messages; (4) Kongzi's chosen disciples showed no special aptitude for learning the Way, or discipline in their commitment to it, which suggests that Kongzi was hardly an inspiring teacher; and (5) Kongzi offered no proper pedagogical model, nor did he push his students to clarify their own thoughts about ethical or practical matters.

To illustrate his second point, Wang Chong cited a famous passage recorded in the *Analects*, in which the disciple Meng Yizi asks the Master about filial piety. The Master replied, "Never offend." Meng Yizi, like later readers, assumed that Kongzi meant, "Never disobey one's parents." On another occasion Fan Chi was driving the Master, and the Master, when asked about the earlier exchange, finally explained what he meant when he used the phrase "Never offend": "Serve them in life according to ritual; bury them upon death according to ritual." Evidently the phrase "Never offend" meant "Do not go against ritual," rather than "Always obey one's parents." Wang Chong quite rightly concludes that if Fan Chi had never asked for an explanation, Kongzi would in all likelihood never have explained his meaning. In giving the sketchiest of instructions to his least able students, Kongzi violated the proverb, "Small talent should be instructed in detail, and for great talent a rough outline suffices."

THE MODERN WORLD sometimes seems consumed by an epic struggle waged between reason and emotion—or, as some would put it, between the Enlightenment, which rid the world of the gross superstitions obscuring an intelligible order of marvelous design, and Romanticism, which sees human beings as the sole architects of their own fates. Neither impulse wholly satisfies, for it is not altogether clear that the light of reason can dispel all confusion, or that intoxication with life leaves more behind than rubble. Straddling these two models lies Kongzi, who found quiet pleasure in the contemplation and practice of a myriad human exchanges, who consistently opposed using "other people as things," as mere objects to an end. The distinctive character of Kongzi's teaching—in contrast to that of his critics—lies in its consistent appeals to the value of the human scale and to sweet reason, appeals lodged most convincingly by his self-proclaimed disciples.

Every one of Kongzi's critics charges the Sage with being too unimaginative and conventional, too old-fashioned in his approaches, or too ready to compromise. In the eyes of Jie Yu, for example, Kongzi had the potential to be like the soaring phoenix, but "his clarity had fallen" because of his endless entanglements with a corrupt world. Kongzi *was* a phoenix, however. This legendary figure rose from the ashes of defeat to persuade people of the practical virtues of everyday existence, while releasing them from those dreaded conventions that prove "unwieldly, slow, heavy, and pale as lead." That surprising triumph is the story of the following chapter on the Master.

SUGGESTED READINGS

For the characterization of Kongzi as a man of humor, see Christoph Harbsmeier, "Confucius Ridens," *Harvard Journal of Asiatic Studies* 50, no. 1 (June 1990): 131–61.

Arthur Waley, *Three Ways of Thought in Ancient China* (New York: Doubleday Anchor, 1956).

Readers of Chinese may wish to consult Li Ling, *Sang jia gou* (Beijing: Shanxi chubanshe, 2007).

Kongzi, the Uncrowned King

In the Annals (Chunqiu), *the record of the former kings of past ages, the Sage derives meaning [from events] but does not appear disputatious.*

— ZHUANGZI, CHAPTER 2

Kongzi was only a commoner, but his name is so illustrious that when you come to his grave mound, those of high rank are offering oxen, sheep, chickens, and pigs in sacrifice, and those of lesser status, wine, dried meat jerky, and winter implements, in the utmost reverence before they go on their ways.

— HUAN TAN, *XIN LUN*

IF KONGZI WAS A SAGE—WHOSE SUPERIOR TEACHINGS BECAME all the more obvious owing to the jibes of his critics—why did he fail to gain adherents quickly in his own lifetime and thereby become a sage-ruler? After all, according to the legends, men of such infinite wisdom and compassion regularly rose to positions of supreme power. Moreover, a Central States savior was due to appear during Kongzi's lifetime, since it had been five hundred years since the Duke of Zhou's civilizing efforts. What had gone wrong? "He had no land," said one popular theory, and hence no basis and scope for his enormous talents. "Bad timing," others suggested, or "insufficient breeding." Kongzi was destined, others believed, to provide in his own person the perfect model for noble spirits forced to accept cruel fates. He was slandered by petty people, and thus prevented from achieving his rightful place, some concluded sadly. Early Chinese thinkers clearly felt they had to come up with *some* explanation, if the early theories about charismatic virtue were not to collapse in the face of the obvious counterevidence presented by the case of Kongzi-the-failure.[1]

Each and every portrait of Kongzi drawn during the first stable empires of Western and Eastern Han (the two last centuries BCE and the two first centuries CE) implicitly or explicitly addressed this single issue. Perhaps that was because society's moral calculations were rocked off kilter with the founding of the Han empire—the greatest the East had ever known—by a mere commoner, Liu Bang (r. 206–195 BCE), who began life in a rural backwater "without a patch of land" to his name. This chapter considers in turn several portraits of Kongzi produced during the two Han periods, in which the land-less Sage, in seeming desperation, devised a realm of the imagination where he reigned unchallenged in his writings. The Han saw Kongzi, above all, as the author of the *Spring and Autumn Annals* [hereafter *Annals*].[2] That Kongzi had gone to his grave unreconciled to his failure to achieve high office meant that cosmic justice would only be served if Kongzi somehow predicted the Han victory that came nearly three centuries later, and reigned, as was his right, through the Han rulers, as a virtual "uncrowned king" or power behind the throne. Hence the proliferation of Han literary portraits of Kongzi that made him the chief architect of the stunning Han success, centuries after his death. By the end of the Han period, Kongzi's signal lack of illustrious forebears and reputable descendants would be posthumously reme-died: Kongzi was awarded his own place among the ranks of the star gods, and appointed First Ancestor to a long line of Kong family members who had been ennobled.

As noted earlier, on the eve of the Han dynasty, in the early third century BCE, it was far from certain that Kongzi's multiple portraits would ever lessen the stigma of "loser" that clung tenaciously to his name. In 200 BCE, no one could have predicted that Kongzi would become the most celebrated figure in all of Chinese history, let alone a god. Kongzi's ultimate triumph should probably be traced to the di-rect appeals different parts of his legends made to different groups within society; their collective membership together eventually raised the Master to unprecedented heights of fame. It may also have helped that the hated Qin dynasty, which had managed by force and intimidation to unify the separate kingdoms, collapsed within months after the death of the First Emperor, Qin Shihuang, in 210 BCE. So speedy a demise of such a vast empire seemed to prove that a more mixed system of direct and indirect control—one that would allow subjects greater autonomy within a system of political vassalage and laissez-faire economics—would enhance a dynasty's chances of survival in the face of internal and external pressures. Kongzi, as a *legendary* chronicler of the pre-unification period, was a suitable candidate for the role of patron saint for a less centralized system (with "patron saint" a more apposite term than it might seem at first glance). After four centuries of steady growth in the numbers of legends attesting to Kongzi's unique preeminence within classical culture, especially marked in the first century CE, Kongzi even managed somehow to survive the collapse of the Eastern Han throne in 220 CE, in part because the roles ascribed to the Sage in Han were so many and so various.[3] In traditional Chinese terms, Kongzi had become a god (*shen* 神), meaning "an unseen force that transforms itself and others easily, without overt coercion." Or, to adopt a metaphor famous in Han, the "thorns" that had impeded entrance to the Kong house had been cleared by hundreds if not thousands of ardent adherents over the ages.[4]

Very much like the *Han History*, composed about 100 CE, many modern histories of China generally presume Kongzi's prescience and godlike perspicacity, no matter whether they are produced in the People's Republic of China, in Taiwan, in Singapore, or in the United States. By such accounts, Kongzi bided his time, knowing that with the first great dynasty he would eventually rise to become "uncrowned king," thanks to increasing patronage by the Han. Almost invariably they devote long pages to the reign of Emperor Wu of Han (r. 141–87 BCE), portraying him as the strong ruler who "canonized" the Five Classics and hailed Kongzi as the protective deity behind the first stable dynasty to rule an area nearly as extensive as that of China today. These histories identify the single greatest achievement of Wudi's reign—if not that of the entire Han—as the creation of a state ideology called "Confucianism" whose chief tenets they seldom bother to define. They say that the young Wudi, restive under the supervision of the dowager empress's circle of senior advisers, made three momentous decisions that were to shape the course of Chinese history forever, constructing it as an "empire of texts" that would be Confucian in all its essentials: in 136 or 135 BCE, Wudi decided to close the ranks of court Academicians to advisers not specializing in the Five Classics, probably because that would block one major avenue for advancement to allies of the domineering dowager. A decade later, in 124 BCE, Wudi decided to establish an Academy in the capital, whose job it was to supervise potential candidates for the civil service in a standard curriculum. At about the same time, Wudi also dramatically expanded the library holdings at court, offering substantial rewards to those who brought archaic and new texts to his attention. These three initiatives, when combined with his selection criteria for scholar-officials, supposedly lent immense cultural capital to the collection, compilation, study, explication, and reproduction of the "Confucian" canonical texts in particular and all writing in general.

Careful scholars bringing no biases to the subject can easily refute all three parts of this myth,[5] using Han sources. A Han proverb talks of "seeing a tail and imagining the whole dog." It means that bits and pieces of information, accurate enough in themselves, are often pieced together by fallible humans to make a picture that is patently false. For example, several of the court Academicians were ritual specialists who, by contemporary reports, could not explicate the authoritative texts at all. In any case, the Five Classics were hardly the preserve of the ethical followers of Kongzi. They functioned as the common cultural coin for all educated people, male and female, regardless of their political leanings and ethical persuasions. And the court Academicians, contrary to the standard narratives that make them an important proto–think tank, could hardly have propelled Han Wudi and his successors to adopt Confucian teachings in policy making. They were so unimportant at court as advisers that they do not appear, collectively or singly, in the key events recorded by the standard histories for nearly a century after Wudi's reign. And while the Academy did test some candidates for the bureaucracy on their ability to retain the clas-

sical tropes needed to lend the court's most brutal acts and extravagant
pageants an aura of high culture, the Academy was never the primary
route to office-holding under Han. Entry to many offices was re-
stricted to the sons and younger brothers of high-ranking officers.
Then, too, while text-learning was a precondition to elite cultivation,
it never sufficed to define cultivation. Too many upstarts, including
palace eunuchs and private slaves, were highly educated at the time,
and eunuchs were among the first to be honored as specialists in exquisite calligraphic forms.

To complicate things further, some of the most prominent figures
in Han went on record condemning what they regarded as an over-
preoccupation with book learning. Late in Eastern Han, for instance,
Xu Gan 許幹 (170–217 CE) wrote, "Those classical scholars who
only practice book learning are not worth looking up to." True men
of worth aspired to be more than mere scribes and scribblers; the
careful professional's preoccupation with details often worked against
that desirable breadth of understanding associated with wisdom and
worth. Moreover, no coherent system of thought that may be labeled
"Confucianism" existed until a *foreign* dynasty, the Mongol Yuan,
enshrined one conservative strain of Song thought called "True Way
Learning" (*Daoxue* 道學) as the single basis for the civil service examinations in 1313, though these same conservatives were already
seeking to control the content of examination questions earlier, in
Southern Song. Equally significant, each item on the usual laundry list
of values now dubbed "Confucian" (filial duty; widow chastity; an
emphasis on family over the individual; a strong work-oriented discipline) predates Kongzi or may be traced to his critics.[6]

Plus the historical records demonstrate that elevation of Kongzi to
Supreme Sage and god was neither as quick nor as automatic as some
post-facto promoters would have it. An oft-repeated tale depicts the
Han founder, in his role as Gaozu, the "High Ancestor," offering the
grand sacrifice or *tailao* to Kongzi in 195 BCE, when he happened to
pass through Queli soon after the empire was pacified under his command. If he did so—and this is not an event inserted into the historical
record until centuries after 195 BCE—it seems unlikely that Gaozu intended by this act to signal a special alignment between his ruling

house and Kongzi, since the standard histories for Han show a throne intent upon establishing its ritual supremacy in the customary way, by supporting and coopting as many local cults as it could reach out to. Quite inexplicable, if we buy the standard line, are two curious facts: (a) no descendant of Kongzi was awarded high rank purely on the basis of his descent from Kongzi until 1 CE; and (b) no sacrifices, so far as we know, were offered to Kongzi outside of Kongzi's hometown for the first two centuries of Western Han rule (206 BCE–8 CE). Only in 1 CE, with the throne in the process of crumbling, did the Western Han line, then under the control of the regent (and later usurper) Wang Mang, enfeoff as marquis a certain Kong Jun, supposedly a direct lineal descendant of Kongzi, on the understanding that he would conduct regular sacrifices to his illustrious ancestor on behalf of the throne.

After the defeat in 23 CE of Wang Mang's short-lived Xin dynasty, the Eastern Han founder was too busy to offer sacrifices in person at Queli, which was more than a thousand miles from his new capital at Luoyang. Instead he sent Song Hong, a high official and relative by marriage, to pay his respects to the Sage. In 29 CE the founder of Eastern Han did give precedence at a court audience to another descendant of Kongzi, one Kong An, though that may well have been simply a gracious gesture to honor a guest who had journeyed such a long distance from the northeast. In 59 CE services were established to the Duke of Zhou and to Kongzi in all the commandery and county seats under Han, and most historians presume that these state sacrifices, once established, were offered regularly until the fall of Han in 220 CE. But only three emperors, the second, third, and fourth to reign over Eastern Han, are known to have personally invoked the aid of Kongzi in support for their dynasty, rather than sending emissaries to Queli to make offerings. We know, too, that in 178 CE, shortly before the end of Eastern Han rule, the portraits of Kongzi and his "seventy-two" disciples of legend were painted on the walls of the Hongdu Palace to serve as models for its eunuchs and serving maids— a dubious honor. When, a few years later, a fire damaged a temple or shrine dedicated to Kongzi (probably at Queli), destroying all the relics of the great man believed to retain some aura of his efficacious presence, including his carriage, robes, and hat, it was taken as an omen that popular support for the "restored" Han ruling house was on the wane.[7]

Such accounts allow us to reconstruct an early time when the figure of Kongzi was periodically invoked by the court, but only as part of a much larger group of worthies and gods, to shore up the legitimacy of Han rule. Kongzi, after all, had articulated principles of governing, and he might be worth propitiating: centuries before Han, the so-called Shanghai corpus of manuscripts (ca. 300 BCE), one of the earliest excavated writings on bamboo now in our possession, summarized Kongzi's political philosophy in the slogan, "Do not go against the people's needs and desires." And yet another pre-Han text, this one compiled during Qin (221–210 BCE), praised Kongzi by drawing an unexpected analogy between his policy proposals and the techniques used by the best charioteers, who know how and when to wield the whip so as to regulate their horses' movements without hurting the horses. Still, the Han government, like any good PR agency today, supplied very different accounts of itself suited to different audiences, so that historians of today cannot always be sure of the principles it operated upon.

But if from the *Analects* and the writings ascribed to Mencius and Xunzi, Kongzi's two most important disciples (see chapter 2), we glean a "Confucian" political program, it would have to include the following measures: (1) a host of redistributive mechanisms by which surplus wealth would be transferred from the very richest to the very poorest, based on the understanding that stable government depends upon the provision of economic and educational opportunities to the populace; (2) a general bias against war, unless all diplomatic methods have failed to remove a dictator from office; (3) a combination of sumptuary regulations and penal laws that identify and reward the most virtuous members of society, but punish with corresponding severity those privileged members of society who engage in self-interested and antisocial conduct; and (4) the general principle that all "others were to be approached as if treating an important guest." (Some clearer indication of Kongzi's attitudes toward gender and class would be welcome, but the extant traditions contradict one another on these matters.)

No part of the foregoing political program was advanced in Western Han or Eastern Han. Indeed, the Han founder was famous for having pissed in the hat of a classical scholar spouting pious injunctions at him, and Han Wudi—the emperor most credited in Chinese history with the exaltation of Kongzi—also went down in history as the ruler whose foreign wars of aggression bankrupted the Han house and turned many locals against the idea of a centralized empire. Nonetheless, Han rulers could readily see the advantages of invoking the name of Kongzi to justify meting out very severe punishments for any misconduct by members of the nobility. Happily, the *Annals* ascribed to Kongzi provided all the rationale the throne needed to charge such nobles with treason, since the *Annals* outlined the gradual usurpation of legitimate power at the royal courts of Zhou and Lu. Imperial patronage sometimes went to the classicists for factional reasons as well. For example, the young Wudi, anxious to retire the senior advisers to his domineering mother, favored the classicists' activist approach over the laissez-faire economic policies associated with a rival classic, the *Laozi Daode jing*. Then, too, Wudi, as an amateur versifier of some talent, surely appreciated the literary effects that could be achieved by those who had mastered the exquisitely formulaic language of the Five Classics. .

If it is wildly anachronistic to see "Confucianism" serving as the primary or only ideology promoting the dignity and legitimacy of the Han ruling house, as conventional accounts would have it, what, then, do the Han records themselves reveal about the place of Kongzi in Han? On what bases were appeals made by the Han throne to its subjects? As the lessons drawn from the Five Classics were so varied and contradictory that they could be cited in support of almost any ethical or political position (in this being like the omen theories of the day, or like the Bible), how did the Han throne actually treat the antique Sage so as to elevate its own position?

KONGZI AS AUTHOR OF THE ANNALS

Good reasons underlie the decision to begin with the story cycles that make Kongzi "uncrowned king": the story about his compilation of the *Annals* seems to drive all the other stories about Kongzi, making possible the lesser-known portraits of Kongzi as seer-prophet and as Black Lord. These portrayals existed not only in Han times; they have come down to the present day, as famously demonstrated in the writings of Kang Youwei (see chapter 7) that focused on Kongzi as an object of religious veneration.[8]

The *Annals*, like all histories of early China, tabooed certain facts and names, thinking them too shameful or awe-inspiring to set down in ordinary writings. But the legend grew up that there were patterns in Kongzi's use of taboos that conveyed his "subtle wording" about events in the future. This legend had the Master—whose political advice was flagrantly ignored in his own lifetime—foresee that the Han dynasty would provide the "right moment" in which he, Kongzi, would receive due appreciation as prophet, patron saint, and guardian of the new dispensation. Liu Bang, the Han founder, had managed to do what no one else in living memory or legend had ever done: rise in the space of a mere three years from the rank of commoner to that of Son of Heaven ruling all of the Central States. By contrast, the legendary sage-kings Shun and Yu had each painstakingly built up a reputation for virtue before being raised to ministerial rank at court; then, as ministers, each was tested for decades before his final elevation to the status of heir to the throne. Shun was married into the royal family, as well. Divine providence must have supported Liu Bang in his spectacular success, for he reunified the empire very quickly after the sudden death of the First Emperor of Qin. It made sense that another man of low rank, Kongzi himself, would have prepared the way for the rapid ascension of the Liu clan, in return for which the Lius would promote his teachings, first by instituting a form of government that relied more on the rites than on punishments, unlike the short-lived Qin dynasty, and second by establishing a cult in honor of the Sage in Kongzi's hometown and in the capital. Two ditties written about Kongzi merged into a single tale. In the first, Kongzi laments his own signal failure to secure patrons:

> *When the Great Way is dormant,*
> *The Rites are the only foundation.*
> *The wise run for cover,*

> Prepared to wait for the right moment.
> Everywhere it is the same,
> So where, oh where, should I go?

In the second, the people of Lu rhapsodize about Kongzi:

> He is dressed in imperial robes
> and bears an emblazoned cap.
> He is our true benefactor.
> He bears an emblazoned cap,
> and is dressed in imperial robes.
> He is kind to us and not selfish.

In one sense Kongzi's appearance in imperial robes with an emblazoned cap—his very elevation to the role of uncrowned king—derives in large part from the belief that Kongzi authored and edited the *Annals*. As Sima Qian writes,

> Kongzi realized that his words went unheeded, nor were his doctrines ever put into practice. So he made a critical assessment of rights and wrongs over a period of 242 years, in order to provide a standard for rules and ceremonies for the ages. He criticized emperors, reprimanded feudal lords, and condemned the high officials so that the business of a true ruler could be known.

Thus what appeared, upon first reading, to be the straightforward chronicle of Lu describing court activities during the reigns of the twelve dukes of Lu was read as a programmatic text, whose subtle language was carefully crafted to instruct worthy rulers in later generations looking to establish just institutions.[9] It was surely not irrelevant that these dukes of Lu claimed descent from the illustrious Duke of Zhou, brother to the Zhou founder and regent for the young King Cheng after the founder's untimely death, for the duke purportedly inaugurated a golden era some five hundred years before the birth of Kongzi, in which peace and cultural unity emanated from a stable ritual center. Judging from the admittedly scanty archaeological record, the first century of Zhou rule was indeed a period of extraordinary cultural efflorescence. But a mere three centuries after the duke, when the *Annals* chronicle begins, the Duke of Zhou's reprehensible descendants in Lu had become unwitting participants in a series of palace intrigues encouraged by royal and ministerial family members with far greater brains, guts, and ambition. Duke Yin (r. 722–712 BCE), the first duke to have his reign chronicled in the *Annals*, was accordingly murdered by his disgruntled brother less than a decade after his accession, and the twelve reigns documented in the *Annals* mirror the appalling decline of the Lu state, whose rulers were too weak to maintain the implicit covenant and customs they had inherited from the Duke of Zhou. In consequence, the *Annals'* seemingly bland retelling of events in Lu conveys a surprisingly compelling vision of order and disorder, detailing the increasing corruption of political life and the reckless squandering of Lu's early potential.

Mencius, ever the faithful advocate of Kongzi (perhaps because he came from Zou, only a few miles from Lu's capital), was apparently the first thinker to argue that his local hero was no ordinary teacher, nor the *Annals* an ordinary work of history. Here is how Mencius put it:

> As the generations declined and the Way became obscure, perverse teachings and violent practices arose. There were even instances of ministers killing their rulers and children killing their fathers. Kongzi was distressed by this, and so he composed the *Annals*. To write such a chronicle is the prerogative of a true king, a Son of Heaven. This is why Kongzi said, "Those who understand me will do so through the *Annals*, and those who condemn me will also do so because of the *Annals*."

In an ideal world, as this passage indicates, chronicles were reportedly commissioned by the Son of Heaven and produced under close state supervision, but since the Zhou Son of Heaven could no longer fulfill his duty as overlord of the realm, Kongzi may have felt he had no alternative but to construct a true history of events, despite his low station in life. Those in agreement with Mencius—Dong Zhongshu in mid-Western Han, for example—emphasized the despair Kongzi experienced as he witnessed events unfolding; also the extraordinary scrupulousness which Kongzi brought to his compilation of the *Annals*. Unable to locate a single ruler willing to put his ideas into practice, Kongzi labored long and hard on the chronicle, "configuring it above so as to accord with Heaven's way and fleshing it out below through examples relating to the human condition." What is often overlooked is that Dong, a master in the *Annals* traditions, significantly shifted the content of the message ascribed to Kongzi: initially the *Annals* was regarded as a political statement alerting contemporary rulers to the dangers of the escalating violence, whereas the *Annals* became in Dong's writings a reflection on cosmic harmony, ensuring that perfect principles of requital weave past to present, Heaven to Earth, and microcosm to macrocosm. Kongzi, according to Dong, "compared it [his ideal world] with [the golden eras in] antiquity, and he examined it in light of current events." For Dong, "The great overarching unity of the *Annals* stems from the never-changing structures of the cosmic order of Heaven-and-Earth and its truly fitting ways of tying past to present." The early critics of Kongzi were not to be silenced, however. In their views, Kongzi had committed an act of treason when he arrogated to himself the honor of writing a definitive account of his state. No loyal subject of Lu or Zhou would have revealed the shortcomings of either the Zhou or Lu courts, they insisted. To offer political judgments on historical and contemporary figures was the height of arrogance—and certainly not the work of a sage!

Mencius in another passage describes the profound impact that Kongzi's decision to compose the *Annals* supposedly had on the major political figures of his day:

> In ancient times, [the sage ruler] Yu the Great controlled the flood-
> waters and the realm was thereby settled. [Some time later,] the
> Duke of Zhou united the border tribes and the Central States,
> driving away the wild beasts, so that the people would be secure.
> And when Kongzi completed the *Annals*, he similarly struck fear
> into the hearts of rebellious ministers and violent sons.

Given the very real dangers inherent in "striking fear" into the hearts of power-holders, we can easily imagine why a low-ranking person like Kongzi might have found it useful or even necessary to register his criticisms obliquely through a careful choice of words, thereby "hiding his ideas" within the patently unremarkable text of the *Annals*. Some argued that Kongzi was motivated by a desire to provide "cover" for his superiors, who had acted in such despicable ways. Or perhaps he had intended all along to write for posterity, because he despaired of effecting significant reforms within his own lifetime. For any of these reasons, Kongzi might have written a text whose agenda was veiled in "subtle wording" (*wei yan*), a text that hinted at present abuses in the process of tendering praise and blame about historical figures and events.

For instance, although the rulers of Wu and Chu to the south of Lu had long styled themselves "kings" (implying absolute equality with their Zhou overlord), the *Annals* quietly called them princes. Elsewhere, the *Annals* employed deliberately euphemistic language in an attempt to simultaneously expose and conceal great wrongdoing: for instance, the *Annals* recorded that "the Great King [the Zhou ruler] went hunting at Heyang" when he had, in fact, most ignominiously scurried to obey the summons of the Duke of Jin, who demanded a meeting in that area. Tradition also reports that Kongzi happily consigned some of the worst historical actors to oblivion, simply expunging their names from the record. Kongzi the historian in composing the *Annals* was obviously "pre-constrained," to borrow the phrase of Lévi-Strauss, to select tropes that would alert readers to the complexity of interpreting events through a series of pithy remarks appended to the dramatic narrative of events, and thereby heighten an awareness of moral complexity. By the judicious apportionment of such "praise and blame," Kongzi hoped to guide later generations, awakening them to the dangers of immorality and the blessings that might accrue from righteous behavior. As one Han source puts it, if deeds and talk match in a particular country, with justice done to each, then surely it is the *Annals* that deserves the credit.

Tradition as transformation, the past as future—this legacy handed

down from Kongzi to the rest of imperial history was reportedly heralded by the occurrence of two solar eclipses in quick succession. These
double signs in the heavens, portending dynastic changeovers, occurred
less than a year before the birth of Kongzi on the *gengzi* day, as
recorded in commentaries appended to the *Annals*.[10] The miraculous
image of "two suns" in the heavens reminds us that Kongzi, the uncrowned king, lived at the same time when the Zhou Son of Heaven
still nominally ruled all the Central States. As it happens, the *gengzi*
day, by a pun, meant both "day of the changeover" and "again to propagate," indicating that a renaissance or rebirth would affect an entire
people.

If extant traditions are any guide to Kongzi's real state of mind
when he inserted his "subtle wording" into the *Annals* (which is
questionable on two counts),[11] the Master was by turns burdened
and uplifted by his strong sense of destiny. "Kongzi was different
from others in his divine clarity, but he was the same as others in
having the Five Emotions [of sorrow, pleasure, worry, anger, and
delight]." Thus Kongzi had to grapple with his own demons whenever he was slighted by others. Still, as readers of the *Analects* will
recall, Kongzi summoned up tremendous courage whenever threatened, because of his belief that Heaven had assigned him a unique
place in its divine plan. "Since the death of King Wen, do not these
cultural patterns of the Central States rest in me? If Heaven had
planned to destroy these patterns, I, who come after King Wen,
would not have had the opportunity to partake of them. Since
Heaven has not seen fit to destroy these patterns, what can any man
do to me?"

This was the accepted backstory to Kongzi's compilation of the
Annals, as recorded in the extant Han traditions. The thinker Wang
Chong (27–97 CE), for example, opined,

> Kongzi wrote the *Annals* when the Zhou had degenerated. Thus
> he looked out for the smallest good while criticizing the small
> flaws. He would cast aside the sources of disorder, as he intended
> to restore upright behavior. The Way of the people and their rulers
> was thereby put in order. And so we know that if the way of the

Zhou had not declined, the ordinary people would not have become so uncultivated; and if the people had not become so uncultivated, the *Annals* would not have been compiled.

Clearly, in Wang's view, authors substantially contributed to contemporary order or disorder whenever they made assertions about the past; authors exerted authority.

These tales about Kongzi's compilation should not be confused with Kongzi's appearance no fewer than forty-six times in the *Zuo Traditions* attached to the *Annals*. In these appearances, Kongzi (551–479 BCE), usually called by the courtesy name of Zhongni, comments upon events dating from the recent past—events that Kongzi might conceivably have heard about from the older generations, or even witnessed himself as a young man. In most instances, however, Kongzi weighs the entire behavior of a specific historical actor, rather than singling out a specific act for praise or condemnation. The result is a series of judgments so complex that no clear moral lesson can possibly be drawn from it. Eric Henry, a classicist at the University of North Carolina, cites one example from the *Zuo* to illustrate this: in the record for 625 BCE, Xiafu Fuji (Xiafu "No-taboos"), then director of ancestral sacrifices in Lu, rearranged the order of the ancestral tablets housed in the temple, so that his father's tablet took precedence over that of a half-brother whose standing was rightfully higher. Kongzi argues that because one of the leaders of the three ministerial clans in Lu, Zang Wenzhong, was Fuji's superior at the time, Zang bore the ultimate responsibility for Xiafu's selfishness. That Zang Wenzhong was a byword for probity in Lu at the time seems not to have deterred Kongzi one bit from criticizing him. Indeed, Zang's very stature in prevailing opinion made it seem all the more pressing for Kongzi to criticize him, we presume. But the terseness of Kongzi's trenchant pronouncements naturally set off a round of controversies over possible readings among all the moralists in his thrall.

In a similar entry, Kongzi reprimands another officer of Lu—Zang Wenzhong's grandson, as it happens—for remonstrating so fiercely with the Duke of Lu that the duke condemned him to exile.

Zhongni [Kongzi] said, "It is hard to be wise. Though Zang Wuzhong was usually wise, he was not allowed to remain in Lu, and there was a good reason for it. His deeds put him at odds with people, and he had hardly been considerate of others. The *Xia Writings* say, 'When you think of something, situate yourself within its context [so that you will empathize with the actors].' This means that a person should be accommodating and moderate."

Had Zang Wuzhong put himself in the place of the duke, Kongzi implies, he would never have called his ruler a coward and "a rat." Kongzi has no patience for those who fail to consider how their criticism will be heard by those in power; an officer, not to mention a ruler, could not afford to ignore the realities of the court's life-or-death powers over the lives of its subjects. Besides, outright protest by loyal servants of the court seldom does any good, and then, too, to deliver such "bitter medicine" is contrary to the dictates of ritual courtesy and compassion. Far better to instruct a wayward ruler by the perfection of one's own upright example than to risk provoking him to even greater heights of folly. Only once in forty-six cases does Kongzi criticize a ruler directly—and that is to observe that the ruler, King Ling of Chu (r. 540–529 BCE), would surely have kept his throne if only he had been able to accept any criticism at all. Kongzi, apparently true to his principles, remains absolutely silent on the subject of the king's notorious cruelty.

Many of Zhongni's assessments prove to be confusing precisely because Kongzi practiced what he preached in the pronouncements ascribed to him: he judged a single act both from the point of view of the actors involved and from the standpoint of the larger consequences of the act. Perhaps the most famous instance of Zhongni's ambiguity occurs in connection with a case in 607 BCE, when Zhao Dun, prime minister of the Jin state, failed to stop his own son from joining with the forces fomenting rebellion. Zhao Dun, who had remonstrated with his lackadaisical ruler until he was blue in the face, had already made plans to go into voluntary exile when he received word that the rebels had assassinated his ruler. Zhao returned to the capital, suppressed the rebellion, executed his own son, and saw to it that the rightful heir was duly installed on the throne. Nevertheless, the Lu court annalist wrote, "Zhao Dun murdered his ruler," putting the onus squarely on Zhao for his involvement in the whole sordid affair. As unofficial historian, Kongzi reportedly then had this to say about the official historian:

> Dong Hu was an upright annalist of olden times. The rule binding him was that he should not conceal anything. Zhao Dun was an upright officer of olden times. For the sake of upholding this model [of historical writing], he in essence acquiesced in his bad reputation. What a pity! He might well have escaped that fate if only he had crossed the border [going into exile, as he originally planned].

In a comparable case, recorded for 528 BCE, the prime minister of Jin, Shu Xiang, denounced his younger brother for bribery. To make it abundantly clear to all Jin subjects that he would always be an impartial judge, Shu Xiang exposed his brother's corpse in the marketplace, making all witnesses to his brother's shame. Zhongni intoned,

> Shu Xiang was one of the few who still exemplified the straightforward honesty attributed to the Ancients. In governing the state and administering the law, he did not conceal the evildoing of his near relation. . . . And in killing his brother, he only added to his glory, but was it really his duty to expose the corpse to further ridicule?

Evidently, Kongzi could not bring himself even in this fairly straightforward case to simply dole out unabashed praise or unreserved blame. Thus, interpretation of the *Annals* becomes a subtle art demanding the greatest insight, since "there is in the *Annals* no principle that can be applied equally to every situation."[12] Always the reader who aims to become a reliable moral arbiter must ask whether the person in the narrative acted wisely so as to achieve the best possible solution. This passionate engagement with the ultimate meaning and limitations of a specific deed or event, entailing consideration of the course of an individual life and its role within social history, is entirely consistent with the Kongzi of the *Analects*, who shies away from pronouncing any single historical figure to be completely humane. Nonetheless, so vividly are incidents treated in the *Annals* and its commentaries that the reader feels keenly, as in real life, the sense of profound dislocation occasioned by the serial disasters that ensue.

The great Han historian Sima Qian believed that in writing the *Annals*, Kongzi "recorded what should be recorded and omitted what should be omitted." The *Annals* in particular set the standard for Sima himself, not to mention all subsequent historians. In assessing the significance of the attribution to Kongzi of the compilation of the *Annals*, it may help to remember that (1) in the pre-printing era, before the tenth century CE, the notion of "authorship" was utterly different than it is today; (2) writing was believed to be the sole recourse left to farsighted men who had been prevented from assuming their rightful place in the administration of the realm; and (3) the logically discrete roles of creation and transmission were consequently blurred from the very beginning, despite Kongzi's famous pronouncement, "I transmit and I do not invent from whole cloth." Ever more writings tended to be ascribed to famous authors over time, so long as those writings were "in the spirit" of the author. In short, fame fed attributions of authorship while attributions fed fame. Still, the writing of history was seen mainly as the preserve of those denied true agency in history, as we learn from Sima Qian in his *Records*. Sima Qian used this rationale when explaining why he finally decided to submit to castration in order to finish the great work of universal history begun by his father:

When King Wen was imprisoned in Youli, he wrote the *Book of Changes*, and when Kongzi was humiliated in Chen and Cai, he composed the *Annals*. . . . The three hundred pieces in the *Odes* were written largely by worthies and sages expressing their frustration. In all such cases, men had ideas that were stifled. They could not manage to communicate their teachings to those of their own generation, and so they narrated past events, while longing for the people of later generations. When a person is hard pressed, how can he avoid writing? . . . I grieve lest there remain in my heart something not fully expressed. I dread it that I might die and my writing not be made known to later ages.

According to Sima Qian, his father repeatedly urged him to write as compensation for worldly failure, thereby strengthening the present and future forces for good and linking the self, at least in the imagination, to earlier halcyon days. Doubtless the old records offered valuable insights into how to effect a convergence of the practical and the moral in governing. Sima Tan also noted,

> The capture of the unicorn [Kongzi's death] had already been more than four hundred years ago. [Mencius insisted that a new sage would appear every five hundred years.] . . . Today the Han has arisen and the whole realm has been united. . . . The loss of the realm's archives is deeply to be feared. . . . Our sole aim must be to create ties with the enlightened generations of old.

One difficulty, of course, confronting historians intent upon forging such ties was that of distinguishing the true teachings of the Ancients from the flood of false teachings that proliferated in the name of "preserving the past." All sorts of wild stories circulated about the legendary figures of the past in which outlandish activities and statements were attributed to them, either mockingly or in misguided attempts to provide a usable precedent in policy making. How to separate the false from the true? That is no small problem today when there are much better tools to verify what really happened. Oral histories and purported eyewitness accounts constituted the chief sources available to Han historians, despite wide consensus among the learned that these sources were patently unreliable. Thinking subjects of Han were generally apt to conceive writing about the past in much the same spirit as Thucydides: the good historian is to put into the mouths of his chief actors the speeches that they would have made, had they been as articulate as the historian. History was true so long as it conveyed the full range of options available to the actors in a given situation, the leaders' motives when determining their courses of action, and the fates of their many subordinates. Thus Zisi, the grandson of Kongzi, offered the standard defense against critics who charged that his writings were filled with sayings falsely attributed to his illustrious forebear:

> Zisi replied, "Among my grandfather's sayings, which are recorded in my writings titled the *Constant Mean* [*Zhongyong*], there are some that I have personally heard and some that others brought to my attention. So even though my text consists of words that are not precisely the same as those of the Master, it does not fall short of the Master's ideas.[13]

Would-be moralists and historians alike garnered evidence from as many sources as possible, including the story that Kongzi consulted with the Old Master Laozi, who was then purportedly the head keeper of the Zhou archives. By gathering and sifting through all the available insights, one could hope to fashion a true history that, like Kongzi's *Annals*, had applications far beyond a single time and place.

History is neither a transparent record of events nor a patchwork of snatches of tales and scraps of evidence. Histories are consciously worked creations into which are poured hopes and dreams. Some have seen history as a dialogue between remembering and forgetting. Others have remarked upon the human propensity to insist that a larger meaning be retrieved or constructed via history, as humans fight the sense of incoherence and futility engendered by unfolding events that seem just like one damn thing after another. Then, too, when capturing a mood, a feeling, or an insight and inscribing it onto the past, the historian becomes by turns a jeweler and a conjurer. Perhaps this explains why the Kongzi of legend sought to become the foremost historian of the Central States civilization.

We, who live in an age filled with books and overloaded with information, tend to forget how stunningly alive the written word must have been in an age when few compositions were set down on expensive silk scrolls or bamboo bundles. Some idea of writing's power may be gleaned from the preface to a Han work, which makes the following extravagant claims for writings of all types:

> Now those who would assess the importance of writings say that they are the means by which to order the main lines of the Way and Virtue, and establish the warp and woof of human affairs. Above, they are examined in light of Heaven, and below, they are measured by Earth. With humans in the middle, it is their writings that comprehend all principles. Even when they cannot quite draw out the inherent qualities of the Mystery, in their complexity they certainly suffice to contemplate everything, from beginning to end. They gather in the essentials; they raise the general outlines. And if the lines fail either to crack open the pure primeval unity or to dispense [the sublime wisdom of] the Great Progenitor, then human muddle remains . . . and there is no way to roam or abide in change and transformation. . . .
>
> In general, to compose a text is the means to glimpse the Way and to open barriers for succeeding generations. . . . It allows the person to have contact with things without being bedazzled or befuddled. It facilitates a person's settling of his inner spirits and nourishing of *qi*, so that . . . the person learns to take real pleasure in his endowment from Heaven-and-Earth.

Under Han, then, Kongzi's *Annals*, as a work of the Supreme Sage, became the main classic to be used when interpreting laws, imagining better worlds, and ascertaining the relation between the powers of the microcosm and macrocosm. Yes, the *Annals* justified the severe punishments meted out to high-ranking traitors. But students of the *Annals* did not act only as unthinking agents for the throne's ambitions. Reportedly, a scholar of the *Annals*, one Kong Xi (a direct descendant of Kongzi, as it happens), was the principal architect of the devastating critique launched against Han Wudi's expansionist policies in Central Asia.

KONGZI, SEER AND PROPHET

Men of learning read into the *Annals* this extraordinary insight into things seen and unseen that made Kongzi the favorite protagonist in anecdotes where an expert was needed to expose the falsity of popular accounts. One tale recounts an encounter between the Duke of Lu and Kongzi in which the duke asked Kongzi to explain why Master Kui, a legendary court musician, had only one foot. (Cutting off a foot was one of the five mutilating punishments in early China, and dismembered and disfigured people, being "inauspicious," were seldom hired at court.) Kongzi explained that the duke had simply misunderstood the phrase *yizu*, which could mean "one foot" but also "one was enough." One excellent musician was "enough" to foster an age of reform dominated by music and rites.

Other Han stories had Kongzi, as amateur historian, consulting old texts. From these he learned the ancient etymologies of many old characters in use long before his time. The earliest extant word list of archaic graphs in China, the *Shuo wen* compiled by Xu Shen about 100 CE, includes twelve analyses of graphs, two based on *Analects* passages and ten on apocryphal sources. Below are three typical examples. Note the popularity of punning glosses in Han times, visual and verbal, which are thought to exhibit the tight correspondences threading through all phenomenal existence:

Mu 木 , "tree," means *mao* 冒, "to issue forth." A tree issues forth from the ground when it grows. It is the cosmic phase corresponding to East. The graph has "vegetation" as its signifier, and the lower part [of the graph] represents the roots.

Shi 士, "man of service," means *shi* 事, "to serve." In counting one begins with 一 ("one") and ends with 十 ("ten," pronounced *shi* also). Kongzi said, "One who can add ten and one is the man of service" [the bureaucrat].

kong 孔 [NB: Kongzi's family name signifies "parturition" and "great"]: It is graphically derived from *fu* 孚 (to brood eggs) and *ya*, the name of the dark bird . . . that comes with the spring equinox and departs with the autumn equinox. It is a migratory bird that causes birth. [NB: All sage-rulers supposedly were born via an immaculate conception following a "mysterious" ("dark") encounter between a virgin and an unidentified "spirit lord" who descended to earth in the form of a bird.]

The early writing system was composed of many parts, each of which was thought to be a true reflection of one or more cosmic patterns. Therefore, every topic now pertaining to the modern disciplines of linguistics, metaphysics, and philosophy was seen as the study of the natural patterns that ideally served as the basis of society. To be able to "read" the graphs by deciphering their etymologies was to discern, then, by a powerful combination of discipline, learning, and intuition, the underlying order that determined the origin, essence, and end of humanity.

Tales that may strike modern readers as downright bizarre or pointless held deep significance for people in Han as they seemed to prove beyond a reasonable doubt that Kongzi had divine powers of special insight into the relationship between past and present events, an insight that informed his writing of the *Annals*. Kongzi had some sort of "celestial light, shining inward," that could "purge or disperse" all obscuring mist, so that he might see and tell "of things invisible to mortal sight." For example, when a fire struck a temple in the Zhou capital, Kongzi immediately divined that it was the ancestral temple erected to King Li that had burned down. When the Duke of Qi asked him how he could be so sure of this, before a detailed report was even received, Kongzi replied that he knew it because King Li (whose posthumous name means "disaster") was so extravagant. By this logic, Heaven refused to strike down King Li directly, lest the king's demise threaten the regular offering of sacrifices due his distant ancestors, Kings Wen and Wu, two paragons of virtue. "Therefore, Heaven destroyed King Li's temple to make his fault clear." After another sign, Kongzi predicted that a ministerial clan would perish "within three years." When it did, a disciple asked Kongzi how he could predict what would happen. He replied,

The *suo* in the family name means to "exhaust." A filial son will exhaust his possessions, if need be, to conduct sacrifices to his ancestors. But the head of this clan begrudged the animals for sacrifice, so the clan's other losses were bound to multiply.

According to his biography in Sima Qian's *Records*, Kongzi had the power not only to read men and their failings, but also to interpret other anomalies:

When Kongzi was forty-two years [in 510? BCE], Duke Zhao of Lu died in Ganhou [his place of exile], and Duke Ding ascended the throne. In the fifth year of Duke Ding, in the summer, Ji Pingzi [head of one of the three ministerial clans who virtually ruled Lu and the key figure in the ousting of Duke Zhao] died and Ji Huanzi took his place as head of the family. When Huanzi happened to have a well dug, the diggers found an earthen container with a sheeplike creature inside. When Huanzi asked Zhongni about it, he described the creature as some kind of dog. Zhongni replied, "From what I have heard, it's a sheep. They say that the spirits of stone and wood are called *kui* and *wangliang*; those of water are the dragon and the *wangxiang*; and the spirit of earth is a hermaphroditic sheep."

This prodigy Kongzi then related to a preceding outrage in which the rightful Duke of Lu was exiled while the disloyal minister who had ousted him died peacefully in his bed in Lu. As the roles of superior and inferior had become confounded with the duke and his minister, an animal that was neither male nor female was an apt omen for the situation.

Still another time, an enormous bone was found—part of a woolly mammoth, we may presume, or perhaps a rhinoceros. In any case, the bone filled an entire cart. The discussion naturally turned to giants, and Kongzi was able to recite a history that had a race of giants peopling the Central States in earlier times. At a later date, when hawks that had gathered in the court of the small state of Chen suddenly died, the breast of one of them was found to have been pierced by an arrow with a flint arrowhead of a certain length and style. Thinking this an augury, Duke Min of Chen (r. 501–478 BCE) sent an envoy to ask Kongzi for his interpretation of it. The Supreme Sage was able to divine that the hawks had flown a great distance, from the Shushen people far to the south, who once, long ago, had been powerful allies of the Zhou founders. Since the *Analects* says quite plainly that Kongzi never discussed weird prodigies, feats of strength, instances of disorder, or the spirits, readers may wonder how, when, and why traditions arose concerning Kongzi as the infallible "seer" into other worlds. What was the source of the story that Kongzi was born with a five-character legend inscribed on his chest proclaiming his destiny as a seer and paragon of erudition? Perhaps the tale derives from his preoccupation with the distant past, enabling him to read strange objects and events, as well as archaic graphs, with an ease born of long familiarity.

KONGZI SCION OF THE BLACK GOD OR DARK LORD

Nearly all the Han legends contributed to the sense that Kongzi was a creature set apart from birth, a man of extraordinary insight who could see into both past and future, unlike common men, who are incapable of seeing what is before their eyes. If, as the Han proverb put it, "gods perceive future events, mere mortals contemporary ones, and the wise sense those events about to happen," Kongzi's role as an astral deity, a Black God in command of miraculous powers, was but a short step from his unblemished record as seer and prophet. China, unlike the Mediterranean world, never devised a hard-and-fast dividing line between divine and human. A person who fulfills his or her potential is a virtual god. Kongzi, as one of those exemplary persons with a profound love of learning and mature human kindness, was considered a god by many in Han and later times.

In legend and myth, the sage rulers of antiquity were all said to have been born of a mysterious connection between young virgins "aroused" and "moved" (*gan* 感) by sky gods who descended to earth in various disguises, most typically that of a dark swallow. Likewise, Kongzi had been conceived "in the wilds" after his mother successfully petitioned the local gods of Hillock Mount to permit her to bear a son. To his contemporaries, Kongzi's paternity evidently was unknown or in dispute. After all, his father, the aged warrior-turned-prefect, died when Kongzi was still an infant, without ever installing Kongzi's mother in his official town residence. So apocryphal tales had Kongzi's mother meeting a Black Lord in a dream-journey to the stars, and this lord impregnated her after bathing her in "fragrant dew," the boon of the gods. The Black Lord said only that he "longed to give birth to a sage." So Kongzi, recalling the Christ child, was at once the son and incarnation of his astral Father.

At least two miracles, those double eclipses, were said to have heralded the birth of Kongzi at the vernal equinox, the time of a fine balance of forces and a harbinger of lush growth. The same mysterious dark birds—ravens or swallows—that figured as totems for the Shang and Zhou overlords of the Central States announced Kongzi's birth. Born in the hollow of a tree, Kongzi was likened to the mulberry itself, whose unisexual seeds are pollinated by the wind so that it sprouts as a result of a curious sympathy between earth and air, a self-generating propensity that obviates the need for the ordinary mechanisms required for reproduction. The hollow mulberry, according to apocrypha, was also "the place whence the sun issues and where the constellation Fang is located. And when the light from it is at its height, the god—the patron spirit of Zhou—will be in force as well . . . so that its essence will cover the sun." Note the references to the sun, symbol of the emperor, and to the light of Kongzi issuing from it, invigorating and yet superseding ["covering"] the Zhou ruling house. Kongzi's birth was said to be miraculously painless, as it invariably is with saviors, and from the first it was obvious to the observant that the boy was precocious. And then there was Kongzi's extraordinary height of some eight feet, not to mention the extraordinary protuberance like an inverted crest of a hillock on his forehead. All this marked him as a spirit. (From this protuberance Kongzi took his style name, Zhongni, which means Middle-Son Hillock, and his personal name, Qiu, which means Mound.)[14]

> He was ten feet tall [in Chinese measurement, or about eight Western feet], with a hillock head, a square face, a nose like the sun, and ears like a river, the forehead of a dragon, and lips shaped like

the Dipper . . . a water sprite's body, a tortoise spine, tiger's paws, and long forearms. . . . His eyebrows and the space between them had twelve colors; his eyes had sixty-four veins. . . . His chest looked like a carpenter's square . . . and there were designs on his palm. The inscription on his chest said, "He will create the evolutions of the Mandate as set forth by celestial tallies that are to fix the future ages."

One contemporary of Kongzi supposedly compared him to the mythical sage-kings:

To me Kong Zhongni seems to have all the outward manifestations of a sage. The flowing shape of his eyes and the rise of the forehead make him look like the Yellow Emperor, the divine ancestor of all the Chinese people. His long arms and arched back, along with his height, make him as tall as Tang, the founder of the Shang dynasty. Yet his speech is deferential and his personal demeanor is extremely tolerant. He is a man of broad learning and good memory, and his knowledge of things in general seems inexhaustible. Don't these characteristics together mean that we are witnessing the advent of a sage?

Understandably, his mother tried to stifle or hide such a bizarre creature at birth, but to no avail. Animals tended him until he could survive on his own. "Sages," as one apocryphal text intones, "are not born in vain. Kongzi served as a warning bell who would fashion the laws of the empire." In any case, when Kongzi's mother died, did he not bury her at the Crossroads of the Five Fathers, a sure sign that he was conscious of his divine ancestry (since the gods were worshipped at crossroads), that he would have difficulty establishing his paternity, and that somehow he belonged to all earthly people who followed him on his Way or path?

Obviously, all the forces of nature, terrestrial, celestial, and temporal, were conjoined in this one physical body. This Kongzi would prove when facing a series of trials at least as impossible as those of Hercules. Unlike Hercules, however, Kongzi's destiny would be to bring a code of morality to men, not to overpower them through sheer physical strength. By such tales, Kongzi's divine origin and special destiny ensured the continuance, and eventually the prosperity, of his earthly line after the Kong family line had almost died out during his lifetime. Readers will recall that Bo Yu, Kongzi's only son and heir, died long before him, along with Kongzi's most beloved disciple, Yan Hui. Kongzi seems not to have rated Bo Yu highly, and indeed, by all accounts, he was a man for whom the word "slacker" seems to have been invented. All the more reason that Kongzi would bemoan the untimely loss of his associates Yan Hui and Ran Geng. Lacking true biological and spiritual heirs at his death, Kongzi left behind only disciples of lesser worth to elevate him to a cult status. Although these disciples failed to comprehend the full depth, tenor, and import of Kongzi's message, they tried in their way to be faithful to his memory, as we know from Sima Qian's account in the "Hereditary House of Kongzi":

> Kongzi was buried by the River Si, north of the capital in Lu, and his disciples mourned for him for three years. When those three years of heartfelt mourning ended, they bade each other farewell. But then they wept loudly again, and each returned to completely express his grief, and some lingered by the grave. Among them only Zigong built a hut beside the grave mound where he remained for three more years. But because more than a hundred of Kongzi's disciples and other men of Lu settled near the grave, the district was named Kong Village. And so in Lu there persisted, generation after generation, the custom of offering an annual sacrifice at the grave mound of Kongzi.

As is the way in legends, the number of disciples who purportedly participated in the solemn rites of mourning miraculously multiplied over time, so that by late Eastern Han the Master was said to have had some eight thousand loyal disciples, not the little band of six or eight who attend Kongzi in the *Analects*. Especially significant, no genuinely early account tells of grieving relatives at the dying Master's bedside, nor are there depictions of the Kong family mourners gathered at his grave. Only a single grandchild, Zisi, may have survived Kongzi, and through this young boy, apparently, the line of Master Kong passed down. Evidently the legacy of Kongzi was in every sense too large to be confined to the Kong direct line of descent, though Zisi is the putative author of one influential digest of Kongzi's teachings, the *Constant Mean* (see chapter 4), which together with the *Great Learning* came to be read as faithful transcriptions of the Master's mature teachings. A Han story provides an insight into the nature of the family business the members of the Kong family were in by Qin and Han times. One Kong Ziyu, head of the Kong family at the time of the death of the First Emperor of Qin, served as ritual adviser to the rebel Chen She, whose uprising hastened the downfall of the Qin.[15] When Chen She died before defeating Qin, Kong Ziyu "passed on everything he knew" to one Shusun Tong, in recognition of that man's fine "grasp of the nature of change and expediency." Shusun Tong had willingly served two masters— Qin and Han—and Shusun Tong, not a member of the Kong family, undertook to adapt the old Qin state rituals for the court of the Han founder. Knowing that the upstart Gaozu feared that he could not master the elaborate rituals of antiquity, Shusun Tong devised a set of pseudo-antique rituals that proved to be easy enough for a country bumpkin.

Such stories hardly prevented people who claimed membership in the Kong family patriline from seizing their chance for fortune and fame. The Kong family narrative highlighted their flesh-and-blood ties as the sole key to a magical patrimony of wisdom inherited from the Sage. All the messiness of the Kong family history would then be obscured, as the historian Lionel Jensen has noted, by "the presumptive continuity of sacrifice to Kongzi at the clan temple," thus emphasizing the eternal character of the "natural" moral supremacy of the Kong family line over others. Thus began the lucrative "Kong family business," in which the Kongs positioned themselves as *the* experts in one branch of classical learning (curiously, not the *Annals*, but the Archaic Script version of the *Documents*). Kong Anguo was the most famous of these classical scholars in Western Han, and Kong Rong in late Eastern Han.[16]

This is such patent nonsense (hagiography as genealogy, in Chinese fashion) that we might well consider how the Kongs, relentless self-promoters to a man, managed to survive the downfall of the Han rulers whose patronage they had enjoyed. The Kong family was able to distance itself from the debacle in large part because the wily Kongs had long seen that it would be in their interest to emphasize ties with the legendary rulers of antiquity. Hence the apocryphal stories showing Kongzi as spiritual heir to the ancient sage-kings. No sooner had Eastern Han fallen in 220 CE than the founder of the short-lived Wei dynasty (220–266 CE) reinstituted sacrifices to Kongzi in repaired temples in its local administrative seats. Each temple contained an image of the Master within its precincts, and the adjacent temple schools taught morality in addition to reading, writing, and arithmetic. Meanwhile the Kong family was busy keeping their famous ancestor's flame alive via pronouncements on the importance of maintaining ancestral sacrifice, as the following late passage ascribed to Zisi shows:

> Zisi, grandson of Kongzi, asked the Master about a person who refused to carry out mourning for a distantly related clansman. "This is a denial of one's debt to the ancestral bounty," Kongzi answered. "The honorable heritage of a given clan cannot be extinguished if its various members keep their clan roots intact. . . . Even someone as exalted as a ruler must not renounce his blood relations, but rather treat them with reverence and affection. Clan members should associate with each other at feasts, their places defined and distinctions made among them by their order of descent. . . . This is the definition of true faithfulness. The hallmark of culture and refinement is said to be 'to treat relatives with proper deference.'"

Any lowering in the caliber of the Kong family members, any decline in the strength of their vocation, could be offset by the impressive length of the Kong family genealogy. But the portrait of Kongzi-as-ancestor perpetuated by succeeding generations of Kongs is a story taken up in later chapters of this book.

WAS KONGZI A KING, a historian, a prophet and seer, *and* also a deity? Rather than conclude, as one modern scholar has done, that the name Confucius was "a free-floating signifier" for all the hopes, desires, and impulses of the Chinese throughout imperial times, this chapter suggests that by Han times, Kongzi had become the legendary historian, king, diviner, and deity, because each of these roles led seamlessly into the next. In other words, the roles accorded Kongzi during the Han reflect the single underlying drive to see Kongzi enthroned among the gods. The praise and blame registered in the "subtle wording" of the *Annals* chronicle delivered morality veiled as history and highly crafted to maximize its lasting impact. No wonder that students of the *Annals* were apt to conflate Kongzi the historian with Kongzi the divine sage and seer who had predicted and then endorsed the rise of the first stable empire in China, that of the Han. The Han claims of Kongzi as virtual "ancestor" were part and parcel of its many initiatives to secure dynastic legitimacy and impose its rule on newly conquered regions by any means available. Why not enhance these claims by alluding to the divine origins and infallibility of Kongzi? For the more divine Kongzi became, the greater the authority of his teachings, especially as regards history and law; the more miraculous his foresight, the more magnificent his choice of the Han emperors as his legitimate successors.

Fame in early China, as now, was constructed by interested parties hoping to gain both tangible and psychic benefits. Kongzi's growing fame reflected well on the ruling house of Han as long as the Kong family classical scholars never sought to challenge its authority. Kongzi's transfiguration and apotheosis, his journey from failed itinerant adviser to protector-deity, was accomplished within the four centuries of Western and Eastern Han. If Kongzi was a historian/seer who not only predicted the rise of Han but also provided it with a sound plan to secure its mandate, Kongzi, the local hero, became the spiritual ancestor for all the Central States, the virtual "uncrowned king" of all visionaries in service to the ritual order. We may sense Kongzi's exalted spirit from an anecdote repeated often in Han times:

> Once, when Zigong was having an audience with prime minister Pi, the latter asked him what Kongzi was like. Zigong replied that

he was not capable of answering that. The prime minister shot back, "Why serve him, if you don't know the answer to that simple question?" Zigong replied, "It is precisely because I don't know the answer that I serve him. That man is like a great stretch of mountain and forest, in that people take from him all that they require." "Don't you add to his capacities through your service?" Zigong replied, "That man's capacities cannot be added to. I am like a heap of earth. If a person tried to use a heap of earth to add to the mountain, the height of the mountain would remain the same, and the attempt condemned as folly." "Well," asked Pi, "do you gain anything at all by your association with him?" "Suppose there was a great tankard of wine in the realm, and you were the only one who didn't drink from it. Whose fault would that be?"

Kongzi was best compared, therefore, to a delicious wine which all could quaff. Zigong added, "I only know that when it comes to quenching my thirst, Kongzi can be compared with the rivers and seas." In this passage, how ardent the admiration and how different its portrait of Kongzi from the dry-as-dust pedant we have grown accustomed to!

Lu Xun and other May Fourth writers (see chapter 7) tended to ascribe all the lapses of Chinese imperial history to a "distorted morality" foisted on unwitting souls by "professional Confucians" during Han and post-Han:

> The fact is that after the Han Dynasty most public opinion was in the hands of professional Confucians. . . . There was hardly a single book not written by these orthodox scholars; they were the only ones to express opinions. . . . To do anything unorthodox was taboo . . . and that is why there has been no change up till now.

Han sources tell a different story, however, one in which professional classicists and Confucian moralists alike worked, for different motives, to ensure that Kongzi exemplified that marvelously protean propensity to transform the self and others that for the Chinese has defined the gods. Once ignored, disparaged, and derided, Kongzi was well on his way to securing himself a place of honor in the pantheon of cultural memory.

SUGGESTED READINGS

Eric Henry, "The Motif of Recognition in Early China," *Harvard Journal of Asiatic Studies* 47, no. 1 (June 1987): 5–30.

Françoise Bottéro, "Revisiting the *Wen* and the *Zi*: The Great Chinese Characters Hoax," *Bulletin of the Museum of Far Eastern Antiquities* 74 (2002): 14–33.

Benjamin A. Elman, *A Cultural History of Civil Examinations in Late Imperial China* (Berkeley: University of California Press, 2000).

For filial duty predating Kongzi, see Michael Nylan, "Individualism and Filial Piety in Han China," *Journal of the American Oriental Society* 116 (January–March 1996): 1–27; Anne Cheng, "Filial Piety with a Vengeance: The Tension between Rites and Law in the Han," in *Filial Piety in Chinese Thought and History*, edited by Alan K. L. Chan and Sor-hoon Tan (London: Routledge Curzon, 2004), 29–43.

On omen interpretation, see Hans Bielenstein, "An Interpretation of the Portents in the Ts'ien Han-shu," *Bulletin of the Museum of Far Eastern Antiquities* 22 (1950): 127–43; and Martin Kern, "Religious Anxiety and Political Interest in Western Han Omen Interpretation: The Case of the Han Wudi Period," *Chūgoku Shigaku zasshi* 10 (2000): 1–31.

Lionel Jensen, "The Genesis of Kongzi in Ancient Narrative," in *On Sacred Grounds: Culture, Society, Politics, and the Formation of the Cult of Confucius*, edited by Thomas A. Wilson (Cambridge: Harvard University Asia Center, 2002) and *Manufacturing Confucianism* (Durham: Duke University Press, 1997); but see also Nicolas Standaert, "The Jesuits Did Not Manufacture 'Confucianism,'" *East Asian Science, Technology, and Medicine* 16 (1999): 115–32.

Julia Murray, "The Hangzhou Portraits of Confucius and Seventy-two Disciples: Art in the Service of Politics," *Art Bulletin* 74, no. 1 (March 1992): 7–18; "The Temple of Confucius and Pictorial Biographies of the Sage," *Journal of Asian Studies* 5, no. 2 (May 1996): 269–300; "Varied View of the Sage: Illustrated Narratives of the Life of Confucius," in *On Sacred Grounds*, edited by Wilson, pp. 222–64.

4

The Canonical Confucius from Han through Song

CONFUCIUS MOURNED THE LOST WAY. IN ANCIENT TIMES IT was practiced by sages who ruled the world. No ordinary men, the sages wielded cosmic powers. They possessed profound insight into the mysteries of the cosmos and were the catalyst that enabled everyone to realize the full potential of their inborn capacity for goodness. The sages promulgated the rites, which perfectly accorded with the patterns coursing through all things, so that reverent lords could honor the gods and filial sons could render feast to their ancestors. The sages were once hailed as true kings. Exalted above other men, the sage-kings imperceptibly aided in the cosmic transformation of all creatures and reigned over the world as equal to Heaven and Earth: expansive and bountiful, they sustained life; lofty and brilliant, they embraced all things.

Not everyone possessed the same capacity to perfect what Heaven gave him. Yet the potential to realize this latent quality lay within each person's grasp. Unlike the sage, who effortlessly manifested the Way in his every deed, most people had to labor tenaciously to hold on to the good without ever relaxing their grasp, lest they fall into errant ways. As men gradually lost hold of goodness, the ancient Way declined. Men no longer recognized the sage and failed to call him king. So Confucius grieved for the Way. He worked tirelessly to awaken the world to this immeasurable loss and to show men the right path toward goodness. His message was simple, yet his teachings proved remarkably difficult to put into practice.

To instruct the lords of his day how to restore the Way, the Master outlined a cultivation program, which is recorded in a text called the

Constant Mean (*Zhongyong* 中庸), sometimes translated as the *Doctrine of the Mean*. Ostensibly addressed to a prince in advanced stages of his education before assuming the throne, the *Constant Mean* envisions a mode of governing that requires far more than maintaining social order or collecting taxes. The Prince, according to this work, must aspire to the attainments of the ancient sage-kings who wielded the very cosmos to create perfect government and to bring harmony to all who lived under Heaven. The Prince must follow his Heaven-endowed nature, Confucius taught, and reach deeply within himself to find a state of inner equilibrium unaffected by the emotions. When he "honors the moral nature and follows the path of inquiry and learning," the *Constant Mean* proclaims, "the Prince realizes the Way's greatness and fulfills its refined, hidden essence." When he masters inner equilibrium and harmonizes his actions with all that is correct, then "Heaven and Earth assume their proper places and all living creatures flourish." By following this path of cultivation, the Prince governs in concert with Heaven and Earth and rules with the Mandate of Heaven.

The moral order of the cosmos envisioned in the *Constant Mean* revolves around the central concept of *cheng*. Sometimes translated as "Sincerity," *cheng* 誠 is perhaps more aptly understood as "Integrity," which, like the Chinese word, conveys both a state of being complete, undivided, or whole and also uncompromising adherence to the good. According to the *Constant Mean*, the Sage possesses Integrity in its most sublime form—"Integrity itself" (*chengzhe* 誠者)—and fully realizes his innate potential for goodness without relying on any external sources. When he unleashes the moral power of his Integrity, the Sage acts as an agent of Heaven's Way by "uniting his internal self with external things" and enabling all people to fulfill their Heaven-endowed nature. Only the Sage is born with his Integrity already fully formed, whereas everyone else must follow man's Way and work tirelessly to attain it (*cheng zhizhe* 誠之者) through learning.

Though it bears unmistakable markings of an age centuries after Confucius died, the *Constant Mean* was commonly accepted in imperial times as an authentic record of Confucius's teachings as recorded by his grandson.[1] During the Han dynasty (206 BCE–220 CE) it was incorporated in a compilation of ritual texts called the *Record of Rites*, one of the Five Classics. Not until the Song dynasty (960–1279 CE), however, did it occupy a central status in the Confucian canon called the Four Books, along with the *Great Learning* (also from the *Rites*), the *Analects*, and *Mencius*. From the Song through the Qing (1644–1911 CE) dynasties, Confucians regarded these works as the purest expression of the Dao transmitted by the ancient sages. While they never displaced the Five Classics, the Four Books constituted the core of the civil examination curriculum as early as the fifteenth century (see chapter 5). Putting aside considerations of what modern philologists might regard as the historically verifiable words of Confucius, this chapter attempts to reconstruct the voice of another figure, that of the *Canonical* Confucius. The authoritative words of the Canonical Confucius were piously recorded in such works as the *Constant Mean* and painstakingly interpreted in commentaries by Zheng Xuan 鄭玄 (127–200 CE) and Zhu Xi 朱熹 (1130–1200). Confucius's words found in critical editions of the *Constant Mean* circulated in government schools and private academies in the Ming and Qing dynasties and thus loomed large in the imaginings of the Sage among all classically educated men for the last six hundred years of imperial Chinese history.

THE CONSTANT MEAN *AND ITS COMMENTARIES*

The text of the *Constant Mean* comes to us today replete with layers of textual commentaries. Inscribed between lines of the classical text, commentaries were literally an integral part of the Classics themselves. Students and scholars as well as modern translators all used them to understand the Classics. Commentators themselves learned from earlier commentaries, often quoting their predecessors at length in their own remarks. And yet, while they clarify the meaning of the canon, commentaries also constitute normative interpretations of classical texts as understood by the commentators who wrote them. A commentary is thus both a necessary tool for understanding the Classics and a prism through which we today can discern how scholars of a given period in imperial times interpreted a classical work. A comparison of different commentaries on a particular classical work opens onto a conceptual horizon of possible interpretations of that work and of the scriptural tradition within which it was interpreted.

This chapter approaches the *Constant Mean* through two of its most important commentaries. Written a thousand years apart—one in the second century and the other in the twelfth—these commentaries illustrate how the ideas that scholars bring to a text change over time and in turn produce distinctive insights. Though their interpretations of the *Constant Mean* are not everywhere at odds with one another, these two commentaries nonetheless demonstrate that a canonical text's meaning is neither singular nor static. Approaching the *Constant Mean* through its commentaries illuminates how a canonical work can acquire new meaning and authorize different and, at times, conflicting interpretations, depending upon the changing historical contexts in which it is read. The ability of a classical work to accommodate a range of distinctive readings is perhaps the most important quality determining the longevity of any scriptural tradition.

A prolific classical scholar in the Eastern Han dynasty (25–220 CE), Zheng Xuan, wrote one of the most influential commentaries on the *Constant Mean* as part of his larger corpus of commentaries on the Five Classics. Centuries later, the Tang court (618–907 CE) used Zheng Xuan's version as the basis of its imperial edition, which was distributed to government schools where students trained for civil-service examinations; Zheng's commentaries were engraved onto stone and placed outside the gate of the Directorate of Education in the capital as testament to their authority. When it moved the capital to Lin'an (present-day Hangzhou) in the twelfth century, the Song court did the same. Parts of Zheng's edition survived into the eighteenth century, when court scholars reconstructed it to compile a new edition of the Thirteen Classics that remains the standard to this day.[2]

The China of Zheng Xuan's day was a once great empire on the verge of collapse. Built upon a political foundation brutally forged by the short-lived Qin empire (221–209 BCE), the Han dynasty ruled in part through an emerging court-appointed civil bureaucracy, which replaced the ancient nobility that had previously governed feudal states by hereditary privilege. Individual merit became increasingly important in court appointments during the Han, which curtailed the ancient nobility's influence at court, even while a consortium of newly empowered families came to exert great influence. The founding emperor of the Han came to power enormously indebted to his kinsmen and generals, to whom he granted extensive domains. A practical outcome of dynastic conquest, their domains inevitably became locations of resistance to imperial authority. After a half century of the central court's strategic expansion of civil administration, these domains, including those under imperial princes, were virtually eliminated. Also, the Han empire was composed of diverse regions populated by peoples of different ethnic backgrounds who spoke a dizzying array of local dialects and regional languages only tenuously united under a writing system used in official documents. The Han emperors were urged by their court advisers to embody universal rule over this enormously diverse empire by emulating the ancient sage-kings exalted in classical texts such as the *Constant Mean.*

A thousand years after Zheng Xuan, Zhu Xi composed a set of commentaries on the emerging canon called the Four Books. Zhu Xi traced his own doctrinal lineage to the great masters of the Northern Song (960–1127 CE), who, he claimed, apprehended Confucius's Dao, which, as contained in the *Constant Mean,* had been "lost for nearly 1,400 years." In doing so, Zhu Xi bypassed the commentarial traditions from the Han through the Tang dynasties, which, he maintained, failed to transmit the ancient Dao. The *Constant Mean*'s metaphysical exploration of human nature and self-cultivation led Zhu Xi to regard it as the most esoteric work of the Confucian canon. Fearing his students might not correctly understand this work's profound meaning, Zhu Xi advised them to study it only after mastering the other texts in the Four Books. Although he relied heavily on Zheng Xuan's commentary for the precise meaning of most passages in the *Constant Mean,* Zhu Xi explicitly departed from it at critical points where, he was convinced, Zheng and other earlier commentators had missed the Supreme Sage's deeper meaning. The imperial court first required Zhu Xi's interpretation of the Four Books in the fourteenth century, and by the fifteenth century the Ming court established it as the core of the civil examination curriculum. From then until well into the nineteenth century, Zhu Xi's version of these works was the dominant authority in the education of classically educated men and women.

Chinese society in Zhu Xi's day differed from that of Zheng Xuan in many important respects. China's population had nearly doubled and had spread out from the banks of the Yellow River and northeast China to the coastal provinces in the southeast as well as inland to the southwest. Cities, which until the Tang dynasty were primarily administrative centers, had developed robust commercial sectors, where paper currency circulated in the world's first money economy. Trade along the inland silk routes still thrived in much the same way as it had for more than a thousand years, and seafaring trade with Indian and Arab merchants, which had begun as early as the eighth century, flourished in Zhu Xi's day, long before Portuguese ships rounded Africa's Cape of Good Hope in 1488 CE. Buddhism, first introduced into China along inland trade routes, profoundly affected religious life at all levels of Song society. The earliest extant printed book, which dates from 868 CE, was in fact a Buddhist sutra. By the tenth century, a new kind of ruling elite filled the political vacuum left by the decline of the hereditary families, which had dominated court and society from the Han through the Tang. This new Song elite, referred to as the "Confucian gentry," enjoyed prestige through success in government civil examinations based on the Confucian Classics. The growing importance of classical education created new incentives in the Song for large-scale printings of books, and for the emergence and growth of private academies. Most academies prepared young men to take civil examinations, but many became centers of classical scholarship that reinterpreted the ancient canon in ways that made it relevant to the concerns of the nonhereditary elite. This resurgence in Confucian learning produced a number of schools of thought, which coalesced around such prominent masters as Zhu Xi, who taught distinctive philosophical doctrines and attracted large numbers of disciples.

Zheng Xuan's and Zhu Xi's understanding of the *Constant Mean* differed in a number of ways that will be examined in this chapter. Two points of difference bear mentioning here: their understanding of the work's title and its purported audience. For Zheng Xuan, this work examines the "practice of inner equilibrium and harmony." According to the text's opening passage, to follow the Way, one must guard against one's own hard-to-perceive shortcomings and master one's latent emotions, maintaining a state of equilibrium so that the emotions expressed in one's interaction with others accord with what is proper. Zheng Xuan's understanding of the title might thus be rendered as the *Practice of Equilibrium*. *Constant Mean* aptly captures Zhu Xi's emphasis on the immutable or constant principles of the middle way between two erroneous excesses. To avoid confusion, the title is rendered as the *Mean* in the section on Zheng Xuan and as the *Constant Mean* elsewhere in the chapter.[3]

Zheng Xuan believed that this text originally addressed a prince (*junzi* 君子) or hereditary lord of the ancient Zhou dynasty. He nonetheless insisted that its lessons applied to the imperial rulers of his own dynasty. Zheng thus placed his hope in a virtuous sovereign who aspired to emulate the ancients. Conversely, Zhu Xi clearly construed the way of the *junzi* as an injunction that applied to members of the Confucian elite like himself, who commanded moral authority, usually at the local level, in or out of bureaucratic positions. The "Way of the *Gentleman*," as Zhu Xi would have it, guided those who followed the teachings of Confucius and devoted themselves to a life of service, either to the throne as an appointed civil official or to the community as a moral exemplar who embodied the Way.

In order to capture ways that commentaries produce new meaning in classical texts, the remainder of this chapter reads the *Constant Mean* according to these two commentaries. The next section follows Zheng Xuan's interpretation and abides by his glosses wherever the original wording is ambiguous. Because Zheng Xuan understands this text as addressed to his sovereign, the key term *junzi* is rendered as "Prince." The section that follows reads the *Constant Mean* according to Zhu Xi's commentary and translates the term *junzi* as "gentleman" in order to convey his sense of an educated man who aspires to moral perfection. The section on Zhu Xi focuses on key points where he differs from Zheng Xuan's interpretation.

ZHENG XUAN AND THE PRACTICE OF EQUILIBRIUM AND HARMONY

The Way of the Prince

Zheng Xuan understood the *Mean* as a cultivation text in which Confucius exhorts the Prince to strive for the greatness of the ancient sage-kings. To undertake this task, the Prince (or sovereign) must resolve to cleave to the Mean with unrelenting vigilance over himself in order to master inner equilibrium and harmonize his actions with what is correct. If he chooses this path, he can assume the duty of the true Prince: to assist Heaven and Earth in nurturing all things, so that they too realize their full potential; only then can the Dao flourish in the world. The *Mean* begins by affirming the innate potential for human goodness: Heaven endows us with an inborn quality or nature, proclaims an anonymous voice. To diverge from one's nature even for an instant violates the Way. Zheng Xuan amplified upon the meaning of Heaven-ordained nature by illustrating how particular types of endowment engender specific personal dispositions: "When Heaven bequeaths the spirit of wood, the nature is benevolent; when it bequeaths the spirit of metal, the nature is righteous; with fire, it is ceremonious; with water, it is trustworthy; with earth, it is wise."

The voice of Confucius, identified simply as the Master in the *Mean,* then decries, "Alas, the Way is not practiced!" The small man opposes the Mean because he has no shame. The learned man thinks he knows the Mean, but exceeds (*guo* 過) it; the ignorant man also thinks he knows it, but can never reach (*buji* 不及) it. "The practice of the Mean is sublime,"[4] the Master continues, and yet "people can rarely hold on to it very long" because they fail to follow their Heaven-endowed nature (2–5).[5] In a nearly identical passage recorded in the *Analects* (6.27), the Master proclaims the Mean's moral power to be sublime. The consistency of the Master's remarks on the Mean in various canonical works such as the *Analects* served to affirm in the minds of his readers during imperial times the image of a singular sagely figure and his teachings.

To illustrate the basic conditions in which most people, in contrast to the sage-kings, must pursue the Way, Confucius compares his most illustrious disciple, Yan Hui, to the paragon Shun, an ancient king who wielded the very cosmos to create perfect government.[6] Shun was supremely wise, Confucius says, for he inquired into everyday speech, restrained evil, promoted the good, and applied the Mean by employing both the learned and the unschooled. In this way he was a sage (6). In contrast to Shun, on whom Heaven endowed the unerring nature of a sage, Yan Hui exemplifies virtue because he *chose* the good and never faltered in his perseverance: "When he chose from the Mean," the Master says, "Yan Hui cleaved to a single good so tightly that he never lost it" (8). People do not cleave to the Mean long enough, he warns (7). The Master thus teaches the Prince that to achieve perfection he must emulate Yan Hui's resolve to cling to the good, and, in so doing, follow the Way of the Prince.

Mastering the Dao requires strength of moral will, which is far more difficult than using force to unify the realm. In response to a disciple who inquired about strength, Confucius distinguishes between the strongman, who sleeps with sword and shield beside him and is unafraid to die, and the Prince, who gently admonishes his subordinates and does not visit fierce retribution on minor transgressions. Admonishing his disciple's fondness for strength, the Master says, "the Prince harmonizes without wavering. Is this not strength? He stands upright in the middle of the path without leaning on anything" and remains true to his ways whether or not the Dao prevails in the world (10). Rustic shamans and practitioners of strange arts that please the world will quickly abandon the Way whenever they encounter trouble. "Only the sage," he says, "relies on the Mean without any concern for fame or worldly recognition" (11).

The way of the Prince can be applied broadly, the Master explains, but it is very subtle. A simpleton may gain partial insight into it, and to a limited extent put it into practice. The sage, too, finds that he is unable to fully grasp the subtle depths of the Way (12). And yet it is not far removed from practical experience. "Hew the axe handle according to wood's grain," the Master quotes from the *Odes* (*Mao Ode* 158); the Way is fashioned according to readily discernible patterns of everyday life. Yet it is often hard to fulfill one's obligations to others. The Master admits, for example, that he was unable to serve his father in the same way that he expected his own son to serve him. By the same measure, he says, he fell short in serving his own lord, his elder brother, and his friends. So one must be vigilant, and, the Master says, "When there are shortcomings in my daily conduct or if I bungle routine interactions with others, then I always make an extra effort to mend; I dare not leave anything left undone" (13).

One's ability fully to realize one's Heaven-endowed potential rests upon one's resolve *not* to rely on external resources. To illustrate the necessity of drawing upon one's own resources in pursuing this goal, Confucius likens this quest to a seemingly external skill: "The Way of the Prince can be likened to archery. If the archer fails to penetrate his mark, he seeks the cause in himself" (14). Mencius similarly said, "The benevolent man is like the archer. The archer corrects himself before letting his arrow fly. If he misses his mark, he does not blame the winner, but only seeks the cause in himself" (2A.7). The figure of the upright archer who perfectly embodies the qualities necessary for realizing perfection can be found in other classical sources, such as the "Meaning of Archery" chapter of the *Rites* as well as in the *Odes* (e.g., *Mao Ode* 220). The possibility of fully realizing the Dao lies within oneself and requires only that one choose to undertake the quest and never slacken in one's resolve: "It is like embarking on a long journey—it begins here, at home—or ascending a high peak—it begins at the foot of the mountain" (15). Success in following the Way of the Prince requires that one reach for the lofty Dao by choosing the good, steadfastly adhering to it with unrelenting resolve, and maintaining vigilance over one's own shortcomings.

The Ancestors' Boundless Moral Power

In Zheng Xuan's reading, the *Mean* has so far stressed the Prince's everyday interactions with other living people as a measure of goodness and as the means by which he realizes it. The next several sections of the text explore the sources of human goodness and moral action by weaving an intricate cosmological web of the Prince's cultivation, his Heavenly mandate to rule, and his pious devotion to his ancestors. These passages provide one of the clearest explanations in the Classics of the necessity of venerating ancestors in one's quest to realize human perfection. Rites of sacrifice to one's ancestors are not merely the effect of preexisting piety; rather, the unfathomable spirits draw people everywhere to the good and reinforce their resolve. The purification rites one observes before the sacrifice, as we shall see presently, form part of an array of cultivation methods that draws inspiration from the exalted object of one's pious devotion: the ancestors, who are neither external, in that we inherit their *qi*, nor internal, being physically distinct from us.

Sages like Shun unerringly hit squarely upon the Mean without external inducement or even premeditation. For the rest of humanity, however, other sources of inspiration become necessary. Foremost among them, according to the *Mean*, are the unfathomable spirits who induce us to do good. "The spirits' and ancestors' exercise of their moral power is indeed boundless," the Master says. "While they cannot be seen or heard, they give birth [*ti* 體] to all living things, and induce [*shi* 使] people everywhere to fast and purify themselves and to don proper garb in order to continue the sacrificial rites" (16). Zheng Xuan remarks, "All things are born by the *qi* of the spirits."[7] As our own ancestors, spirits are a part of our being in that they give birth to us; their *qi* flows within us.

Two other texts included in the *Record of Rites* elaborate upon the importance and meaning of sacrifice. The "Fundamentals of Sacrifice" (*jitong* 祭統) explains that sacrifice to one's ancestors expresses the inner feelings of the filial heart: "Sacrifice is not produced by an external thing, it comes from within and is produced from the heart. The heart is moved by the ancestors and is expressed by means of rites." This chapter then explains how fasting purifies the self, thereby enabling one to commune with the ancestors: "Upon attaining purity, one resists depraved things and stops desires. . . . The heart that does not dwell on frivolous things always follows the Dao. Hands and feet that do not move recklessly always follow the rite. For this reason, the Prince's purifications obtain the moral power of his acute perception [*jingming* 精明]. . . . Upon achieving the utmost purity, one attains acute perception and only then communes with the spirits." As a filial son, the Prince devotes his every thought to his ancestors during purification rites. If he observes such rites wholeheartedly, and nothing distracts him from his purpose, he will see them as when they lived: "During purifications, think of the ancestor's daily activities," explains the "Meaning of Sacrifice" (*jiyi* 祭義), also in the *Record of Rites*, "think of his smile, daily thoughts and pleasures, and routine diversions. After the Prince purifies himself for three days, he sees what he has purified himself to see. On the day of the sacrifice, he certainly catches faint glimpses of the spirits when he enters the shrine and a gentle sense of their murmuring at every point during the rite until he turns to leave."

"Spirits abound as though above us, as though to our left and right," the Master continues in the *Mean*. "The *Odes* says, 'When spirits come, they cannot be fathomed, yet we tire of them not.' When the indistinct spirits appear, integrity cannot be suppressed!" (16). Heaven imparts the possibility of human goodness at birth, but to realize it fully requires the extraordinary resolve to choose the good in every instance. This usually occurs in one's everyday interactions with friends, family, and associates, but the arrival of the unfathomable spirits inspires a transcendent resolve: it produces integrity, an internal disposition that overcomes all obstacles and enables one to realize fully one's Heaven-ordained nature.

The sage-king Shun most perfectly embodied the self-realization of his Heaven-endowed nature. "Shun was greatly filial," the Master says. "He possessed the moral power of a sage and so people revered him as the Son of Heaven. . . . He received sacrifice in the ancestral temple of the ancient kings and his descendants continued the rites that he began. . . . From this we know that men of surpassing moral virtue certainly receive the Mandate" (17).[8] The early Zhou kings continued the rites of their ancestors and so never worried about the Mandate: "Sons followed the rites that their fathers created" (18). Confucius similarly draws a direct correlation between filiality and following the ritual precedents of one's forebears; in *Analects* 4.20, he says, "If for three years a son does not alter his father's ways, he may be called filial." The consistency of the Master's views again serves to affirm the image of a singular Confucius speaking throughout multiple canonical sources.

Though filiality might typically be construed as pious love of one's living parents, the Master explains it in the *Mean* almost exclusively in terms of devotion to one's ancestors. He repeatedly draws parallels between the world of the ancestors and the world of the living, linking them in overlapping spheres that mitigate barriers which might otherwise separate them. The ability to see and serve the dead as living requires the acute perception attained through purification rites and marks the attainment of filiality in its highest form. "Filiality," the Master says, "is to piously continue the wishes of one's ancestors by following their sacrificial services. The filial son prepares the ancestral shrine each spring and autumn, lays out his ancestors' sacrificial vessels and clothing, and offers them ripe fruits and freshly harvested grains."

Rituals that bring proper order to the spirits also order living men by distinguishing high from low: "The sequence of ancestral tablets distinguishes between father and son," the Master continues, "rank separates noble from humble; services distinguish among worthies; low-ranking celebrants in the toasting rotation raise their cups to their superiors, which serves to include the humble; and banquet feathers rank guests according to age. To follow the ancestors, to perform their rites and music; to revere what they honored and love what they held dear; to serve the dead as one serves the living: this is the supreme realization of Filiality." The Prince attains Supreme Filiality, and thus realizes human perfection, by serving his ancestors with the same piety with which he serves his living parents. The Master similarly said in the *Book of Filiality* (*Xiaojing* 孝經), "In filiality nothing surpasses revering one's father. In revering one's father nothing surpasses his receiving rites as Heaven's correlate."

The Art of Governing

Governing, as envisioned in the *Mean*, endeavors to bring about the universal realization of the Dao, a state in which all creatures fulfill their innate potential endowed by Heaven. To accomplish this ideal state, the Prince must hold on to the Mean with unrelenting resolve, master his inner equilibrium to ensure that his actions accord with what is correct, and extend the piety he exhibits toward his own living kin and ancestors to everyone under Heaven. The art of governing envisioned in the *Mean* aims to maintain tranquillity throughout the realm, to be sure, but to construe it as principally secular would overlook the multiple ways in which social, political, ethical, and religious activities constantly overlap. The very idea that seemingly secular acts such as laboring in the fields, interacting with others, or governing could be separated from religious activities is more a product of the eighteenth-century Enlightenment than of the world conceived in the *Mean*. To import it into this text risks unraveling the richly textured lives that show no evidence of distinguishing between secular and sacred.

The Master portrays understanding of ancestral rites and sacrifices to High God (*shangdi* 上帝) as a prerequisite for understanding governance. He says, "The suburban rites and soils altar serve High God, and rites at the ancestral temple serve the Prince's ancestors. He who understands these rites will govern the state as easily as pointing to the palm of his hand" (19). He who masters equilibrium and harmony possesses power over the cosmos, because, through his own cultivation, Heaven and Earth will assume their proper places and all living creatures will flourish. The Prince's success in following the Way hinges on his ability to master equilibrium and harmony and extend their beneficence outward to those around him and eventually to everyone throughout the realm.

To ensure that his government extends to everyone and continues well after he dies, the Master says, the Prince must treat his subjects as his own kin and choose wise counselors who follow the Dao by cultivating benevolence (*ren* 仁) in themselves and extending it to others. Five cardinal relationships that affect everyone, regardless of rank or station, appear repeatedly throughout the *Mean*: lord-minister (or subject), father-son, husband-wife, elder and younger brothers, and friends. The wise man understands those cardinal relationships from birth and conducts himself properly through them with ease. The benevolent man comes to understand them through learning and conducts himself properly because he sees that it is beneficial to do so. The brave man understands the cardinal relationships after some difficulty and conducts himself properly through considerable effort.

"Whether one understands the Dao from birth, or realizes it with ease or with difficulty, they are one."

Making explicit this principle of extending the Dao outward, the Master says, "One who knows how to cultivate the self, knows how to govern others." He then enumerates a sequence of stages called "Constancies," which, when the Prince carefully abides by them, produce what might be thought of as a Confucian version of utopia. These Constancies emanate outward from the Prince through the ranks of the nobility and courtiers to the common folk who till the land and labor in shops. The Prince must first cultivate himself, which he "accomplishes by fasting and purifying himself" before performing sacrifices to the gods and spirits, "donning proper garb and never contravening the rites." The Prince's performance of his religious duties to the gods and ancestral spirits constitutes the first Constancy, or step, toward realizing the Dao in human society. The Prince also upholds these Constancies by maintaining concord within his family and among his ministers and officers, by honoring the worthy man, treating his subjects as his own children, and welcoming those who come from afar. Then people will flock to him and the world will hold him in awe (20).

The Prince's own cultivation establishes the moral foundation of the art of governing. He must initiate moral rectification in his own person first in order to set the other Constancies into motion, culminating in the universal realization of Dao throughout his realm. Success at any one point in the sequence requires successful completion of the prior one. The beneficial effects of his own cultivation emanate outward from the Prince through concentric domains that ultimately encompass the entire world. Once the Prince realizes Integrity himself, he will be compliant with his kin, then he will gain the trust of his friends, and his subordinates will have access to their superiors. Then he governs the people as a true Prince.

Integrity, the Sage, and the Way of Heaven

This lengthy discussion of the moral foundation of governance concludes with a careful analysis of Integrity (*cheng* 誠), one of the most important concepts of the entire text. The *Mean* distinguishes between the Way of Heaven, exemplified by the Sage who possesses Integrity from birth, and the Way of Man, the path that everyone not born a sage must follow to acquire Integrity through learning. "Integrity *itself* [*chengzhe* 誠者] is the Way of Heaven," an unidentified speaker proclaims. "To attain Integrity [*cheng zhizhe* 誠之者] is man's Way." In his interlinear commentary on this passage, Zheng Xuan explains that "Integrity itself is Heavenly nature," which sages alone possess at birth. "To *attain* Integrity means to acquire it through learning."[9]

The anonymous speaker in the *Mean* continues, "He who [originally] possesses Integrity, hits upon the Mean without forethought; this is the Sage who effortlessly hits squarely upon the Dao. To *attain* Integrity [through learning] requires that one choose the good and steadfastly hold on to it [*ze shan er gu zhi* 擇善而固執]," as exemplified by the Master's disciple Yan Hui. In contrast to Integrity itself, possessed by such extraordinary men as Shun, who invariably hit upon the Mean, to *attain* Integrity "one must study it broadly, inquire into it thoroughly, reflect upon it carefully, distinguish it clearly, and practice it earnestly. If others master it after one attempt, then do it a hundred times; if others master it after ten attempts, then do it a thousand times; in the end you will master this Dao." Learning in the *Mean* clearly entails something more than acquiring facts or accumulating information. Learning, rather, amounts to a moral quest to attain perfection through emulation of the sages. Although the sages tower above all humanity throughout the ages, the passage concludes, "even the ignorant can gain wisdom and the weak can become strong" (20).

That an unidentified speaker pronounces on the concept of Integrity facilitates a crucial if subtle shift in the text's perspective. The *Mean* hereafter speaks increasingly of the Sage rather than the Prince, and where the Prince appears in the text, Zheng Xuan usually refers to him as a sage in his commentary. More important, the canonical voice of Confucius dominated the first half of the text as though it were an actual record of the Master's audience with a Prince, whereas Confucius speaks only three times from this midpoint on. The Master's relative silence does not diminish his stature. To the contrary, he becomes the text's central object of veneration. Both Zheng Xuan and

Zhu Xi read the latter half of the text as a proclamation of Confucius as the Sage. This claim anticipates the *Mean*'s dramatic conclusion, which explicitly exalts Confucius as the Sage and heir to the legacy of the ancient sage-kings.

While the amorphous figure of the Sage was subject to ongoing debate throughout Chinese history, most early sources agree that sages had penetrating insight into the mysterious operations of Heaven and Earth and devised ways to harmonize human life with those mysteries. The earliest sages showed the people how to build houses, till fields, and domesticate animals. Sages also fashioned the eight trigrams used in the divination found in the *Book of Changes*, and devised the rites and music. The *Analects* shares the view in the *Mean* that Heaven chooses the sage. One is born a sage because Heaven favors that person with the nature of a sage, which cannot be acquired through any amount of effort. Confucius in the *Analects* says that Heaven bestowed upon him the underlying patterns of the Dao (9.5). But unlike the sage-king Shun, Confucius was thwarted in his quest to spread his penetrating insight, and never gained the throne. Mencius nonetheless proclaimed that Confucius's accomplishments surpassed those of the ancient sage-kings: "Since the birth of the people, no one has surpassed the Master" (2A.2).

The *Mean* continues its examination of Integrity by distinguishing between sages, who possess it at birth, and worthies, who acquire it through learning: "To illuminate one's virtue on the basis of Integrity is called nature; to attain Integrity from one's brilliant virtue is called the teaching" (21). Zheng Xuan explains in his commentary, "The Sage gains brilliant virtue from his Supreme Integrity—Integrity in its most sublime state—because it is already integral to his nature, whereas the worthy man attains Supreme Integrity from brilliant virtue through learning." Nature, then, according to Zheng Xuan, is not a universal "human nature," innately shared by everyone. Rather, the quality of Supreme Integrity is innately possessed only by sages. Whereas the worthy man possesses the capacity to realize the full potential of the sage, Supreme Integrity is not an inborn attribute of his nature; he must work relentlessly to acquire it by studying the sages. Zheng Xuan thus positions the Sage—and, less so, the Prince—in the exalted cosmic

role of assisting Heaven and Earth in their creative, nurturing transformations.

Zheng Xuan's view of nature differs from those of his predecessors
Mencius and Xunzi. The Confucius of the *Analects* remains neutral
on the question of innate goodness (17.2); Zheng suggests that there
is no single, universal nature shared by all people, but that people's
natures show gradations of quality. Mencius, however, argued for a
universally good nature that was corrupted through habitual views or
improper cultivation practices (*Mencius* 6A.1–9). Xunzi argued for a
single, universal but defective human nature, which, he said, produced evil and contention as people strove to satisfy their selfish desires (*Xunzi,* chapter 23).

The *Mean* continues, "Only he who has achieved Supreme Integrity
can fulfill his own nature." Such a man can in turn "fulfill the nature of
others and all living creatures," and in so doing, "assist Heaven and
Earth in the nurturing transformations of all things and become equal
to Heaven and Earth" (22). Continuing the distinction between the
sage, who possesses Integrity, and all others who must work to acquire
it, the text says: one "can attain Integrity by first working on small instances of it. With minor accomplishments, one gradually manifests
greater accomplishments and affects others who will then be transformed into good people" (23). "Those who possess Supreme Integrity
have foreknowledge" because "they understand the portents of a
newly emergent state or one on the verge of collapse as revealed in the
milfoil [used in divination]. . . . Men of Supreme Integrity are thus like
spirits" (24). Zheng Xuan and other early commentators substantiate
the bold claim that sages, like spirits, can augur the fate of states, by
listing specific occasions when prescient men of Supreme Integrity actually foretold the rise and fall of dynasties.

Like the "Dao, which always follows the correct path, the man of
Integrity [*chengzhe*] realizes his innate goodness of his own accord."
Such a man and the Dao are both self-sufficient and are thus able to
realize goodness without conscious effort or external assistance.
While the man of Integrity possesses the capacity to achieve his innate
potential for goodness, he can realize it only by transcending the
boundaries of his own physical self: "Integrity is the beginning and

end of all creatures . . . and so the Prince holds it in high esteem." The Prince prizes it as a venerable object yet to be realized in himself. "The man of Integrity not only fully realizes his potential, but is himself the very means by which all creatures are brought to completion. To complete oneself is benevolence, and to complete others is wisdom. The moral power of this nature unites the internal self with external things, and thus all things obtain their proper place" (25). The man of Integrity establishes a profound bond with all living creatures by serving as a vehicle that enables them to realize their full potential and, through this common endeavor, obliterates distinctions between the self and other. Herein lies the awesome power of the sage, which a ruler must strive to emulate in order to govern with the Mandate of Heaven.

Continuing in this same cosmological vein, the text expounds upon the ever more lofty purpose of the man of Supreme Integrity: "Supreme Integrity is ceaseless, permanent, and clearly in evidence everywhere; it extends far and wide." The man of Supreme Integrity is said to be equal to Heaven and Earth because, like Earth, he is expansive and bountiful and sustains living creatures; like Heaven, he is lofty and brilliant and envelops them. "In this way, he is imperceptibly manifest and transforms things without moving; he accomplishes his aims without acting" (26). Like Heaven and Earth, whose transformative effects are both profound and beyond human comprehension, the Sage effortlessly changes those around him without anyone realizing that he has acted at all. "Great and flourishing is the Sage's Way. It nurtures all things and towers up to the very pinnacle of Heaven. The sublime rites must await such a man before they can be put into practice. For this reason, the Prince honors the moral nature and follows the path of inquiry and learning; he realizes the Way's greatness and fulfills its refined, hidden essence; and he ascends to lofty brilliance and follows the path of the Constant Mean" (27).

At this point in the text the Master interrupts the anonymous voice speaking at length on Integrity. A dialogue ensues. Disaster, Confucius warns, will certainly be visited upon scurrilous, self-aggrandizing men and antiquarians who promote outmoded policies.

The anonymous voice concurs with the Master, as if the two were preoccupied in intense conversation, "One who sits on the throne dares not promulgate rites and music if he does not possess moral power. And if he possesses moral power but not the throne, he still dares not promulgate rites and music."

Commentator Zheng Xuan joins this colloquy to add, portentously, "This means that only a Sage who sits on the throne promulgates rites and music." Only a sage-king like Shun possesses the qualities necessary to set the rites and music.

Recognizing that he can only follow the rites made by kings, the Master rejoins, "I may speak of the rites of the Xia," but even the ruler of the Xia's successor state Qi "is unable to understand them. I've studied the Shang rites that are still preserved in the state of Song . . . but I follow the Zhou" (28), reiterating a nearly identical passage that appears in the *Analects* (3.9).

The anonymous voice resumes, "Even a good ruler commands no allegiance of his subjects without showing evidence of his goodness."[10] Proper governance hinges on the Prince's abiding personal commitment to goodness, which he must exhibit in his every action. "Thus the Prince's Dao is rooted in his person and is fulfilled by the common folk. He aspires to revive the ways of the former kings and does not violate the cosmic order founded upon the sustaining power of Heaven and Earth. No doubts remain when he submits [his acts] to the ancestors for approval, and the generations who await the sage will not be deluded. . . . The Prince's acts become the Dao for later generations; his actions become the model, his words become precepts" for all to follow (29).

The Apotheosis of the Sage

The closing passages of the *Mean* identify Confucius as the Sage who possesses Supreme Integrity and who has attained the cosmological powers to enable all creatures to fulfill their innate potential described throughout the work. The anonymous voice of the text says Confucius "followed Yao and Shun and upheld the regulations of kings Wen and Wu. He adhered to Heaven's seasons above and followed the course of land and waterways below. He may be likened to Heaven and Earth, which envelop all things; to the four seasons because of their orderly succession; and to the sun and moon, which shine brilliantly" (30). Zheng Xuan explains that Confucius "embraced the surpassing moral power of the ancients to compile the *Spring and Autumn Annals*," said to establish the institutions of the Han dynasty. He quotes Confucius's remark that this work "contained his entire life's purpose." Zheng Xuan and other Han scholars regarded this work—not the *Analects*, compiled by Confucius's disciples and later followers—as Confucius's most outstanding achievement, and used it as the cornerstone of Han institutions. They read the *Spring and Autumn Annals*, moreover, on the basis of the *Gongyang* commentary, which claimed that Confucius used the lofty standards of the ancient sage-kings to condemn rulers of his own day for violating the exalted ways and institutions bequeathed by the sage-kings.

"Only the Supreme Sage," the anonymous voice of the *Mean* continues, "possesses the clear brilliance and upright wisdom worthy of one who sits on the throne." Zheng Xuan explains: "One whose moral power does not match this cannot rule the world." Then Zheng makes explicit the key point of this part of the text: "This passage laments that Master Kong possessed the Prince's moral power but not his mandate" (31). Notwithstanding that the king has the station to govern men, he commands the moral authority to do so only if he is virtuous. In the absence of the king's mandate to rule, which was incontrovertibly the case in Confucius's day, true moral authority to create the institutions to govern the world lay in the hands of the "uncrowned king"—Confucius—discussed in chapter 3.

Reiterating the cosmic effects of the Supreme Sage's impact on the world, the *Mean*'s anonymous voice proclaims, "Vast like Heaven, deep like the ocean. He is seen and all revere him; he speaks and all invest their trust in him; he acts and all are persuaded. His reputation sweeps across the Middle Kingdom as far as the barbarians in remote lands, to wherever boat or cart may carry, and to the farthest place that human strength can reach, to all that Heaven envelops and that Earth sustains; to all that sun and moon shine upon, and all that glistens in the morning dew. Whoever has blood and breath reveres him and regards him with affection. Thus it is said that he is equal to Heaven"

(31). The man of Supreme Integrity achieves such feats by drawing from his incomparably profound wisdom (32): "Only he can comprehend the great patterns under Heaven, establish the great foundation of the world, and understand the nurturing transformations of Heaven and Earth. What need does he have to rely on anything or anyone? Supreme is his benevolence! Profound his depth! Pervasive [his knowledge of] Heaven! Can one truly understand the Sage's wisdom unless one is himself a sage?"

This "man of Supreme Integrity is Master Kong," Zheng Xuan explains. "The 'great patterns' the Master comprehended refers to the six arts in the *Spring and Autumn Annals*." Classical sources describe the arts of rites, music, archery, charioteering, calligraphy, and mathematics as necessary training for members of the nobility. "The great foundation he established," Zheng Xuan continues, "is the *Book of Filiality*." This work, using the question-and-answer format found in several chapters of the *Record of Rites*, records the Master's conversation with a disciple celebrated in the *Analects* for his filiality (8.3). Regarded in the Han as a repository of basic lessons on filiality, the *Book of Filiality* draws parallels between the son's reverence toward his father and mother and the king's sacrifices to Heaven and Earth. In doing so, the voice of the Master as recorded in this work establishes a continuum linking family, the sovereign, and the guiding forces of Heaven and Earth.

The final section of the *Mean* draws from the *Book of Odes* to reinforce the profound simplicity of the Sage's moral power to imperceptibly transform the people. The Way of the Prince "disdains complexity and opts for refined subtlety like 'a pure white robe'" (*Mao Ode* 57). The Prince reflects inwardly, and his moral power "shines forth from the ocean depths" (*Mao Ode* 192). Nothing surpasses his moral power, and all take him as the paragon (*Mao Ode* 269). High God said to King Wen, who rose against the corrupt king of the Shang to seize Heaven's Mandate for the Zhou, "I am moved by your brilliant moral power, yet you make no show of it in your demeanor" (*Mao Ode* 241). The text then quotes the Master one last time, as if to acknowledge his own unheralded transformative effects on the world: "Never announce your intention to transform the people." The *Odes* (235) proclaims, "Exalted Heaven works without sound or smell!" The true king merely exemplifies goodness without fanfare in order to sustain his subjects in the same way that Heaven and Earth silently nourish all creatures.

In sum, Zheng Xuan reads the *Mean* as Confucius's urgent call for his sovereign to emulate the ancient sages and rule with the Mandate of Heaven. The Prince must accordingly follow the Way of Man by continuing the ritual precedents of former kings, cultivating his Heaven-endowed nature, and mastering equilibrium and harmony. He must draw from his ancestors' surpassing moral power the strength of his resolve to hold steadfastly to the good. Once he understands the ancestral rites and extends the same sense of filiality and reverence that he exhibits toward his own kin to everyone throughout the realm, he will govern All-under-Heaven. Although Confucius never ruled as a king, he possessed Supreme Integrity in its most sublime state, and, like Heaven itself, noiselessly worked to transform the people. The rulers of the Han dynasty, according to Zheng Xuan, must emulate the Master and rule silently, imperceptibly, in order to transform the people.

ZHU XI AND THE WAY OF THE GENTLEMAN

Confucianism of Late Imperial China

Zhu Xi's reading of the *Constant Mean* a thousand years later does not so much contradict Zheng Xuan's normative understanding as build a new metaphysical edifice on top of it. While he relies heavily on Zheng Xuan's exegesis of most of the text, Zhu Xi introduces at least three novel interpretations that reflect Confucian thinking during the Song. First, while he, too, reads the text as Confucius's discourse on cultivation, Zhu universalizes its message and applies it not just to the sovereign, but to all classically educated men—to the gentleman. Indeed, Zhu Xi places his greatest hopes not in the ruler, but in men who resolve to practice the Dao outside of government with the hope of transforming the world. Partly in response to Buddhism's claim about the universality of enlightenment, most Confucian thinkers in late imperial times sought to apply the teachings found in ancient canonical works to all classically educated men. Because Zhu Xi understood the *Constant Mean* in this greatly enlarged sense, the term *junzi*, translated as the "Prince" in the first section, will hereafter be translated as the "gentleman."

Second, Zhu concurs with the long-standing claim that Confucius's grandson Kong Ji (aka Zisi) authored the *Constant Mean*, and identifies Kong Ji as the speaker in much of the text's latter half. This point is crucial for Zhu Xi, who maintained that Confucius alone inherited the Dao from the ancient sage-kings and transmitted it to Mencius. Widely believed in Song times to be the last sage of the ancient world, Mencius was unable to transmit the Dao to a disciple, so it was lost. For Zhu Xi, the *Constant Mean* forges a vital genealogical link between Confucius and Mencius because he believes that its reputed author, Kong Ji, transmitted the Dao to Mencius in the form of the *Constant Mean*. For 1,500 years, Zhu Xi said, the ancient Dao lay precariously in the words of this text until men in the Song dynasty received the transmission of the Dao.

Third, Zhu Xi diverges from Zheng Xuan most explicitly in his understanding of the question of human nature. He believed that Heaven endowed everyone with the same nature, which he identified as Heavenly Principle. The imperative to cultivate one's nature therefore applied to anyone able to undertake it according to the principles laid out in the *Constant Mean* and the other works of the Four Books, not just the prince. Zhu Xi furthermore draws out key terms from the text to build a metaphysical framework in which to pursue self-cultivation methods not found in a literal reading of the canon. He adheres to the principle that people differ in their capacity to realize their innate potential, but maintains that everyone possesses the same sagely nature. No mere contrivance, Zhu Xi's unmistakably innovative understanding of the *Constant Mean* derives from his strategic selections from the Four Books to formulate a teaching well suited to an age profoundly changed by Buddhism.

Two features of Buddhism particularly resonated in Confucian thinking during Zhu Xi's day. Chinese schools of Buddhism posited a universal truth or principle underlying all phenomena of the sensible world, called *Dhárma*. Wisdom, they said, lay in apprehending the impermanence of all things, that one's own soul was merely transitory, and that even the Dhárma was ultimately empty of all content; it was nothingness itself. Song Confucian masters posited Principle (*li* 理) as the underlying creative force of all things. Although Zhu Xi and his successors argued that the doctrine of Principle could be traced back to the ancient sages, they were hard pressed to cite specific passages in the canon that explicitly stated as much. This doctrinal innovation makes more sense, rather, as a Confucian response to Buddhism's universalizing pronouncements based on Dhárma. Contrary to the Buddhist notion of Dhárma as nothingness, however, Song Confucians identified Principle with Heaven, the ultimate source of goodness, particularly benevolence and righteousness. The Confucian understanding of Principle resembles Plato's theory of forms in that it posits a general, immutable truth that informs all particular instances. Confucian Principle and Platonic form are also accessible to human scrutiny, if one knows how to seek them in particular instances. Confucian Principle, however, produces—literally gives birth to—particular things through an animating force called *qi* 氣, which defines individual endowments of goodness. Confucian Principle, moreover, is ultimately a single, generative truth identified with Heaven, and the source of individual goodness conferred through human nature. The *Constant Mean*'s opening declaration that "what Heaven confers is called nature" figured largely in Zhu Xi's understanding of human nature. Zhu Xi comments on this passage that "human nature is Principle."

Some schools of Buddhism, particularly Chan, advocated the doctrine of sudden enlightenment based on the Mahāyāna idea that everyone possessed innate wisdom called the Buddha nature, or Buddha mind. Consistent with long-standing Mahāyāna teachings, they maintained that this nature was ultimately empty and furthermore that one could achieve enlightenment suddenly through meditation on it. Confucian masters from the Song through Qing periods maintained that everyone possessed a singular human nature, which, they maintained, was innately good and bestowed by Heaven. They disagreed dramatically, though, on the methods necessary to gain enlightenment. Zhu Xi's position that self-cultivation must begin with investigating the Principles of particular things, especially matters contained in the Classics, became the dominant position endorsed by the imperial court in the fourteenth century. Dissenting Confucians maintained that one's original nature was already replete with the goodness necessary to achieve enlightenment, and that externally directed investigation of Principle diverted attention away from the self. Zhu Xi and his adherents vehemently opposed this unmediated approach as falling into the error of the Chan Buddhist doctrine of sudden enlightenment.

The Sages' Mind Transmission

Zhu Xi believed that earlier commentators had missed the true meaning of the *Constant Mean*. In a preface to his version of the text, Zhu Xi entwines the history of the sagely transmission of the Dao and metaphysics to formulate a moral imperative to cultivate the self. He sees a tension between latent and expressed emotions mentioned in the *Constant Mean* and authorizes an approach to self-cultivation that shifts the metaphysical ground upon which it takes place. In Zheng Xuan's reading, the Prince resolves to master equilibrium and harmony and attain Integrity through a concerted act of will. Zhu Xi, conversely, concentrates on the cultivation of the mind, a word that does not appear in the original text and appears only rarely in Zheng Xuan's commentary. The mind, according to Zhu Xi, exists precariously between two possible states of consciousness that determine the moral choices one makes: the Mind of Dao (*Daoxin* 道心) and the human mind (*renxin* 人心). Zhu Xi grafts these two states of consciousness onto the text of the *Constant Mean* by equating his concept of the Mind of Dao with Heaven-ordained nature as the locus of pure latent emotions, which exist in a state of equilibrium, and equating the human mind with expressed emotions, which, he says, are capable of harmonizing with the Mean but are also prone to err. The *Constant Mean* counsels vigilance against hard-to-perceive inner shortcomings that threaten to lead one astray; Zhu Xi formulates a method of self-cultivation premised on a dread of external deceptions. He was utterly convinced, for example, that the captivating allure of Buddhism's "spurious truths," as he called them, had already seduced the most brilliant minds of his generation. For Zhu Xi, the human mind, which is the locus of possible error, also has the capacity to examine the inner self and guide one through a process of self-cultivation toward sagehood.

The ancient sage-kings, Zhu Xi's preface states, transmitted the "lineage of the Way" (*Daotong* 道統) at the coronation of each new successor to the throne. When Yao announced that Heaven ordained Shun to succeed him, he taught Shun to "hold fast to this Mean." When he ceded the throne to his successor, Shun added three sentences to formulate what became known as the "mind transmission" of the sages, which, according to Zhu, resonates throughout the *Constant Mean*: "The human mind is precarious, the mind of Dao barely perceptible. Be discerning and single-minded; hold fast to this Mean."[11] The ancient sages transmitted this Dao as part of the royal succession, Zhu Xi says, but "alas, our Master never sat on the throne. He continued the former sages and inaugurated later learning, thus his accomplishment surpassed that of Yao and Shun." This sentiment echoes Zheng Xuan's earlier lament that Confucius never ruled China. Yet Zhu Xi maintained that the Master rose above the ancient kings because he transmitted the Dao to his followers, who authored the Four Books. Once the privileged domain of kings and the Master, the Dao, in Zhu Xi's account, is attainable to commoners.

By availing the Way to everyone, Confucius became the teacher of all ages. "By Kong Ji's day, much time had passed since the time of the Sage," and heterodoxies (*yiduan* 異端) arose. Kong Ji feared that under such circumstances the Dao would be lost, so he wrote the *Constant Mean*, in which he "substantiated the teaching transmitted from Yao and Shun on the basis of what he had heard from his father," who received it directly from the Master. Zhu Xi then buttresses his understanding of the text by matching key passages in the *Constant Mean* with the wording of the ancient sage-kings' mind transmission: To "follow one's Heaven-ordained nature," taken from the opening lines of the text, "is the 'Mind of Dao.' To 'choose the good and steadfastly hold on to it,'" exemplified by Confucius's disciple Yan Hui (20), "means 'to be discerning and single-minded.' The phrase 'the gentleman [aka Prince] always hits upon the Mean' [2] means to 'hold fast to this Mean.' With another generation," Zhu continues, "we have Mencius, who further illuminated this book to continue the lineage of the early sages. When he died the lineage was lost." Overtly missing in Zhu's neat pairing of phrases is any passage in the *Constant Mean* that corresponds to the precarious human mind—a problem in Zhu Xi's explanation that persisted in subsequent debates on his reading of the text for centuries after his death.

Cultivation of the Mind and the Attainment of Integrity

Having constructed a canonical foundation for the sages' mind transmission, Zhu Xi turns to the question of how the Dao was lost after Mencius and then recovered by his own immediate predecessors in the Song dynasty. "Our Dao existed precariously in nothing more than words," Zhu Xi laments, "while heterodoxies grew with each passing day." Daoists and Buddhists greatly corrupted the Way with their spurious teachings. Fortunately, the text of the *Constant Mean* survived so that it could be "used to retrieve the sages' transmission, severed for more than a thousand years . . . and rebuke the specious doctrines taught by the two schools" of Daoism and Buddhism.

People are susceptible to such deceptions, according to Zhu Xi, because the human mind is prone to err, making the imperative to cultivate the mind properly all the more urgent. All people originally possess the "one mind of pure consciousness," but some minds "are produced by individual endowments of selfish *qi*,[12] whereas other minds arise from the correctness of their endowed nature and thus operate differently." The mind is not inherently evil in Zhu Xi's understanding, but some people are more susceptible to deceit. The precarious human mind and the pure mind of Dao "indistinguishably crowd a small space in the self and we no longer know how to distinguish them." The solution, Zhu Xi maintains, lies in the self-cultivation methods described in the *Constant Mean*, understood in light of the sages' mind transmission: Be discerning (*jing* 精), he says, and one can scrutinize the human mind and the mind of Dao without confusing them. "Be single-minded [*yi* 一], and one can preserve the original mind's correctness without departing from it. To pursue this without the slightest interruption will certainly enable the mind of Dao to forever govern the entire self and the human mind to always do its bidding."[13] In Zhu Xi's formulation in his preface to the *Constant Mean*, the mind of Dao and the human mind constitute two different modes of consciousness rather than two distinct minds, contrary to his critics' claims. The former is pure and thus inherently recognizes the good, whereas the latter is susceptible to desires that cloud its moral judgment. The principal objective of Zhu Xi's method of self-cultivation centers on rectifying the human mind so that it always abides by the mind of Dao.

In his lengthy preface, Zhu Xi effectively incorporates the *Constant Mean* into a method of self-cultivation largely unknown before the introduction of Buddhism into China. In his edition of the *Constant Mean* itself, Zhu Xi divides the main body of the text into three parts. He says the opening lines establish the basic teachings of the text as a whole: the Dao is an immutable truth originating in Heaven. Heaven confers on all people a nature—the innate source of goodness possessed by everyone—which must be properly cultivated. According to Zhu Xi, the next twenty sections, or chapters as he calls them, compose the Master's explanation of the opening lines as recorded by Kong Ji, his grandson. These twenty chapters are roughly evenly divided between the Way of Heaven, fulfilled by sage-king Shun, and the Way of Man, which directs the gentleman in his quest for sagehood through acquiring Integrity in himself. The final part, Zhu Xi says, comprises Kong Ji's own comments on the Master's teachings. Zheng Xuan had not divided the text so neatly, and says little about the organization of the work or who purportedly speaks in the text, except those passages explicitly attributed to the Master. The earliest extant version of Zheng Xuan's redaction of the *Constant Mean* is divided in half, roughly near the halfway point, which falls in the middle of chapter 20 in Zhu Xi's edition.

In his interlinear commentary, Zhu Xi interpolates philosophical claims into the *Constant Mean* that, in effect, overlay earlier interpretations. Zheng Xuan distinguished the Heaven-ordained nature into five personal dispositions: benevolent, righteous, ceremonious, trustworthy, and wise. A thousand years later Zhu Xi introduced new terms to subordinate Zheng Xuan's understanding of human nature to a cosmology governed by Principle: "Nature is Principle," Zhu Xi comments, succinctly establishing a key premise of his belief that nature is a commonly shared universal essence endowed by Heaven on everyone. "Heaven gives birth to all things with yin and yang and the Five Phases." Things "acquire particular form by means of *qi* [animating force] and are invested with Principle, which is like [Heaven's] command." Though it comes into existence simultaneously with *qi*, Principle determines a person's innate potential. Particular endowments of *qi*, however, determine a person's capacity to realize his full potential. "Although Principle and the Dao are the same [in that they are universal], allotment of *qi* varies [from one person to the next] and so some people exceed [*guo*] their proper allotment and others fall short of it [*buji*]."

Like Zheng Xuan, Zhu Xi distinguishes sages from everyone else. Unlike Zheng Xuan, however, Zhu Xi upholds sagehood as a universal ideal, somewhat more like his Buddhist contemporaries whom he vilifies.[14] "Sages," Zhu Xi states, "cultivated their Heavenly allotment on the basis of what is proper and became models for the world." Because "the Mean is perfect," and because "everyone alike receives it, it is initially not difficult to cultivate. But some people exceed [*guo*] the perfect Mean and lose its equilibrium, whereas others fall short of it [*buji*] and so do not realize perfection," owing to different allotments of *qi* (Zhu links this to a nearly identical passage in *Analects* 6.26). Most people differ from sages, according to Zhu Xi, not because they lack the innate potential, but because of mistakes in judgment that cause them to miss the Mean. Classical scholars of the Han and Tang, he said, never reached the Mean because they failed to penetrate the surface meaning of the Classics to apprehend the essential Principles they contained. Others, deluded by Buddhism, exceeded the Mean because they sought sudden enlightenment without following the proper steps outlined in the canon. The *Great Learning*, another of the Four Books taken from the *Rites*, specifies a multistep process of self-cultivation, which begins, according to Zhu Xi's not-uncontroversial understanding, with the investigation of the Principles of things. Zhu

Xi's systematic method proceeds from the extension of knowledge to ensuring that one's thoughts have Integrity (*cheng*) and that one's mind is rectified in order to cultivate the self. One can then bring order to one's family and to one's kingdom, and only then will peace prevail throughout the world. Much like the Constancies described in chapter 20 of Zhu Xi's version of the *Constant Mean*, the beneficence of the multistep process of cultivation outlined in the *Great Learning* expands outward from the perfectly cultivated self in ever larger concentric circles to eventually include everyone.

Seeking to attain Integrity, Zhu Xi explains in his commentary on the *Constant Mean*, is the only sure method of avoiding errors that lead one away from the Mean; Integrity "is the original state of Heavenly Principle." Only the Sage already possesses Integrity in its most sublime state, whereas the Way of Man works to rectify the fallible human mind by showing ordinary people how to attain it: "The Sage's moral power binds Heavenly principle and perfect authenticity to effortlessly hit upon the Dao without concerted premeditation; this is the Way of Heaven. Until one has attained sagehood," holding out the ultimate goal, "one cannot be without selfish desires nor can one be entirely authentic in one's moral practice. One can understand goodness only after prior reflection and choosing the good. One can attain Integrity for oneself only after forcing oneself to steadfastly hold on to it; this is the Way of Man." Integrity and attaining it, Zhu says, is the crux of the entire text (20).

The Way of Heaven, the Way of Man

Zhu Xi divides the second part of the *Constant Mean* into chapters devoted to Heaven's Way and to Man's Way. Chapters on Heaven's Way concern the Sage's innate embodiment of perfect Integrity and his ability "to use his perfect nature to fulfill the nature of all other creatures" (23). In his comment on the passage that likens those who possess Supreme Integrity to spirits (24), Zhu says, "Men who realize Supreme Integrity and are utterly without the slightest selfishness or bias in their mind's eye can apprehend the incipient state of Principle before it becomes manifest. 'Spirits' refers to ancestral spirits and other gods," he says. "Only with the Sage's limitless impartiality and utter lack of selfishness can one possess Supreme Integrity without relying on anything." Only the man of Supreme Integrity can "be the model for all the world" (32). Zhu Xi stresses that "only the Sage can use his perfect nature to fulfill the nature of all other creatures."

On the surface, Zhu Xi's understanding of sagehood parallels Zheng Xuan's idea of the Prince who has fully realized his innate potential. But in fact they differ in a number of respects. As noted previously, Zheng Xuan conceives of the Prince as the king or a hereditary lord, whereas for Zhu Xi, a sage, who was no doubt born an extraordinary man, constituted an ideal goal for those who followed the correct path. Taken in historical context, Zhu's claim might be construed as a Confucian alternative to the Mahāyāna promise of universal Buddhahood. To respond to this Buddhist doctrine, Zhu Xi and many of his contemporaries looked to Mencius's position that human nature is innately good (6A.1–6), succinctly articulated in the statement, "Everyone can be a Yao or Shun" (6B.2). While formulating a position that differed from universal Buddhahood, Zhu Xi read the *Constant Mean* as a method for classically educated men and women to achieve a level of human perfection not present in Zheng Xuan's reading.

In contrast to Mahāyāna's universalistic aspirations, the *Constant Mean*, in Zhu Xi's reading, envisions what one scholar terms the "fiduciary community." This is an interdependent community in which the Prince, the Sage, or the gentleman follows the path of self-cultivation, which simultaneously establishes objective conditions that in turn enable all creatures to fulfill their Heaven-endowed potential. Although the Confucian community makes no pretense of bringing anything akin to permanent universal enlightenment for everyone in this or the next life, it nonetheless engages the afterlife through veneration of the ancestors. Hardly a mere symbol or an expression of humanism, pious sacrifice, as we have seen, facilitates the filial son's "communion with his ancestors." The *Constant Mean*, according to both Zheng Xuan and Zhu Xi, makes clear that the ancestors' boundless moral power over the living "induces people everywhere to fast and purify themselves" and thus aspire to become good. Any characterization of Confucianism as a this-worldly humanism, then, sees only half the picture.

The gentleman who follows the Way of Man may gradually attain Integrity and eventually participate in the cosmic process of Heaven and Earth's nurturing of all things. Adopting a gradualist approach to perfection, Zhu Xi says, "after the sage, lesser men must extend their partially manifested goodness in order to realize their full potential. . . . After concentrating on such work they begin to transform others. This partially manifest Supreme Integrity," Zhu states in an almost ambivalent affirmation of Mencius, "is no different from the Sage" (23). Later Zhu Xi reiterates the claim that we can all become sages through learning and emulate the ancient sages' ability to engender the fiduciary community: "Once he completes himself, the man of Integrity naturally extends it to others and the Dao extends to others as well. Benevolence preserves nature's essence, and wisdom functions to issue it forth. Our nature certainly possesses these qualities so that there is no distinction between internal and external. Having attained it in oneself, this will be manifest in external things, which will all assume their proper place" (25).

A key passage in the *Constant Mean* that has attracted considerable attention states: "The gentleman honors the moral nature and follows the path of inquiry and learning; he realizes the Way's greatness and fulfills its refined, hidden essence; and he ascends to lofty brilliance and follows the path of the Constant Mean" (27). Zhu Xi interprets this passage as a validation of an essential element of his method of self-cultivation. The "moral nature" in this passage, he explains, "refers to the perfect Principle that we receive from Heaven. . . . 'To honor the moral nature' is the means to nourish the mind-heart in order to realize the greatness of the Dao itself. To 'follow the path of inquiry and learning' is the means to extend knowledge and fulfill the fine points of the Dao itself." Honoring the nature and following the path "constitute the great beginning of cultivating virtue and collecting the Dao. Nourishing the mind-heart entails immersing oneself in knowledge already acquired and earnestly practicing abilities already mastered without allowing the slightest self-deception or selfish desires to enter in."

In a marvelous rhetorical flourish, Zhu manages here to tie together his doctrine of Principle with the *Constant Mean* and another text of the Four Books, the *Great Learning*. In one of his boldest exegetical moves, Zhu Xi reworded the text of the *Great Learning* to authorize the multistep process of moral self-cultivation beginning with the extension of knowledge, which he defined as the investigation of Principle. "The extension of knowledge," he explains in his commentary on the *Constant Mean*, "entails the daily acquisition of knowledge of previously unknown principles and daily reconsideration of textual passages that one previously did not fully understand, without the slightest error in analyzing Principle and without the slightest mistake of 'not reaching' or 'going beyond' [*guo buji*] in managing one's affairs. There is no knowledge to extend without nourishing the mind-heart; one must extend knowledge if one is to nourish the mind."

In sum, Zhu Xi reads the *Constant Mean* as Kong Ji's faithful transcription of Confucius's urgent call on everyone to resolve to perfect the goodness of his Heaven-ordained nature. The ancient sage-kings affirmed this innate goodness, Zhu Xi argued, but they also warned the world in their mind transmission to exercise great vigilance because many people are constitutionally susceptible to the deceptions of heterodoxies. Confucius understood this teaching of innate goodness and the dangers inherent in the fallible human mind, Zhu maintained, and taught it to his disciples. Kong Ji, in Zhu Xi's telling, wrote the *Constant Mean* to instruct the world how to cultivate the self properly in order to avoid errors, because he was distressed that heterodoxies already flourished in his day. Mencius received this teaching from Kong Ji, but could not transmit it to a disciple, so it died with him. After Mencius, the sages' mind transmission languished beneath the surface of the words of the *Constant Mean* until the Confucian masters in the Song dynasty finally apprehended the totality of Confucius's message and taught it to their disciples. But Zhu Xi perceived among some of those disciples the narrow scholar's mistakes of "not reaching" the Mean and the Buddhistic scholar's error of exceeding or "going beyond" it by seeking sudden enlightenment. Zhu Xi's reading of the *Constant Mean* outlines the process of interdependent steps one must follow to cultivate the self: honor the moral nature, which means to nourish the mind-heart, and follow the path of inquiry and learning, which means to extend knowledge.

CONCLUSION

This chapter on the canonical Confucius found in the *Constant Mean* spans the millennium from the Han to the Song. Zheng Xuan of the Eastern Han and Zhu Xi of the Southern Song largely agreed on several of the text's most important points. They understood it as a cultivation text, which outlined a path that would empower men in positions of moral authority who followed it to perfect themselves and, in the process, enable everyone to realize the potential that Heaven ordained for them. They agreed that one could achieve perfection only by working through the complex web of relationships with other creatures and with the spirits of the dead. They both distinguished the sages, perfect from birth, from those who aspired to follow the Way of Man and acquire Integrity. Zheng Xuan and Zhu Xi shared a conception of human perfectibility based on specific principles of filiality, benevolence, and righteousness. They recognized the central role of properly venerating one's ancestors as an integral part of the process of self-perfection and upheld the necessity of extending the sense of filiality that one shows to one's parents and ancestors outward to others who reside in their domain. Finally, they understood the *Constant Mean* as exalting the Master as the canonical Sage who singularly embodied Supreme Integrity and thus became a paragon for ten thousand generations.

They differed primarily in Zhu Xi's inclination to universalize its message and to interiorize the work of cultivation. Zheng Xuan read the *Mean* as a method for the sovereign to rule with the Mandate of Heaven, which hinged on the ruler's ability to sustain his cultivation efforts. Zhu Xi read it as a method for all learned men to cultivate the deepest interior of their being—the mind—in order to ensure that the self was always guided by the Mind of Dao. This process of self-perfection begins with careful study of the sages and culminates with the establishment of objective conditions in which all people fully realize their potential as human beings.

The crisis of loss and the hope of recovery run throughout the *Constant Mean* and its two commentaries. The Master despaired for the demise of an ancient time when sages ruled the world and all creatures realized an inborn potential for perfection. Kong Ji soon thereafter reiterated the Master's sense of loss when he composed the *Constant Mean* and asserted that the Master himself was a sage who possessed Sublime Integrity, but that tragically he never gained the throne from which to promulgate the Way. Zheng Xuan, too, held out hope that the *Mean* could enlighten his own lord, who might reverse the imminent demise of the once mighty Han Empire. Looking back a thousand years, Zhu Xi in the Song despaired that his predecessors failed to restore the Way in the world of men. But Zhu Xi, too, never lost hope that the Way might one day be practiced again. Impatient, though, that his sovereign might not cultivate the Way properly and cognizant that a foreign teaching had already deceived so many earnest minds, Zhu Xi appealed to gentlemen of proper classical learning to seek this inner goodness latent within everyone and enlighten those around them. Zheng Xuan and Zhu Xi may have differed on many particulars, but on this they agreed: the Way is not practiced, and yet the source of human goodness was originally given to everyone by Heaven.

SUGGESTED READINGS

Translations of the entire text of the *Mean* include James Legge's thoroughly annotated *The Doctrine of the Mean* in The Chinese Classics (London: Trübner & Co., 1876), 383–434; Wing-tsit Chan, *A Source Book in Chinese Philosophy* (Princeton, NJ: Princeton University Press, 1963), 95–114, which largely follows Zhu Xi's version, though, like Zhu, Chan cites Zheng Xuan's commentary; Andrew Plaks, *Ta Hsüeh and Chung Yung* (London: Penguin, 2003), 23–55; Roger T. Ames and David L. Hall, *Focusing the Familiar: A Translation and Philosophical Interpretation of the Zhongyong* (Honolulu: University of Hawaii Press, 2001); and Daniel Gardner, *The Four Books: The Basic Teachings of the Later Confucian Tradition* (Indianapolis: Hackett, 2007), 107–129.

For an important and influential philosophical treatment of the
Mean, see Tu Wei-ming, *Centrality and Commonality* (Albany,
NY: SUNY Press, 1989).

Sources used for the Chinese text: Zheng Xuan and Kong Yingda,
Liji zhushu (Sibu beiyao, ed., Taibei: Zhonghua shuju, 1965);
Zhu Xi, *Sishu zhangju jizhu* (Beijing: Zhonghua shuju, 1983);
Qian Mu, *Sishu shiyi* (Taibei: Xuesheng shuju, 1978), which com-
pares Zheng Xuan's and Zhu Xi's commentaries; and Ōtsuki
Nobuyoshi, *Shushi shiso shūchū tenkyō kō* (Tokyo: Chubun,
1976), which traces the origins of Zhu Xi's commentaries.

Critical studies of commentaries in classical Chinese texts include
John Makeham, *Transmitters and Creators: Chinese Commentators and Commentaries on the Analects* (Cambridge: Harvard
University Press, 2003) and Daniel Gardner, "Confucian Commentary and Chinese Intellectual History," *Journal of Asian Studies* 57, no. 2 (May 1998): 397–422.

5

The Supreme Sage and the Imperial Cults: Ritual and Doctrine

TWICE A YEAR THE CHAMBERLAIN HAD NOTICES POSTED ON *yamen* gates instructing officials not to prosecute criminal cases for the next three days and to observe a vegetarian diet. The Office of Imperial Sacrifices prescribed such measures to enable civil officials to purify themselves for the ceremony to venerate Confucius. Summoned by the slow, steady beat of the large drum inside the Confucius Temple, officials and other degree-holders gathered in order of rank at the gate before dawn and filed into the courtyard to observe the ritual feasting of the spirits of Confucius and his followers, held in the first week of every second and eighth lunar month. For more than a thousand years officials in the capital and in administrative cities and towns throughout the empire performed this rite at temples devoted to the man known as the Supreme Sage. Court authorities in Korea, Japan, and Vietnam also sang this rite in sinified renderings in their native languages. According to official sources written in classical Chinese—the oldest written language of East Asia—this sacrifice included a feast of meat, wine, and other foods laid out in carefully measured containers in front of the altars.[1] The spirits of the Supreme Sage and more than 150 of his most renowned followers and masters of the ancient canon sat at wooden tablets bearing their names while officials offered them the feast, accompanied by refined music, a dance in slow, measured stances, and hymns proclaiming the Supreme Sage's virtue.

The figure of Confucius as an object of cult veneration might not be familiar to many readers today, yet most Chinese in the late imperial era (960–1911 CE)—and all classically educated males—encountered him in the Confucius Temple. To understand why the court expended such great care in venerating the cultic Confucius, it is important to consider how this ceremony fits into the larger pantheon of gods and spirits venerated by court authorities in thousands of temples and shrines throughout the capital, across the empire, and beyond. Civil officials in late imperial times drew upon the Classics to compose the rites celebrated at these temples. As the Son of Heaven, the emperor alone raised the wine vessels to the highest gods of the pantheon. Yet the liturgies he followed, the myriad supplemental acts that accompanied his supplications at the main altar, and the many lesser rites performed outside the Forbidden City fell wholly within the purview of his court ministers educated in the Confucian Classics. These liturgical matters—scarcely mentioned in most books about late imperial China—remained an abiding concern among Confucian scholars inside and outside of the court. Approaching the cult of Confucius in the context of this larger imperial ritual system of gods illumines the fundamentally religious orientation of Confucianism and the understanding of spirits it shares with virtually everyone in late imperial times, irrespective of education or social status.

In addition to hosting sacrifices, the Confucius Temple also served to enshrine Confucian teachings and doctrines. After the imperial court integrated the cult of Confucius into the imperial pantheon in the Tang dynasty (618–907 CE), civil officials never ceased to debate the cult's meaning. In the early years of the cult, the court wavered on the central question of who was its principal sage, for, perhaps surprisingly, Confucius did not always hold this status. In subsequent years the court also added spirit tablets of other scholars, in effect endorsing the doctrines they taught. As a cult devoted to the spirits of men of surpassing classical learning, its rituals were necessarily bound up with the curriculum used to educate men preparing for civil examinations based on the Confucian Classics. One hundred ninety-eight carved stone tablets that still stand in front of the main gate of the Temple in Beijing best illustrate the Confucius Temple's integral connection with the examination system: they bear more than fifty thousand names of men who passed the highest examination beginning in 1313, date of the first examination to be held in the capital city of Beijing, to 1904, when the last civil examination was held there. The Libationer of the Directorate of Education led the new degree-holders who had passed the Palace Examination to the Temple to pay obeisance to the Supreme Sage.

This chapter considers the imperial cult of Confucius in its ritual and doctrinal contexts. The first section considers the highest cults—those of Heaven and Earth, the imperial ancestors, and the gods of soils and grains—in order to examine the basic logic of the pantheon and the fundamental principles of cult sacrifice. This section illustrates two key points: First, the cult of Confucius occupied a space within a vast cult system maintained by officials whose primary source of liturgical expertise was mastery of Confucian rites based on the Classics. Second, the basic elements of all imperial cult rites were essentially the same; they differed largely in the amount of food offered and details distinctive to each cult, such as the words of the hymns and prayers that praised the virtues of individual deities. This chapter then examines the court's definition and approval of Confucian doctrine by enshrining classical scholars and Confucian masters in the Temple to receive sacrifice alongside of Confucius. This next section shows that in the early years of imperial patronage of a temple cult located at the Imperial University, Confucius's status was at times subordinated to that of the Duke of Zhou. Once the Tang court committed itself to Confucius as the principal sage of this cult in the seventh century, the imperial court played an important role in the identification of an officially sanctioned body of Confucian doctrines. Although proponents of Zhu Xi's (1130–1200 CE) relatively narrow vision of the Confucian tradition grew steadily in the thirteenth and fourteenth centuries, the court institutionalized this interpretation only in the early fifteenth century, when it codified these doctrines in a new version of the Confucian canon and required candidates sitting for civil examinations to base their answers on this version.

PANTHEON

Principles of Cult Veneration

According to the Five Classics, ancient kings sacrificed to the gods and spirits that governed the natural and human worlds. Ritual scholars in the Tang dynasty systematized these cults as a pantheon divided into a three-tiered hierarchy as described in the Classics. The emperor led Great Sacrifices in and around the Forbidden City to the most exalted gods. High-ranking ministers performed Middle Sacrifices to the lesser gods and spirits of the second tier. Local officials offered Minor (or miscellaneous) Sacrifices at the county level. The emperor and civil officials followed a detailed calendar, which arranged the sacrifices to these gods according to a regular cycle set to the lunar months.

Cult sacrifice venerates gods and spirits with ritual feasts. It nurtures the gods and enhances their power while simultaneously fostering the well-being of their patrons. Cult sacrifice constitutes a means of exchange that benefits gods and their patrons. Precisely what is exchanged in cults varies among world religions. In Pure Land Buddhism, for example, the rite of enunciating the Buddha's name with complete faith and devotion—an immaterial sacrifice, to be sure, but an offering nonetheless—brings the supplicant the promise of rebirth in the Western Paradise at death. The imperial cults in China sought neither personal blessing nor salvation for him who made the offering; indeed, personal salvation was not in the offing from these gods—not even from Heaven—because they were never seen as exercising this kind of power. Rather, the person who offered sacrifice acted on behalf of a larger constituency (e.g., the imperial family, officialdom, farmers, etc.), beseeching the appropriate god to requite an offering with blessings for all those within his constituency. By acting on the behalf of subjects who deferred the performance of such rites to those with the authority to conduct them, the civil official who offered sacrifice deployed an essential instrument of governing the world—a world conceived of as encompassing humans, planetary and astral gods, nature deities, and ancestral spirits. The *Constant Mean*, discussed in chapter 4, makes clear that governing required something more than a secular bureaucrat's cool efficiency, because the efficacy of these rites hinged upon the supplicant's purity. As Confucius states in the *Analects*, an offering not given with reverence is no offering at all (3.12). Having observed the purification fast in the days before the ceremony, the celebrants gained the state of reverence necessary so that they, in the words of the *Record of Rites*, "certainly caught faint glimpses of the spirit upon entering the shrine." Only in seeing the spirit can the one who offers sacrifice serve it, and he can see it only if he attains true inner reverence.

The court scrupulously managed the gods' awesome powers by carefully regulating who had access to them according to a hierarchy believed to inhere in the universe itself. Only the emperor, as we have seen, could offer Great Sacrifice to the gods and spirits of the highest tier. Ritual codes of cults celebrated at lower levels of the spirit hierarchy, such as Soils and Grains, differentiated the emperor's offerings from those of lower-ranking civil officials in conspicuous ways. In Great Sacrifice, the twelve containers corresponded in number to the twelve insignia on the emperor's robes, which in turn derived from the number of months in a year, the span of a complete ritual cycle. Only the emperor or his surrogate ascended the altars in the Forbidden City and its suburbs; and not even his surrogate could invoke the spirit of the dynastic founder to share in the feast offered to the gods of Soils and Grains unless he was himself an imperial kinsman. The ritual codes even differentiated ancestral cults according to status, by limiting the generations of ancestors one could invoke at ancestral shrines of kinship groups and at family altars inside the home (ostensibly beyond the gaze of imperial authorities). The emperor sacrificed to seven generations—the dynastic founder and the six most recent generations of his ancestors—whereas a high-ranking official could sacrifice to his lineage founder and the five most recent generations, and an official of the fourth grade and below sacrificed to his lineage founder and the three most recent generations. The social prestige associated with offering cult to more generations of ancestors must have been considerable, but these religious rituals should not be reduced to mere demonstrations of social status. Ancestral rites held enormous cultural capital precisely because emperors, officials, and commoners alike revered the spirits, in whose immense power they believed.

Heaven and Earth

On the morning of the winter solstice, Ming (1368–1644) and Qing (1644–1911) emperors concluded a three-day purification fast, which they observed while secluded in a purification dormitory, and ascended a circular platform to present a single calf and other foods to "Exalted Heaven, High God" (*Hao Tian shangdi* 昊天上帝), which occupied the pinnacle of the ritual hierarchy. Heaven above exerted the greatest power in the cosmos, but did not rule alone; it required the nurturing power of Earth to sustain life, and so the ritual statutes prescribed a similar offering to the deity called "August Earth" at the summer solstice on a square platform. Properly built ritual structures accorded with the forces that governed the universe: Heaven was round, thus its altar was placed atop a circular mound, and Earth was square, as was the platform where August Earth received cult feast.

Known since ancient times as the Son of Heaven, the emperor enjoyed unparalleled status in the human world and exclusive access to Heaven through the imperial cult celebrated at the Altar of Heaven. The geographic orientation of the capital city facilitated the emperor's privileged cosmic bond with Heaven by providing him unhindered access along Beijing's broad avenue extending from his throne room to the enormous walled complex of the Altar of Heaven, south of the Forbidden City. Whereas they performed sacrifices to Heaven assiduously, emperors in late imperial times often dispatched surrogates to the northern suburbs to offer sacrifices to Earth, or simply performed a dual service on the winter solstice, based on the thinking that Heaven and Earth were coeval deities that circulated through the cosmos according to the contingent principles of yin and yang.

Yin and yang function in ritual contexts less as things in themselves than as the state or movement of things. Things in their yang state are light and luminous; in their yin state they are heavy and dark. Animated yang things are active, ascending, and so catalyze movement of things in their yin state, which are heavy, descending, dark, and receptive. The ascending yang and descending yin thus describe all phenomena, such as the workings of the body's inner organs that determine one's health; the king's policies, which, to succeed, must be appropriately attuned to seasonal change; and the movements of the gods, planets, and all things through the cosmos. Yin and yang operate in complementary ways when attended to properly, and in destructive ways when they are not. As we shall see in chapter 6, the bodily actions of the rites and the sonic qualities of the music of sacrifices to Confucius are carefully orchestrated to resonate according to the principles of yin and yang.

Imperial Ancestors

A cult of the imperial ancestors also held exalted status within the highest tier of the ritual hierarchy. Five times a year the emperor offered a carefully prepared feast of an ox, goat, pig, and other foods to the dynastic founder and his empress, accompanied by as many as six generations of the reigning emperor's most recent ancestors, in the Great Shrine inside the high walls of the Forbidden City. The emperor's ancestors exerted auspicious power over the throne and imperium, and afforded him access to the larger spirit world. At least since the Tang, the spirit of the dynasty's founder shared a portion of the ritual feast offered at the Altar of Heaven, even before similar offerings were extended to Sun, Moon, and Five Planets. Before leaving the palace to perform any Great Sacrifice, the emperor went to Revering Ancestors Hall to inform the ancestors of his intentions and to beseech them to intercede on his behalf to ensure the ceremony's success. Although the imperial cult system divided the cosmos into ostensibly discrete spheres over which the gods ruled, this principle of the interaction of spirits—particularly ancestral spirits—across intersecting spheres informed the entire cult system.

The ancestors' omnipresence during the emperor's contact with the highest gods underscored the central importance of filial piety, or filiality (*xiao*)—an abiding reverence toward one's forebears—in all imperial sacrifices. Manuals on imperial rites often invoked the canon to describe the purified state of reverence and piety with which the filial son entered the temple, even when a person performed rites to nonancestral gods. Filiality imbued an ancient king's every move in the ancestral hall; "on the day of the sacrifice," the *Record of Rites* says,

> . . . he certainly catches faint glimpses of the spirits upon entering the shrine and a gentle sense of their murmuring at every point

during the rite until he turns to leave. He listens after leaving the hall and indistinctly hears the spirits sigh. In this way the filiality of the former kings is such that they never forget the sight of their ancestors' visages, nor the sound of their voices.

Ritual purity of the filial son can be characterized as an undivided state of concentration on the spirit. According to ancient statutes still observed during the Ming and Qing, ritual celebrants observed a simple diet of food and drink without strong flavor or intoxicating effects, and secluded themselves for two or three days to prepare for the ceremony and to think of nothing other than the spirit. The Ming ritual code affirmed the filial son's unfaltering cognizance of the spirit's constant presence as the ideal state of the person who offers the sacrifice:

To concentrate and unify the mind with solemn reverence and meticulous care; if one has any thoughts, one visualizes the spirit that is to receive the sacrifice as he is immediately above or on one's left or right; pure and with complete sincerity, without a moment's lapse: this is what purification accomplishes.

Even when offering cult to Confucius, the celebrants must concentrate on the spirit as living, in the same way that descendants imagined their deceased kin. As the only rites practiced by Chinese of every social status and educational background, the cult of ancestors informed ritual practices in other imperial cults performed by civil officials, as well as in cult offered to popular gods venerated in community shrines and in the home. Belief that the manes of one's ancestors lingered for a period of time after death—usually the span of at least three generations—and rites to nurture them in exchange for whatever blessings they could bestow can be found everywhere in China as well as in Korea, Japan, and Vietnam.

Gods of Soils and Grains

Unlike ancestral spirits, which always took feasts indoors, the gods of Soils and Grains—the final cults in the highest tier of the imperial pantheon—were seated at parallel altars on an open square platform. The square platform established a connection with August Earth at the square platform in the northern suburb; a connection made explicit in the prayer sung during the Soils and Grains ceremony, which proclaimed the "assistance they rendered to August Earth in nurturing the auspicious cereals that sustain the people." Owing to their organic association with the soils of every locality, Soils and Grains also received offerings from local officials, a practice that dates back at least to the Zhou dynasty (ca. 1100–256 BCE), when hereditary lords maintained such altars. Local Soils and Grains cults, categorized as Middle Sacrifices, were distinguished from the emperor's Great Sacrifice by the smaller portions of the offerings and the titles used to honor them. As an agricultural society, China celebrated other overlapping cults devoted to the powers that affected the harvest, which effectively saturated this sphere of the cosmos with an abundance of ritual activity. The court observed services for spirits that influenced the human role in agriculture: plowing, sowing, and reaping. Ancient prayers to Field Ancestor (*Tianzu* 田祖) evolved into an elaborate agricultural cult devoted to First Farmer (*Xiannong*), or Spirit Farmer (*Shennong*), who, one hymn proclaimed, "planted the auspicious seeds and instructed the common folk who eternally relied upon this for ten thousand generations." The Manchus, who conquered the empire in the seventeenth century and established the Qing, elaborated on this rite with a grand ceremony at which the emperor personally plowed the first few rows of an imperial plot adjacent to the First Farmer's temple outside of the Forbidden City.

The emperor personally offered Great Sacrifices to gods who occupied the highest of the three tiers of the imperial pantheon. He usually dispatched high-ranking members of the court to offer Middle Sacrifices to such gods as Morning Sun at a square platform inside a circular walled complex in the eastern suburb on the spring equinox, and to Evening Moon at an open square platform in the western suburb on the autumn equinox. Unlike the Great Sacrifice, which used twelve vessels of foods, the Middle Sacrifice required only ten vessels. Other civil officials in and around the capital, at provincial and county seats across China, and as far away as Korea and Japan patronized such cults and those of other gods associated with more circumscribed or geographically proximate domains. Gods of wind and clouds, thunder and rain, sacred mountains and rivers, for example, each received ritual feasts from local officials at altars and shrines expressly devoted to them.

The Rites and Late Imperial Society

Rites venerating the gods that governed the cosmos described in the Five Classics evolved slowly during the long centuries of ancient China. Some of the most ancient rites were inextricably tied to the hereditary lineages of kings and lords who ruled early China. At the same time that the sovereign continued to assume the throne by privilege of royal descent, the ancient nobility, which ruled hereditary domains, declined with the expansion in the Qin (221–209 BCE) and Han (206 BCE–220 CE) dynasties of an imperial bureaucracy that assumed administrative control over local resources and ritual responsibility for regional cults. Owing in part to the growing status of classically educated men appointed to the bureaucracy during the Tang dynasty, the court formed a civil cult devoted to Confucius, whom it dubbed Exalted King of Culture (*Wenxuan wang* 文宣王). The word "culture" (*wen* 文) in his title alludes to a passage in the *Analects* where Confucius states that Heaven invested the underlying patterns of the Dao, called *wen*, in him (9.5). The word *wen* also denotes civil as opposed to military (*wu* 武) officials.

Powerful military clans based along the northwestern frontier far overshadowed the influence of civil officials in the Tang. These clans dominated local society through hereditary privileges over extensive manors, and the imperial court through monopolies of court rank. Tang military clans claimed descent from a number of ancient personages, such as Lü Wang, the general who led the Zhou conquest of the Shang dynasty (ca. 1600–ca. 1100 BCE). The Tang court founded a military cult centered on Lü Wang, whom it dubbed King of Military Victory (*Wucheng wang* 武成王); the cult thrived under the military clans' patronage, but eventually foundered as their status waned late in the dynasty. Early in the Song dynasty (960–1279 CE) this cult fell into obscurity, due in part to policies aimed at limiting the power of military clans. These policies were initiated by the founding emperor, himself a former general who seized the throne in a coup d'état. The Ming court (1368–1644) patronized another military figure called Lord Guan, or Guan Yu (160–219), a general said to wield awesome powers over the elements. His cult thrived because he enjoyed popular support as the patron saint of the rapidly expanding merchant class.

The discussion of imperial cults thus far yields at least three key insights into late imperial society. (1) The cosmos imagined in imperial cults was ruled by many gods and spirits, each of whom governed particular, though nearly always overlapping, spheres of the universe or specific human institutions and occupations. In those spheres of the cosmos that society held to be particularly important—such as governing, the harvest, and ancestors—the court did not hesitate to permit a degree of redundancy in cult veneration, resulting in a ritual density in some spheres and comparatively less overlap and concentration of ritual activity in those spheres held to be less important. (2) As the primary means of interaction between gods and rulers, imperial cults accorded with the hierarchical structure believed to inhere in the universe: the Son of Heaven alone feasted the highest and most powerful gods, using liturgies appropriate for his own exalted status, which corresponded to that of the gods. The spirit and human worlds were governed by parallel administrative hierarchies, linked at every level by rites of sacrifice in which celebrants and gods engaged in reciprocal exchange. (3) The cult of ancestors acted as the linchpin of the ritual activities of emperor, civil officials, and commoners alike, because virtually all people venerated their own ancestors and because the basic condition of ritual purity required in all cults was largely characterized by a state of reverence and filial piety.

Imperial cults harnessed the power of reverence and piety to ensure that the rite succeeded and thereby nurtured the gods and protected the interests of their patrons. They also invoked another level of power not usually recognized by their patrons. The formation of the civil and military cults in the Tang dynasty provides ample evidence that cults enhanced the social prestige and political influence of competing sectors of Chinese society. Scrutiny of the civil cult of Confucius demonstrates that cults were internally contested domains, in which patrons vied with one another over how to define the very meaning of the cult to which they were devoted. The issues debated within cults varied depending upon matters of concern to the patrons of a given cult. Controversies regarding the ancestral shrine of the imperial family, for example, touched upon questions of imperial succession. When a Ming emperor succeeded his cousin who had no heir, he insisted, over strident opposition at court, upon posthumously enthroning his natal father and installing him in the Imperial Ancestral Temple. Patrons of the cult of Confucius, who by the eleventh century came to dominate the court and bureaucracy, were intensely concerned with questions of doctrine: What did the Supreme Sage teach? What texts properly record those teachings? Who among his followers correctly understood them? The next section turns to these concerns.

DOCTRINE

In addition to the veneration of Confucius as a powerful spirit in the official pantheon, the temple located in official educational complexes also served an important doctrinal function. Eighth-century debates over who held the primary status of sage in the temple—Confucius or the Duke of Zhou—had important doctrinal implications. By adding new figures to the temple, such as masters of particular canonical works and later followers of Confucius, the court sanctioned the ideas expressed in their commentaries and philosophical writings. Records of debates on whom to enshrine in the temple provide valuable insight into the court's position on which teachings accorded with the classical texts. The growing prominence of Zhu Xi in the temple and of his classical commentaries (discussed in chapter 4) in civil examinations during the Ming indicates the court's increasing willingness to sanction a narrow conception of Confucian doctrine. By the fifteenth century the temple cult and civil examinations provided the court with essential venues from which to promulgate imperial orthodoxy.

The history of the cult of Confucius may be divided into three periods. (1) From some time after Confucius's death in 479 BCE until after the fall of the Han dynasty, generations of his followers and descendants venerated Confucius in a local cult celebrated in Qufu, with only occasional official patronage. (2) With the first sacrifice to Confucius by court officials in the capital in the mid–third century CE, the cult emerged from the local circumstances of its beginnings, to become gradually integrated into imperial institutions. During the next five hundred years, imperial officials performed sacrifices to Confucius at educational sites with increasing frequency, but several key elements of a cult, such as the identity of its principal sage—Confucius or the Duke of Zhou—and the classical precedent that sanctioned it, remained unresolved. (3) A cult devoted to Confucius as its sage, with a regular liturgy based on a widely accepted classical precedent, was fully integrated into the imperial cults celebrated in and around the capital from the mid–eighth century. The cult of Confucius, patronized by classically educated civil officials and Confucian literati, grew in prominence during the late imperial period and thrived until the end of the nineteenth century. During this third period the cult continued to evolve along with fundamental changes in society as well as within Confucian learning itself.

The Early Local Cult

After his death, Confucius's disciples observed three years of mourning, as for a deceased parent. After grieving for three years, says the early chronicler Sima Qian (ca. 145–ca. 85 BCE), "some departed still in tears, while others remained." One disciple, Zigong, whom we encountered in chapter 1, continued a vigil in a hut by his master's graveside for another three years. Centuries later, Sima Qian witnessed annual sacrifices (*fengci* 奉祠) to Confucius beside his grave, where scholars gathered to discuss the rites, perform toasting rituals, and hold archery ceremonies. An ancient chronicle records the eulogy of young Duke Ai, who lamented the Sage's passing by saying, "Alas! What grief! Venerable Ni. I've no model to emulate now." A disciple retorted sharply, "To eulogize a man one ignored in life violates propriety. To invoke his name at all is merely presumptuous. The Duke errs on both counts." Histories of the cult compiled much later merely record the Duke's lament without the disciple's derisive comment, as if to fix the moment of official patronage at the very year of Confucius's death. These later histories also cite several occasions during the Han dynasty when an emperor stopped in Qufu to offer sacrifice to Confucius's spirit or to bestow hereditary titles on his living descendants. Some historians date the establishment of Confucianism as orthodoxy to the Han, which seems unlikely since neither the ruling family nor prominent ministers at the time held a coherent sense of the classical heritage as centered on Confucius or as doctrinally distinct from competing schools or teachings (see chapter 3). Imperial visits to tombs or temples constituted important expressions of court approval, but they were hardly unique to Confucius. Early Han rulers routinely visited many local cults and bestowed posthumous honors on other extraordinary personages. The throne's similar support of the Duke of Zhou—the archetypal loyal minister of the first Zhou king—in particular augured a momentous debate in the formation of an imperial cult centuries later.

Court Celebration of the Cult

Cult veneration of Confucius first emerged from its place of origin after the fall of the Han dynasty. According to the official chronicles of the Three Kingdoms, the emperor of the state of Wei (220–265 CE) explicated the *Analects* in 241 CE, then ordered the Chamberlain to offer a large beast sacrifice to Confucius in the Imperial Academy with Yan Hui as his correlate, who shared the offering. This marks the first recorded official celebration of the cult in the capital. By including Confucius and his greatest disciple in the ceremony, the court effectively established a bond between Confucius and the court's highest educational institution. It furthermore associated the cult with the emperor's personal moral training, such as that described in the *Constant Mean* (see chapter 4) and his mastery of a work solely associated with Confucius. The chronicles record scores of court rites that built upon the 241 precedent, performed by a series of short-lived dynasties in subsequent centuries when China was ruled by regional kingdoms. These rites included a more detailed liturgy, with music and dance appropriate for a duke, painted portraits of Confucius's disciples, a temple expressly devoted to Confucius in the capital, and detailed

instructions on ritual clothing worn by the emperor during his observance of the rites.[2]

Along with its growing commitment, beginning in the third century, to venerating Confucius in the capital, the court extended similar
honors to the towering figure of the Duke of Zhou. Confucius himself
had emulated the Duke of Zhou and venerated him as a cult figure
(*Analects* 3.15). The Duke of Zhou had received offerings in several
cults associated with his varied contributions to early Chinese civilization. A paragon of ministerial loyalty, he assisted his brother in founding the Zhou dynasty and presided over the court when his infant
nephew became king. When the young king came of age, he repaid his
uncle's loyalty by enfeoffing him as the Duke of Zhou in Qufu. According to the *Record of Rites*, the Zhou court charged later lords of
the state of Lu to "sacrifice to the Duke with rites and music appropriate for the Son of Heaven." The *Record of Rites* provides rich details of annual sacrifices to the duke in the royal Zhou Ancestral
Temple, thus establishing clear canonical precedent for an imperial
cult of the Duke of Zhou. According to early historians of the Han dynasty, he continued to receive sacrifices in the Zhou Ancestral Temple,
relocated in Qufu, even after the fall of the Han. Another cult based in
the royal capital of Chang'an venerated the duke, who conceived of the
ancient capital and offered a large beast sacrifice at the Soils Altar
when the foundation stones of the city were laid. A cult venerated him
as a kind of patron saint of the city as late as the sixth century.

In the seventh century, two erstwhile distinct cults, one devoted to
the Duke of Zhou and the other to Confucius, merged in the thinking
of some members of the court. The Tang dynasty greatly expanded
the educational system by admitting to imperial schools the scions of
the imperial family and rank-bearing families in the capital. Sons of
commoners were admitted to commandery and county schools
throughout the empire. The first Tang emperor ordered rites at these
schools honoring the Duke of Zhou and Confucius, each in his own
shrine. "Outstanding virtue must receive sacrifice," he said:

Ji Dan [the Duke of Zhou] ruled the Zhou states, created ritual
precedents, brilliantly illumined institutions and regulations, opened

the eyes and ears of the people, and fathomed the depths of the laws. Profound is Venerable Ni [Confucius], upon whom Heaven conferred deep wisdom; the teachings of the four disciplines have remained constant throughout the ages[3]; the legacy of his three thousand disciples' magnificence never ceased. Only with these two sages has the Dao been manifested among the people.

When the first Tang emperor in 624 CE personally visited the temple at the Imperial University devoted to both men to observe the joint ceremony, the Duke of Zhou held primary status as sage, and Confucius held secondary status as teacher. Court ministers later prevailed upon the second emperor to remove the duke from this temple on grounds that his veneration in school temples lacked proper classical precedent. During this same period ritual scholars first systematized the entire imperial cult order on the three-tiered system by drawing on the recently completed authoritative edition of the canon called the *Correct Meaning of the Five Classics*. On the basis of this new edition of the Classics, the court downgraded cults found to lack a classical basis and determined the appropriate precedent for the cult of Confucius: a passage on the libation sacrifice offered to the Sage and to teachers of schools, found in the *Record of Rites*.[4] Memorialists cited this passage in 628 CE to argue for the duke's removal from the Temple that venerated Confucius, and cited it again under the third emperor after the Duke had been briefly restored there. They argued that since the Duke devised court rites when the Zhou dynasty was founded, his tablet should be moved to the temple that honored the Zhou kings. The emperor concurred, and his tablet remained there as a correlate of the Zhou kings ever after.

In the years after it positioned Confucius as the Sage, the court implemented several other measures that defined this cult as distinctively "Confucian." It enshrined eleven of Confucius's disciples and, in 739, elevated Confucius to Exalted King of Culture, placing his spirit image so that it faced south, the orientation of a sovereign. From this time until the end of the imperial era in 1911, the cult centered on Confucius, his followers, and their teachings. In the millennium that followed, the court periodically changed Confucius's title, revised details of the liturgy of sacrifice, and enshrined later followers of the Sage. But the status of the imperial cult of Confucius remained inviolable from the eighth until the early twentieth century, even while the amorphous figure of Confucius and interpretations of his teachings never ceased to change. Indeed, this was the only imperial cult actually to outlive imperial institutions, which formally ended in 1911.

Why did these disparate events converge in the Tang dynasty to form an imperial cult of Confucius? David McMullen shows that although hereditary elites continued to dominate social and political institutions in the Tang, a classically educated elite gained a degree of independence from them and carved out an important niche at court on the basis of their classical learning. And although the highest academies only admitted the sons of imperial and hereditary rank-bearing families, the system also provided for young men without hereditary privilege. Classical scholarship thrived under court sponsorship in the seventh century, providing an important foundation for a cult devoted to the Sage of that classical heritage. The apparent sharpening of this cult's focus as a distinctively *Confucian* formation, with the ascension of Confucius and his disciples in it, might also reflect the ascendance of another presence on the Tang cultural landscape; in 645 CE, not long after court scholars began work on the *Correct Meaning of the Five Classics,* a monk named Xuanzang (ca. 596–664 CE) returned from India with hundreds of Buddhist scriptures and began the largest translation of Buddhist texts ever undertaken.[5] The appearance at the Tang court of another corpus of sacred texts and the increasing devotion to the Buddha must have surely induced Confucian scholars to clarify their own vision of the Way.

By the eighth century, nearly a hundred Buddhist monasteries dotted the urban landscape of the capital alone. In response to Buddhism's growing influence in Chinese society, Han Yu (768–824 CE) wrote an impassioned defense of the Confucian Dao and a scathing criticism of Buddhism and Daoism. The ancients from Yao and Shun to the Duke of Zhou and Confucius, he said, taught benevolence and righteousness. Their Dao can be read in the Classics and practiced in the rites; it is evident in the different occupations and constant bonds and even in the clothes people wear and the food they eat. "In life one received love and in death the constant norms were fulfilled [through ancestral sacrifice]. Heaven's spirit came to take sacrifice at the suburban altar and the ancestors were sated in the ancestral temple. This is what I call the Dao," Han said, "not what Laozi and the Buddhists call the Dao." Anticipating Zhu Xi's assertions in his commentary on the *Constant Mean* some three hundred years later, Han Yu then declaimed, "Yao transmitted [the Dao] to Shun and he to Yu. Yu transmitted it to Tang and Tang to kings Wen and Wu and to the Duke of Zhou. They transmitted it to Confucius and he to Mencius. When Mencius died, it was no longer transmitted." In other words, Han Yu identifies Mencius as the last person to receive the Dao. The Daoists and Buddhists wrought great destruction by obliterating the Dao taught by the ancients, Han Yu maintained. They destroyed the constant bonds such that "a son no longer regards his father as a father, a minister has ceased to regard his lord as king, and the people don't attend to their proper duties." Han Yu's appeal was unprecedented in its vitriolic polemic against Buddhism and Daoism and in the clarity of his vision of a discrete Confucian tradition that must be upheld against other, evil doctrines.

The Imperial Cult of Confucius

LATE TANG THROUGH THE SONG (NINTH TO THIRTEENTH CENTURIES). The courts that followed the Tang dynasty never departed very far from its basic principles of ritual veneration of Confucius, established by the mid–eighth century. Bureaucratic authorities offered sacrifices to Confucius as a Sage at educational institutions in the capital and at schools throughout the empire. Though it lacked explicit classical precedent, the court authorized the cult on the basis of a passage found in the *Record of Rites* on libation sacrifice to the Sage and to teachers of schools.[6] Two other types of figures received secondary offerings: founders of canonical traditions of the Five Classics and personal disciples of the Sage. In the eleventh century the Ministry of Rites added to these benchmarks when it enshrined four figures who did not meet either criterion. These four—Mencius, Xunzi, Yang Xiong (53 BCE–18 CE), and Han Yu—each in his own way had regarded himself as a faithful disciple of Confucius.[7]

By the Song dynasty, Confucianism's status in Chinese society had risen dramatically. The great military families that dominated the Tang declined rapidly in the aftermath of widespread peasant rebellions in the eighth and ninth centuries. Anxious to forestall a resurgent military class, the Song court expanded the civil bureaucracy and appointed graduates of the civil examinations to positions of power. A Confucian gentry, defined by success in civil examinations and mastery of classical learning rather than by hereditary privilege, dominated society throughout the late imperial era. With the rising importance of Confucian learning, debates on the proper understanding of its teachings became hotly contested. Prime minister Wang Anshi (1021–1086) deployed the power of government-run educational institutions to train and recruit cadres to implement his vision of fundamental social reform. When a protégé followed him as prime minister, Wang Anshi was enshrined in the Confucius Temple, and the writings of his opponents, the brothers Cheng Yi (1030–1107) and Cheng Hao (1032–1085), were banned from civil examinations. The reformers' brazen use of educational institutions and the temple to serve political ends—though only short-lived—set a compelling precedent eventually used by their opponents long after the tumult of Wang's reforms had passed.

Wang Anshi's political adversaries were philosophically opposed to deploying the central government's power to legislate social reform through the proclamation of laws. The Cheng brothers and their large circle of followers preferred to work outside government structures—which was largely necessitated by Wang's control of the court—to transform public norms so that they accorded with canonical principles. Public morality could not be converted by mandate from above, they maintained, but needed to be transformed gradually through moral cultivation under the nurturing care of the gentleman, eloquently expressed in Zhu Xi's reading of the *Constant Mean*. The results of such a grassroots approach, they believed, would be more permanent than any changes through public decree. Much like Han Yu before them, the Cheng brothers and their followers, most notably Zhu Xi, were particularly alarmed by what they believed were Buddhism's growing tangible effects on popular customs and even within Confucian circles. Zhu Xi maintained that a chasm separated their own corrupt age from the golden age of the sages, and called for the revival of the ancient Dao. Recovery of this lost Dao, Zhu argued in his preface to the *Constant Mean,* required an understanding of the mind transmission passed down from the ancient sage-kings to Confucius and finally to Mencius.

Though controversial in his own day, Zhu Xi's claim that after the death of the last sage, Mencius, only the Cheng brothers properly understood the true Dao, eventually became widely accepted. Yet it posed a question: If the last sage who understood the Dao had died 1,400 years earlier, how could the Cheng brothers possibly have retrieved it? The key, Zhu Xi argued, lay in discerning a patterned essence usually translated as Principle (*li*), inherent in all things. Just as the master jade carver follows the subtle patterns of the grain of a piece of jade to carve it properly, one who seeks to understand the Dao must investigate the latent, essential pattern (or Principle) in each thing. Although all things possess an essential Principle, Zhu Xi maintained that such "things" as filiality, righteousness, and benevolence were the most important objects of investigation. The textual legacy of the sages—the Classics—possessed the essential pattern of such "things" in their most refined form. Zhu Xi identified four works in particular—eventually called the Four Books—that provided the gateway to the Dao: the *Analects, Mencius,* the *Great Learning,* attributed to Confucius's disciple Zengzi, and the *Constant Mean.* Merely to apprehend the surface meaning of words in such texts, Zhu maintained, would not apprehend their essential Principle, which is subtle. Han and Tang classicists failed to discern the innate patterns latent in the ancient texts because they explicated the surface meaning of words rather than seeking to apprehend the Dao itself.[8]

Zhu Xi warned that investigating the innate pattern in things could be dangerous. Whereas Han and Tang classicists did not go far enough (*buji*) to inquire beyond, or beneath, the surface meaning of words, others more recently went too far (*guo*) and extracted lofty ideas more consonant with Buddhism than with Confucius's ancient Dao. The proper investigation of innate patterns of things must navigate between the errors of inadequacy and excess—between superficial, literal readings of the sages' words and overly esoteric and subtle imaginings of sublime falsehoods. Understanding of the Dao by investigating essential principles in things was at once accessible to anyone and yet oddly elusive: so many followed their investigations to "spurious truths," which confounded the Sage's Dao by their seeming authenticity. Zhu Xi cited several disciples of the Cheng brothers whose excesses produced error, usually because they had studied Buddhism in their early education and never extirpated its traces from their thinking.

Zhu Xi excised from his genealogy of what became known as Learning of the Way, or the Dao School (*Daoxue* 道學)[9], those scholars who deviated from the primary aim of recovering the lost Way of the ancient sages. Zhu laid out the principles of these exclusions in his influential anthology titled *Reflections on Things at Hand*. Whereas Zhu's complete oeuvre provides ample evidence of his seemingly ecumenical learning, in the century after his death some of his most ardent followers adhered to his more rigid pronouncements. An encyclopedic collection of Zhu's conversations called *Topics of Master Zhu's Conversations* (*Zhuzi yulei* 朱子語類), completed in 1270, reveals an astonishingly profound and widely read man who rigorously divided the major figures of the Confucian tradition into those who transmitted the ancient Dao and those who did not. Lü Zuqian (1137–1181), who co-edited *Reflections on Things at Hand,* emerges as uncritically reliant on Han commentaries and not adequately concerned with passing judgment on moral questions. Zhu Xi criticizes Lu Xiangshan (1139–1193), his most important philosophical adversary in his own day, because he taught what Zhu regarded as a Buddhistic method of sudden enlightenment that skipped over the necessary step of investigating things, and because he sought common ground between Buddhism and Confucianism.

In contrast to the Cheng brothers' opposition (during the Northern Song) to using government institutions to promulgate their understanding of the Confucian Dao in the waning years of the Southern Song dynasty (1127–1279), Zhu Xi's followers agitated in the court to canonize his vision of the Confucian tradition. Until then, only one person—the ill-fated Wang Anshi—had been enshrined by the same dynasty under which he had lived. By this measure alone, the enshrinement in the twelfth century of five Song masters, including the

Cheng brothers and Zhu Xi, constituted an extraordinary act. In announcing this change, the emperor reiterated Zhu Xi's genealogical conception of the Dao and evidently bound the fate of the Song dynasty with that of Zhu's understanding of the Confucian tradition. He cited the Dao's essential embodiment in a new canon called the Four Books, the loss of the Dao's transmission after Mencius, and its retrieval by the Cheng brothers in his own Song dynasty: "Since the restoration [of the Southern Song], Zhu Xi's refined thinking and brilliant analysis harmonized form and content. He used the *Great Learning, Analects, Mencius,* and *Constant Mean* [constituting the Four Books] to completely illuminate Confucius's Dao and enlighten the world." Several years later the Song court canonized the authors of the Four Books by elevating Zengzi, reputed author of the *Great Learning,* and Kong Ji, author of the *Constant Mean,* to the status of correlates in the temple, joining Yan Hui and Mencius.

Yet the Song court refrained from canonizing a narrow orthodoxy based on Dao School teachings as found in *Master Zhu's Conversations.* In addition to Zhu Xi, it also enshrined prominent Song masters who, though not antagonistic to Dao School teachings, nonetheless formulated ideas not wholly consonant with them, either. Nor did it enforce a narrow conception of the Dao in civil examinations. Although writings by the Cheng brothers and Zhu Xi were banned from the examination curriculum for short periods, the Song court never required Dao School commentaries in civil examinations, as its successors would later do. Filling bureaucratic positions on the basis of examination success rather than hereditary privilege had become the predominant administrative practice only a few centuries earlier. As such, mastering the Confucian Classics according to any reading as a criterion for appointment already amounted to a relatively narrow gateway to positions of political authority. Wang Anshi's legacy of heavy-handed enforcement of his narrow understanding of the tradition remained a fairly recent nightmare in the collective memory of many Song officials. Few in the Southern Song desired to replicate his statist methods in imposing political and cultural reforms. Using the throne's authority to promulgate a narrow state ideology was largely unprecedented in the Song, and tended to evoke such infamous policies as Qin Shihuang's (r. 246–210 BCE) book burning and Empress Wu Zetian's (r. 684–705) deployment of Buddhism to counter court resistance to her reign.

YUAN–MING–QING (FOURTEENTH THROUGH NINETEENTH CENTURIES). In contrast to the Song, which never endorsed this exclusionary approach to the Confucian Dao, the three dynasties that followed carefully consolidated the teachings of Cheng Yi and Zhu Xi as Cheng-Zhu orthodoxy. The Mongols—a non-Chinese nomadic people who conquered China and established the Yuan dynasty (1279–1368)—required Chinese candidates sitting for civil examinations to follow Zhu Xi's commentaries on the Four Books, as well as his commentaries on the *Changes* and *Odes*. Song commentaries replaced Tang versions of the *Rites* and *Documents*, and a collection of remarks by several scholars, including Zhu Xi, prefaced the Yuan edition of the *Spring and Autumn Annals*.

It is difficult to gauge the impact of Cheng-Zhu orthodoxy on the court under the Mongols, because they strictly limited the number of Han Chinese eligible to receive an examination degree. The Yuan court preferred to appoint Mongols and their military allies to high positions in order to limit Han Chinese influence at court. But if his tangible effects on Yuan administration and policy remain unclear, Zhu Xi's influence is clearly evident in the teachings of Confucian masters of the early Ming. Not everyone concurred with Zhu Xi's ideas, but virtually all prominent thinkers of the Ming used his writings as a touchstone, either quoting them in support of their own ideas or criticizing them to formulate dissenting positions. Given the pervasive use of Zhu Xi's version of the Four Books in Ming education, Zhu's prominence comes as no surprise. Before Wang Yangming (1472–1529) rescued Lu Xiangshan, Zhu Xi's principal intellectual adversary, from oblivion, virtually no one cited Lu's writings. Indeed, most educated men who had even heard of Lu knew him only through Zhu Xi's oft-repeated criticisms, found in widely available editions of *Reflections on Things at Hand*, *Topics of Master Zhu's Conversations*, and the imperial collection of Dao School writings called *Great Collection on Nature and Principle*.

During the first century and a half of Ming rule, memorialists repeatedly advocated narrowing the criteria for enshrinement in the Confucius Temple to corroborate Zhu Xi's understanding of the Confucian tradition. One set of temple reform proposals, submitted to the throne in 1370, stands out because it established the terms of debates until the court finally adopted most of those proposals 150 years later. They called for the restoration of the ancient practice of using tablets as seats for the spirits rather than sculpted or painted images. They recommended that the current practice of feasting the correlates Yan Hui, Zengzi, and Kong Ji before their fathers, who were also enshrined in the temple as Confucius's disciples, should cease, because it violated the principle of filiality. These reform proposals also argued that since Confucius never ruled as a sovereign, his title of Exalted King of Culture should be revised and his spirit tablet in the temple should face not south but east, as befitted a minister or teacher.

On the question of Confucian doctrine, Ming officials called for the removal from the temple of such figures as Xunzi, Yang Xiong, and others, whom they juxtaposed to the correlates who "carefully transmitted the Dao of Confucius." In the fifteenth century court officials launched an explicit critique of the offenses that Yang Xiong and others had committed against morality, then called for their removal from the Temple. "Now that the learning of Principle [another name for the Dao School] greatly illuminates the world," they said, "why use the confused and unorthodox writings of the Han and Wei periods?" Half a century later, in 1530, the court, with the strong support of the emperor, finally adopted these proposals regarding liturgy and doctrine, reiterating in detail the rationale for implementing them expressed by earlier memorialists. These reforms remained in place for the remainder of the Ming and Qing dynasties. An early Qing emperor insisted upon elevating Zhu Xi's temple rank by placing his tablet among those of eleven of Confucius's personal disciples, contravening an otherwise rigorously observed chronological order of the tablets. The apotheosis of Zhu Xi's learning was complete.

CONCLUSION

Imperial orthodoxy was the product of debates at court on Confucian doctrine, which was nearly always contested. Although authority to make all final decisions on such matters lay with the emperor, even the most autocratic ruler refrained from acting by fiat, preferring instead to promote ministers whose opinions corroborated his own views, if indeed he held any. The first emperor of the Ming dynasty, the very model of an autocrat, implemented far-reaching ritual reforms by relying upon the scholarly opinions of ministers whose positions found some opposition as well as more support at court. Court debates on enshrinement in the Temple directly affected, and were framed by, educational curricula used to prepare candidates for civil examinations. Men who passed these examinations held important positions at court and in the civil bureaucracy. Thus enshrinement, civil examinations, and bureaucratic appointment formed a nexus of power in late imperial times. Institutional enforcement of orthodoxy through civil examinations and the Temple cult perpetuated adherence to the teachings found in Zhu Xi's commentaries on the Four Books, but the court never punished deviation from imperial orthodoxy. Rather, deviation from the court's normative position on orthodoxy, entailed a kind of intellectual banishment; it usually ensured failure in the examination halls and thus no bureaucratic appointment, which was the objective of most examinees. Staunch critics of Cheng-Zhu orthodoxy nonetheless thrived in private academies and informal intellectual circles during the Ming and Qing dynasties, unafraid of government reprisals—unless, of course, their barbs landed too close to the person of the emperor or other powerful men.[10]

The discussion so far has touched upon cult veneration of gods and spirits in a general way. How are we to understand cult ritual, particularly given that it is so far removed from the personal experience of most people today? We can no longer observe the emperor ascending the round altar mound to offer sacrifice to Heaven; a hundred years have passed since the last emperor performed such rites. Nor can we share the filial son's experience as he raises the wine vessel to the spirits of his ancestors, for to fully appreciate such a ritual act requires at the very least that we grew up with the belief that the ancestors linger after death and that spirits surround our every move. Travelers to Taiwan today, however, may still observe government-sponsored sacrifices to Confucius in the brilliantly painted Temple in Taibei or in the simple beauty of the Temple in Tainan. The cult of Confucius thrives along with myriad other cults in this southern city of Taiwan, where government officials and education officers pride themselves on following the authentic rites once performed by imperial officials. Spurred by a thriving tourist industry in the post-Mao era, abbreviated performances of this rite, without real food offerings, can be seen in Confucius Temples in Beijing, Qufu, Jiading, outside of Shanghai, and numerous other temples that survived the repeated onslaughts visited upon them by foreign invasions or rebel pillaging in the nineteenth and twentieth centuries, or by Mao's Red Guards during the Cultural Revolution.

In the absence of personal observation of cult rites, one might still imagine oneself standing near the celebrants and watching them closely as they execute the movements that the ritual texts instruct them to perform. We might consider carefully the ritual master's instructions on why such rites are so necessary, and listen to his admonitions to a young master about to consecrate food and drink to the spirit of the Sage. Such an approach to Confucian rites may well fall short of direct observation of a ceremony, but in the absence of first-hand experience, no better alternative may exist. The next chapter considers what may be the most personal experience of Confucius long after his death: that of serving his spirit in the Temple located in the town where he once walked and taught his disciples.

Suggested Readings

For a general introduction to major themes of Chinese religions, see Stephen Teiser, "The Sprits of Chinese Religions," in Donald Lopez Jr., ed., *Religions of China in Practice* (Princeton: Princeton University Press, 1996), 3–37.

For the rise to prominence of Confucian scholars in the Tang, and their discussions of court ritual, see David McMullen, *State and*

Scholars in T'ang China (Cambridge, England: Cambridge University Press, 1988).

For court debates on the cult of Confucius in connection with the formation of imperial orthodoxy, see Thomas Wilson, *Genealogy of the Way: The Construction and Uses of the Confucian Tradition in Late Imperial China* (Palo Alto, CA: Stanford University Press, 1994).

On imperial rituals in the Qing, see Angela Zito, *Of Body and Brush: Grand Sacrifice as Text/Performance in Eighteenth-Century China* (Chicago: University of Chicago Press, 1997).

On official and popular patronage of the Guandi cult, see Prasenjit Duara, "Superscribing Symbols: The Myth of Guandi, Chinese God of War," *Journal of Asian Studies* 47, no. 4 (November 1988): 778–95.

Chinese sources used for the history of the cult include Jin Zhizhi and Song Hong, *Wenmiao liyue kao* (1691); Kong Jifen, *Queli wenxian kao* (1762); Li Zhizao, *Pangong liyue shu* (1618); Lü Yuanshan, *Sheng men zhi* (1613); Qu Jiusi, *Kong miao liyue kao* (1609); and Zhang Chaorui, *Kongmen chuan Dao lu* (1598).

6

The Cultic Confucius in the Imperial
Temple and Ancestral Shrine

*The Master said, "If I do not offer the sacrifice myself, it is like not
sacrificing at all."*[1]

THROUGHOUT LATE IMPERIAL TIMES (960–1911) CONFUCIUS
figured in two overlapping cults. In the previous chapter we saw
that the imperial court and civil bureaucracy venerated him as
the Supreme Sage at a temple in the capital. The Ming and Qing
courts deployed the enshrinement and placement of scholars in the
Confucius Temple in Beijing as an institutional site for the promulgation of imperial orthodoxy. This chapter moves from Beijing to Qufu,
Shandong, where Confucius's descendants venerated him as their
founding ancestor. The court conferred hereditary noble titles on his
most direct living descendant, who maintained a large fiefdom that
extended well beyond the town of Qufu. This chapter explores the
overlapping practices of the imperial and ancestral cults and poses
two main questions: How was the veneration of ancestors practiced
by this most exemplary Confucian family, and what place did the cult
of Confucius occupy in the great enterprise of governing empire?

To answer these questions, this chapter focuses on Confucius's
seventy-first-generation descendant, named Kong Zhaohuan (1735–
1782), and on two ceremonies that he led as the Duke for Fulfilling the
Sage: an ancestral sacrifice performed on the winter solstice in December 1746, and an imperial sacrifice performed in March 1749. No detailed historical accounts of either of these occasions exists; indeed, few
if any accounts of particular ceremonies were ever recorded, for to do
so would be rather like writing a historical account of a particular

Catholic Mass. Liturgical details of Confucian rites were debated and fixed in advance, and their actual performance rigorously adhered to those details under the watchful eyes of several ritual masters—at least two attended each person performing the service, in addition to two other ceremonial masters who announced each step of the rite. All celebrants rehearsed the rite during the seclusion period in the days before the ceremony. Although no amount of practice and supervisory redundancy could prevent variation or error in every case, we can be reasonably sure that any significant departure from the liturgy would have been caught by more than one officer, and corrected immediately. The descriptions of these two rites thus require an act of historical imagination based on sources that date to within a few decades of one another. In order to illuminate these otherwise esoteric ceremonies, this admittedly idealized account presents what ritual authorities at the time intended to happen.

Chinese typically embraced elements of different religions and rarely devoted themselves exclusively to any one. Because Confucianism, Daoism, Buddhism, and popular religious beliefs and practices overlapped in the everyday lives of most people in myriad ways, it is nearly impossible to generalize about the religion of the Chinese people. For the past millennium, however, nearly all people who lived in China prayed to their ancestors and offered them food and drink. They drew from different traditions—often improvising details—to perform these rites. Yet as virtually the only religious practice shared by people of all walks of life, the veneration of ancestors provides important insights into the religious lives of Chinese in late imperial times. As described in the *Constant Mean,* discussed in chapter 4, the filial son's pious offerings to his ancestors afforded a distinctively Confucian model of this religious practice. Our inquiry into Chinese ancestor veneration begins with a twelve-year-old boy named Kong Zhaohuan on a cold winter morning in a temple that sits in Watchtower District in an ancient town among the hills of northeastern China.

MORNING OF THE WINTER SOLSTICE
QIANLONG EMPEROR'S ELEVENTH YEAR
HALL OF REQUITING ORIGINS, DUKE ZHAOHUAN'S ESTATE
[26 DECEMBER 1746²]

The young master had come to this hall, called Requiting Origins, each morning ever since he could remember. On those occasions the tablets of the ancestors remained shut inside cabinets while Zhaohuan knelt with his two sisters, beloved mother,³ grandmother, and great-grandmother in front of the five altars to pay their respects. On this cold, dark morning of the winter solstice, the tablets of five generations of ancestors were to be taken out of their cabinets and placed on altars. During the hour-long ceremony the spirits were to sit at the tablets bearing their names to partake in a sacrificial feast of meat, grains, and wine.⁴ This occasion was extraordinary, because at the age of twelve the young master was to lead his nearest kin in the ceremony as the Duke for Fulfilling the Sage, for he was the most direct living descendant of Confucius, the one called "Supreme Sage, First Teacher, Master Kong."

The tablets played a crucial role in the sacrifice, but Zhaohuan's attention was drawn to the life-size portraits of his ancestors. In ancient times, grandchildren sat before effigies dressed in appropriate garb and placed on the altars, to "personate" their deceased ancestors by receiving and drinking the wine for them. Now the ancestors were believed to partake of the feast through aromas of the wine and soups, so paintings replaced effigies. They had to be exact in every detail, so that when the duke saw the portraits, he could see his ancestors just as though they still lived and sat there before him, taking food and drink when he held up the vessels. Zhaohuan thus bore the awesome responsibility of acting for his kin in this ceremony, which, to succeed, required his undivided concentration on the spirits.

Having placed incense on each of the five altars to guide the spirits to their proper places, and having washed and filled the wine tripods, Zhaohuan studied the faces of Kong Sihui, the fifty-fourth-generation descendant of Confucius and his wife, to recall what his ritual tutor had told him: "Heaven conferred brilliance upon Sihui, who had learned to read when still quite young." Days earlier, secluded in the temple to purify himself and fast for the ceremony, Zhaohuan sat at a large table where the old tutor unrolled a scroll on which the names of the ancestors were brushed in meticulous calligraphy. The name of the fifty-fourth-generation duke was at the top of the thick sheet of white paper, followed by a single column of names: five generations of Sihui's descendants, each connected by a short vertical line. Below the last of these names—Yanjin of the fifty-ninth generation—four lines spread out to the names of his four sons. Yanjin's four sons all together had five sons who in turn had twelve, and so on. The names quickly spread out across the paper, each connected by a line to his father. The names on the left ended every few generations with notes written in small, neat characters, saying, "Founded separate household." These sons had long since moved out of the manor that Zhaohuan now headed, and had set up other residences across town, or elsewhere in the county, and some very far away. Only the names of the senior line continued without interruption to the lower right corner, ending with Zhaohuan's own. His eyes retraced the seventeen generations back to the top of the genealogy, and his most illustrious ancestor came to mind. He looked up at his tutor and asked, "Why is Founding Ancestor not among these names? Isn't Supreme Sage, Master Kong, seated in the Hall of Requiting Origins?"

"The ancients have said that noblemen keep five altars," the ritual tutor replied, "four to venerate ancestors back to the patriarch's *Gaozu* [great-great-grandfather]. The middle altar is for the founder of the hereditary line. Requiting Origins is the ancestral hall of the family line that has passed down for generations the title of Duke for Fulfilling the Sage, and Kong Sihui is the founder of that line. Other families of the Kong lineage keep their own altars, but they are not dukes, so they observe rites for only three generations of ancestors. Master Kong is the Founding Ancestor of all *authentic* Kongs, who may venerate him in the Ancestral Temple just west of the young master's estate. To see Founding

Ancestor, you will have to wait until the ceremony there. The senior heirs of the other, lesser branches will send representatives."

Zhaohuan contemplated this larger ceremony with some trepidation, but mostly with intense anticipation of the honor of finally serving Founding Ancestor. His eyes widened when he heard the ritual tutor's next words.

"But of course," the tutor continued, "the grandest ceremony of all is held in the largest temple in Qufu, called the Kong Temple, four times a year.[5] That is an imperial temple, which pays homage to the outstanding sages and scholars who exalted and promoted the culture of the ancient sage-kings. All those who venerate the Way may enter: students enrolled at local academies—the most promising among them have the honor of performing the ceremonial dance of the 'Six Rows' on the platform in front of the Hall of Great Completion—as well as their teachers and the magistrate. Members of the imperial court travel from Beijing to attend, and sometimes even the Emperor himself attends. There is talk that the glorious Emperor may honor us with his presence at Great Completion in two year's time."

The old man looked down at the genealogy and said, "There will be time to discuss the other ceremonies later. Let us think only about the ceremony in Requiting Origins. To perform it properly, you need to know the ancestors as they were when they lived. The *Record of Rites* admonishes, 'Think of your ancestors' daily activities, their smiles, their preoccupations, and the things that gave them joy.' This is the most important goal of your purifications now: to devote your thoughts entirely to the ancestors so that when you enter the temple you may glimpse the spirits at the altars. This requires your solemn reverence of the ancestors. To offer the sacrifice without reverence is like not offering the sacrifice at all."

The tutor paused for the young master to consider the weight of these words. Then he turned back to the paper on the table and continued to describe the fifty-fourth-generation duke. Sihui studied with the renowned master Zhang Xu (1236–1302) of Daojiang to investigate the deeper principles of the Classics. The emperor dubbed him Grand Master of Excellent Counsel and gave him the silver seal of the third rank. The ritual tutor's expression turned grave, and he continued, "Soon after he became duke, a man claiming to be a kinsman attempted to enter the Ancestral Temple to pay homage to our ancestors. Sihui conducted an investigation and found that the man was an impostor, a descendant of the villainous Kong Mo, a serf[6] who, soon after the fall of the Tang dynasty [618–907], had killed off nearly all authentic members of the Kong family and seized the estate. Sihui expelled the impostor and then had the correct genealogy engraved in stone and placed outside the Ancestral Temple."[7] Zhaohuan had stopped to gaze at this tablet many times when he passed through the walled courtyard in front of the Temple between the Ducal Manor and the large Kong Temple. The tablet stands nearly ten feet high and is engraved with the names of the ancestors, who are divided into twenty branches. The main lineage of dukes—Kong Zhaohuan's own line descended from Sihui—stretches prominently along the primary or right side of the stone and is easily distinguishable from all of the other branches.

Standing now at the altars in Requiting Origins on this cold winter morning, Zhaohuan was momentarily distracted by his frosted breath. His hands were cold, but he was otherwise comfortable in his heavy winter ceremonial robes. Then shadows of the tablets danced in the flickering candlelight as the spirits beckoned Zhaohuan's thoughts back to them and he recalled the last thing his ritual tutor said of the remarkable Kong Sihui: "On the day he died a flock of cranes on his roof cried out, and a southeasterly spirit light pierced through the house."

Standing behind Zhaohuan, to his right, the liturgist spoke: "Present the wine!" Zhaohuan took the tripod of wine from an acolyte and lifted it up toward the fifty-fourth-generation ancestors' tablets, poured a small portion on the floor so that their spirits could find it, then handed the tripod to an acolyte who placed it on the altar table. Zhaohuan prostrated himself, then rose, with all those present following his movements; then he moved right, to the altar on the Founder's left.[8] He studied the portraits of his great-great-grandparents and recalled what his ritual tutor had said of Kong Yuqi,[9] who was the sixty-seventh-generation descendant of the Sage. He was appointed duke when he was ten, and greatly impressed the emperor with his mature, ceremonious conduct during imperial rites. Throughout his long tenure as duke, Yuqi would rise early and work until late at night. While at leisure, he loved to paint orchids and bamboo. Zhaohuan looked at the portrait of Yuqi's first wife. She was the governor's daughter; the marriage had created close bonds with an important family in the provincial capital. She died when Yuqi was twenty-two, so he married again: the daughter of a high provincial official in Shandong who originally hailed from the famously refined township of Kunshan in Jiangsu province. She was herself an accomplished poet. She bore Yuqi sons, but died when Yuqi was thirty-five, so he married a third time: great-great-grandmother Huang, who was now in her sixties and sat with the women in Requiting Origins Hall.

Zhaohuan served these ancestors just as he had Lineage Founder, then moved left to the altar where his great-grandfather Chuanduo[10] was seated with his two wives in three separate portraits. Zhaohuan recalled that Chuanduo had once opened the family grain reserves in a time of great famine to feed thousands of starving people who came to him for relief. He was an accomplished poet and a scholar of the *Record of Rites*. Zhaohuan was struck by his great-grandfather's portrait. He must have been in his late fifties when he sat for it. That was when he began to suffer from arthritis and found it difficult to walk. The emperor noticed this when Chuanduo was in the capital and instructed him to delegate his ritual duties in the capital to another. Chuanduo's eldest son had died over a decade earlier, so his second son made the journey to the capital to represent the Kongs. Later Kong Guangqi—Zhaohuan's own father—was appointed duke when he reached the age of eighteen. Zhaohuan didn't remember his great-grandfather, who died just several months after he was born. He sensed great-grandfather's pain in his sunken eyes, but all that surrounded them was glorious: a wispy beard hung down to his chest, his right hand held a court necklace of amber jade and rose quartz with short strings of green jade beads. He wore a red silk floss cap with a red and yellow embroidered brim crested with a ruby on a three-tiered insignia. His black robe bore the embroidered five-clawed yellow and red dragon on its breast, a motif repeated on the shoulders, sleeves, and hem. His sheer black surcoat subtly clouded the robe's embroidery underneath. Chuanduo's second wife, Li Yu, gave birth to his son, Kong Jihuo. Li Yu sat on a chair covered with a tiger-skin rug and wore an elaborate blue headdress with inset jewels and sets of triple strings of small beads. Two matching pendants of five strings of red, blue, and yellow precious stones hung from the crown of the headdress and fell to her shoulders. Her hands were clasped in the flowing sleeves of her red robe, which bore embroidered four-clawed dragons and rested across a full-length sleeveless dark blue court vest.

He served these spirits the same way he had done for the others, then moved to the altar of his grandparents. He looked at the young face of his grandfather,[11] who was twenty-three when he died. Grandfather, an avid reader, had composed a volume of poems. He had never served as duke, but was posthumously granted that title years later, in 1735. His wife[12] hailed from the prestigious Wang family of Wanping district in Beijing, whose sons served as grand secretaries and ministry directors. Her father was director of an imperial ministry in the capital. Now in her mid-fifties, Grandmother Wang sat in the hall that morning.

Finally, Zhaohuan looked into his father's kind eyes, which betrayed a slight smile. Zhaohuan had grieved his father's passing for the requisite three years, and he had only several months earlier emerged from the relative solitude of mourning. He was now expected to approach his father in an entirely different frame of mind—with the propitious disposition of the auspicious rites that were the very foundation of ancestral veneration. The seventieth-generation duke, Guangqi (1713–1743), the ritual master had told him, was congenial in his interactions with others, and resolutely forthright. He never harbored prejudice in his deliberations and was loved by all, even his servants, to whom he listened attentively and remained tolerant, even when they were impertinent. His grandfather began to groom Guangqi for his duties when he was very young, bringing him to court in the capital. After succeeding his grandfather as duke at the age of eighteen, Guangqi frequently visited the capital to accompany the emperor during imperial observance of sacrifices at the Imperial University and in the Qianlong emperor's third year (1738) for the Ploughing Ceremony, celebrated in grand scroll paintings. Afterwards, Guangqi wrote two essays on ritual that pleased the emperor. He also traveled to the capital a number of times to attend the imperial lectures on the Classics. These years were the heyday of the Kong family's relations with the emperor, but they were soon to be overshadowed by controversy with the local magistrate—a matter that Zhaohuan quickly put out of his mind. He thought instead of the scholarly pursuits undertaken by his father, who had written eight volumes of essays and several volumes of poems; then he took the tripod from the acolyte to serve his father.

Having served his ancestors for the first offering, Zhaohuan stood while the prayer was read. Zhaohuan then returned to his station at the foot of the steps outside the Hall and waited until he was summoned back into Requiting Origins. After offering the feast to the spirits twice more, Zhaohuan drank some of the blessed wine and received a portion of the meat, which he would share with other family members. Acolytes moved dishes slightly on each altar to signal the spirits that the feast was complete. The spirits were escorted out of the temple, their tablets returned to the cabinets, and all celebrants processed out behind the spirits. Finally the prayer was burned in a brick oven in the courtyard, and the ceremony ended.

FROM ANCESTOR TO DEITY

Chinese of all walks of life have observed some form of ancestral cult since the Song dynasty. Regardless of particular religious affiliation, they shared certain basic beliefs that underlay ancestral sacrifice. Most important among these beliefs was that spirits of the deceased lingered after death and influenced the welfare of their living descendants. According to such canonical sources as the *Zuo Commentary* and *Book of Rites,* the spirit or "soul" is itself a complex entity, comprising "corporeal being," a yin force called *po* 魄, which animates the physical body beginning at conception, and "spiritual essence," a yang force called *hun* 魂, which constitutes a person's consciousness. As the physical body decomposes into the soil after death, corporeal being (*po*) dissipates into the ether. When attended to properly, the spirit (*shen* 神) of the deceased retains its spiritual essence—its thoughts and will— and can exercise a certain amount of power in the cosmos and offer protection to its descendants, both living and dead, joining them all in a mutually beneficial corporate body. The power that an ancestor wielded in the spirit world depended upon his or her status or accomplishments while alive and the extent to which descendants piously maintained the ancestral cult afterward.

Despite this shared conception of soul, Chinese differed in many key beliefs concerning ancestors and spirits, largely depending upon educational background and social status. Inspired by a confidence in the ultimate goodness of the cosmic order guided by Heaven and the canonical gods that inhabit the world, Confucians maintained an abiding reverence toward gods and spirits. Conversely, capricious and malign spirits crowded the religious landscape of popular consciousness. Gods who thought they had been ignored, corrupt underlings of the spirit world, and recently deceased kinsmen sought revenge among the living and therefore became sources of intense anxiety. People employed Daoist exorcists to combat the harmful effects of malign spirits and vengeful ancestors. Such beliefs often crossed social boundaries; fear of the workings of demonic spirits not found in canonical sources existed among cultivators, urban merchants, and members of upright literati families. Graphic Daoist images of the underworld shaped how unlettered people imagined the underworld through which souls passed after death. Perhaps most widespread of all were Buddhist notions of karma and retribution for past sins, which profoundly affected how people in late imperial times understood the nature and causes of death, and how they imagined the tortures their ancestors might endure in hell.

The Kongs of Qufu observed a liturgy based on the classical precedents that governed canonical rites at court and in the homes of literati families. Close scrutiny of the duke, who embodies key elements of the rite as a whole, yields important insights into these rites. In order to consecrate offerings—to render them to the spirits—the duke must himself achieve a state of mental-corporeal purity. To do so, he secluded himself in the temple in the days before the ceremony and single-mindedly devoted himself to the spirits who were to receive the feast. Just before the ceremony, he bathed and changed into clothes worn only for such ritual occasions, washed his hands before handling the wine tripods, then washed the tripods before an acolyte, who had undergone similar ablutions, filled them with wine. Thus purified, the duke consecrated the whole feast by holding up the tripod to the spirits, focusing on their portraits, and recalling their demeanor and accomplishments. After each spirit had been served three times, the duke drank the remainder of the wine, blessed by contact with the spirits. This action distinguished the duke from other celebrants. As consecrator, he stood between the spirits and the assembled body of celebrants and acted for the latter by rendering sacrifice and by leading celebrants through each phase of the liturgy; they followed him in observing the purification fast beforehand, and knelt or prostrated themselves during the ceremony whenever he did so.

When he approached the spirits, he observed a respectful distance and, without actual contact with them, was not himself in any sense consecrated. This respectful distance distinguished canonical rites from what Confucians saw as blasphemous ceremonies performed by shaman priests and exorcists, who, Confucians maintained, desecrated the spirits through inappropriate intimate contact with them. Confucius once admonished a disciple to revere ghosts and spirits while maintaining a respectful distance (*Analects* 6.22). A commentator on this passage explains, "Revere ghosts and spirits without desecrating them."

The duke's prerogative to lead the ceremony derived from his genealogical proximity to the ancestors, not from esoteric knowledge. Indeed, the duke often lacked full ritual knowledge, and so a liturgist always instructed him at each step of the rite. Liturgical sources stressed technical mastery of the rite, but even a boy led the rite when he was the most direct living descendant of the ancestors. Success of an ancestral rite required a reverent devotion to the spirits, engendered by filial piety (*xiao* 孝) imbued in the "blood and bones" of descendants. Having inherited the proper seminal spirit (*jingqi* 精氣) transmitted in the *po*, descendants, especially the most senior lineage heir (*zongzi* 宗子), could establish contact with their own ancestors. Birth sequence, not merit, determined who would inherit the noble title, reside in the manor, and lead the collective body of celebrants in temple ceremonies. As Kongzi's most direct male descendant, Kong Zhaohuan became patriarch at the age of nine, and even his older kinsmen occupied junior positions in relation to him. Descent was not an inviolable principle, however, for on rare occasions clan elders stripped senior heirs of their status on grounds of corruption.[13] The Kongs thus expended great effort through education and proper rearing to nurture the patriarch's capacity to perform competently his ritual and administrative duties.

Like most kinship organizations in late imperial China, the Kong ancestral cult was internally stratified according to the principles of patrilineal descent. The Kongs ordered their ancestors in the temple in a hierarchy determined by generational seniority: the Lineage Founder (*shizu* 始祖) seated in the middle and four generations of the duke's most recent ancestors arrayed on either side according to seniority, alternating between the senior position (*zhao* 昭) on the Founder's left and the junior side (*mu* 穆) on his right.[14] Ordering of the tablets and feasting of the spirits in proper sequence accords with a hierarchy believed to inhere in the cosmos and the gods that rule it. Similarly, all living male descendants occupied clearly designated positions in the patriline as determined by a meticulously recorded genealogy kept in a box stored in the back room of the temple, never to be seen by outsiders.[15] The enormous size of the Kong clan—more than twenty thousand living in the Qufu area alone—necessitated such scrupulous record-keeping. The duke's family, referred to as the patriline (*dazong* 大宗), headed a massive kinship organization subdivided into sixty collateral households hierarchically ranked according to patrilineal principles, whereby the households of elder male descendants held higher ritual status than sons descended from more junior, cadet lines. These genealogical principles translated the natural hierarchical order of the cosmos, which ensured that the ancestors would be fed in proper sequence, into the kinship organization of living descendants. The preface to the Kong genealogy, completed in 1745, attributed to the ten-year-old Kong Zhaohuan, establishes this sacred parallel: "A family's genealogy is like a state's history. A history that lacks credibility is a crime against Heaven. A genealogy that lacks credibility is a crime against the ancestors. The *Rites* says, 'All things originate in Heaven, people originate in ancestors.'"[16]

In addition to Requiting Origins, the duke led sacrifices at the Ancestral Temple. All celebrants who attended ceremonies there either were surnamed Kong or were married to a Kong. The Ancestral Temple catered to all of Kongzi's living descendants and thus had to accommodate a significantly larger populace of spirits and living kin, conceivably numbering in the thousands. Requiting Origins ceremonies venerated ancestors from the duke's father to the founder of his ducal line. Conversely, the Kong Ancestral Temple housed the spirits common to all living kinsmen, beginning with Master Kong—referred to as Founding Ancestor—his son, grandson, and their wives. It also housed the spirit of the forty-third-generation descendant, Kong Renyu, who was referred to as the Restoration Ancestor (*zhongxing zu* 中興祖). According to the story told in clan records, during the chaos following on the fall of the Tang dynasty an upstart serf named Mo assumed the Kong surname and conspired to kill the senior heir, Renyu's father, and all his kin in order to claim the Kong ancestral lands as his own. After an official investigation some years later, the court executed Kong Mo, restored Renyu to his rightful position as senior heir, and gave him the hereditary title of duke. As the sole survivor of those troubled times, Kong Renyu held the status of common ancestor of all authentic Kongs in the Ancestral Temple cult.[17]

Zhaohuan crossed from the ostensibly private domain of ancestral rites to the public sphere of imperial cults when he led services in a third temple in Qufu called the Kong Temple. Situated along an east-west axis, these three temples hosted a series of distinct yet interrelated cults. In contrast to the Hall of Requiting Origins and the Kong Ancestral Temple, where ancestral cult was offered, the Kong Temple was the site of an *imperial* cult to Confucius, his followers, and his descendants. This cult occupied the middle tier among the three tiers of imperial cults that served nature deities and tutelary and ancestral spirits discussed in the preceding chapter. In the eighteenth century the Kong Temple, also known as the Culture Temple, housed 140 spirits, including Confucius's followers, and the most venerated founders of canonical traditions, with Master Kong at its center as Sage. Because of its complex relationship with the *ancestral* cult in Qufu (as headed in the seventy-first generation by Zhaohuan), the imperial cult of Confucius included elements from both imperial and ancestral cults. Whereas in the Ancestral Temple, Kongzi's tablet named him Founding Ancestor, his tablet in the Kong Temple called him "Supreme Sage First Teacher." The duke usually acted as principal consecrator at the Kong Temple in Qufu, but he did so as the highest-ranking civil official in the area rather than as Kongzi's most direct living descendant. At this and other Confucius shrines the consecrator as imperial officer differed from the consecrator as filial son, in that he was not acting as descendant of the spirits he served. The ties that bound consecrator and spirit could not be literally seminal. Ritual sources on imperial sacrifice nonetheless often invoked filial piety as the ideal inner state of the sacrificer, usually characterized as "reverent" (*jing* 敬).

Celebrants at ancestral rites were born into membership in the cult, whereas those who gathered at the Kong Temple in Qufu, at such temples in the capital, and at administrative complexes in other parts of China, as well as in Korea, Japan, and Vietnam, attended because they had dedicated their lives to mastering Confucian learning and had achieved some level of success in the examination system. Members of the Kong family may have predominated, but the celebrants included boys attending local government schools and private academies, the teachers there, and all other holders of civil examination degrees. Celebrants were ranked according to their status in the civil bureaucracy, roughly paralleling the spirit hierarchy in the temple. Classically educated men and boys were marked by distinction in relation to the rest of society, and imperial proscriptions forbade unschooled commoners from attending these ceremonies.

Kongzi's statue today sits at the center altar in the main hall called

Great Completion, behind a tablet inscribed with his title: "Supreme Sage, First Teacher, Master Kong." Because this temple venerates the Confucian Dao, Kongzi, like all figures enshrined here, sits alone in his niche, unaccompanied by his wife. Four correlates sitting in niches are chronologically arrayed two on each side of the Supreme Sage, based on the *zhao-mu* principle of seniority used in ancestral halls. Three of these correlates are Kongzi's most prominent disciples: Yan Hui, said to best exemplify benevolence, sits in the first position on the Master's left; Zengzi, credited with compiling the *Great Learning*, sits on the Master's right; Kongzi's grandson Kong Ji, credited with compiling the *Constant Mean*, sits next to Yan Hui on the left. Mencius, whose writings defending and amplifying Kongzi's teachings are contained in a book that bears his name, sits in the last correlate position. Thus four of the five men enshrined at the pinnacle of the temple hierarchy are associated with the Four Books, which the Ming and Qing courts had canonized as the foundation of orthodoxy and the civil examinations.

The duke offered sacrifice to these five spirits, while secondary consecrators served all other spirits in the temple. Twelve other figures referred to as Savants (*zhe* 哲) were also housed in the main hall. Eleven of these men were Kongzi's most outstanding disciples because they excelled in the four disciplines: personal virtue, oratory, governance, and scholarship. The Kangxi emperor had Zhu Xi (1130–1200 CE) promoted from the status of Worthy to Savant in 1712, on grounds that "only his commentaries on the Classics illuminated the truth" and that "after Confucius and Mencius, Master Zhu's achievements have most benefited this Culture." The tablets of the remaining worthies and scholars were placed in the two long corridors, called cloisters, on both sides of the main hall, forming the eastern and western walls of the temple grounds. These figures included disciples of the Sage, masters of the Five Classics, and the men who recovered the lost Way a thousand years after the death of the last sage.

The connection between the Kongs' veneration of their founding ancestor and the court's veneration of Kongzi among other gods underlay a more than century-long debate in the Ming dynasty. Attempts to clarify this relationship notwithstanding, the ritual reforms of 1530 produced by these debates left an ambiguous legacy. Spirits housed in imperial temples were, like those in ancestral shrines, represented by images, sculptures in the former, paintings in the latter. In the early Ming, the court ordered the removal of images from all imperial temples except Kong temples.[18] Although the 1530 temple reforms removed Kongzi's noble title, as had been done to other gods earlier, these reforms nonetheless retained important connections with ancestral pietism. The feasting sequence in the Kong temples throughout the realm implemented in 1530 clearly illustrates the indelible imprint of ancestral veneration and filial piety upon the imperial cult. Kongzi's father, Shuliang He, had received cult in his own shrine in Qufu since the fourteenth century. As early as the mid–fifteenth century, memorialists advocated similar rites in temples at local schools maintained by the government throughout the empire. Since the fathers of three correlates already received sacrifice in the cloisters for their own accomplishments, they were in effect being served *after* their more prominent sons, which, these memorialists maintained, violated the ancient tenet of filial piety. The *Zuo Commentary* on the *Spring and Autumn Annals*, they reminded the court, said, "Even if a son is a sage, he does not take precedence over his father" (Duke Wen 2.8). As part of the sweeping reforms of 1530, the court erected a new shrine to house these fathers, behind the main hall in all imperial Kong temples. It was called Giving Birth to the Sage (*Qisheng ci*), and it occupied the north end of the temple complex—the primary position—which meant that, beginning in 1530, the spirits in this shrine received cult before the spirits of their sons.

Imperial and ancestral rites operated according to the same basic principles of sacrifice. The spirits invoked into the temple sat at tablets that bore their names and titles. They partook of a feast of wine, meat, and grains consecrated by a sacrificer who had achieved ritual purity. As ethereal beings, spirits took food and drink through their aromas, and thus left no visible or material trace of having done so. Canonical sources admonished against expensive, elaborate feasts, because the spirits preferred a simple fare of unseasoned broth, grains, edible grasses, and meats, which were typically offered raw. Spirits were drawn to the feast when their senses of smell and taste were stimulated by the burial of the fur and blood of the primary victim outside the temple gate, the burning of incense at their altars, and the pouring of some of the wine onto the floor in front of the altars. Neither abstract symbol nor empty gesture, these actions enabled the spirits to partake of the feast.

The success of sacrificial rites also depended upon properly harnessing the power of yin and yang and the five phases.[19] The five colors of the robes worn by consecrators and spirit images, the foods offered as sacrifice, the materials used to make musical instruments and the tones they produced had to be modulated according to ascending yang and descending yin and to correspondences with the five phases. Consider, for example, the bronze bell and jade chime used in the music. The sequence of bronze and jade invoked the powers of yang and yin. Metal is yang, thus the bronze bell, as a yang instrument, initiates a song or measure, just as the male yang power initiates all things in the universe. Stone is yin, thus the jade chime, as a yin instrument, collects or consummates the polyphony of the song, just as the female yin receives and brings to completion all things. Each hymn was perfectly symmetrical: first the sound of wood, then that of metal initiated the song, and jade and finally wood again concluded it. A bronze bell initiated each measure of a song, a jade chime concluded it; a drum—the sound of skin—punctuated each measure. Each note was played by silk strings and by three kinds of wind instrument, made of earth (ceramic), bamboo, and gourd.

The imperial and ancestral cults were distinct yet overlapping. As discussed in chapter 5, the imperial cult situated Kongzi as the Sage of a broad cultural tradition in a pantheon of gods who reigned over natural elements and human civilization, patronized by the court, civil bureaucracy, and ultimately all subjects of the throne. The ancestral cult placed Master Kong in a genealogy of ancestors patronized by their descendants. The spirits in the imperial and ancestral cults were arranged hierarchically, based on the principle of descent. Though their qualifications differed, consecrators in these two cults played analogous roles in relation both to the spirits and to the assembled body who attended. The liturgies of both operated according to the same basic principles, although new elements were added in the imperial rites. The music and dance in the imperial ceremony illustrate how consciously the material and sonic elements of the rite were designed to resonate with the elemental cosmic power of yin and yang. The liturgy, furthermore, fashioned or disciplined the person of the consecrator and other celebrants into the reverent bodies necessary for the rite's success—the obeisances and dance positions represented nothing other than the reverence that gods and spirits would requite with due blessings. Repeated cleansing of hands and ritual vessels also assured them of the celebrants' sincerity.

If sacrifices to Kongzi in the capital resonated with the presences of other gods in nearby temples and altars patronized by the throne, imperial rites to Kongzi performed in his hometown of Qufu resonated with distinctively local spirits. The imperial rite in Qufu penetrated past the Kong Temple gates and across the thresholds of neighboring shrines dedicated to spirits related to the Sage by blood and by marriage, and even to the tutelary spirit of the land. The permeability of cult rites performed at the many altars throughout Qufu was perhaps best illustrated in the first week of the second month of each season, when, at the hour of the tiger, the duke led the sacrifice at Great Completion.

HOUR OF THE TIGER

SEVENTH DAY OF THE SECOND LUNAR MONTH

OF THE QIANLONG EMPEROR'S TWELFTH YEAR

GREAT COMPLETION HALL, QUFU, SHANDONG

[5:00 A.M., 17 MARCH 1749]

Torches cast brilliant red and yellow hues on the painted walls of Great Completion when Zhaohuan entered the temple courtyard through Bell Chime Gate. An usher led him along the walkway past the assembled guests—the duke's kinsmen and other descendants of the Four Families,[20] an emperor's envoy, local officials, and students—to the front of the Apricot Pavilion. The Supreme Sage, it was said, had lectured his disciples in this very place. The dancers waited in six rows of six on the elevated stone platform in front of Great Completion, which stood some twenty meters high and fifty across in the middle of the courtyard.[21] The imperial yellow roof tiles were shrouded in the darkness of the pale morning sky.

Kong Zhaohuan wore a long silk robe, dark blue, fronted with a large, four-clawed dragon (*mang* 蟒) of gold embroidery gazing intently straight ahead. Two more dragons floated just below it; another pair adorned the tops of the shoulders above solid blue sleeves, each with a small dragon on its tapered cuff, which flared slightly at the wrist. Patches of light blue and white clouds dotted the robe's background above a horizon of billowing sea waves. Four gilded mountains surged out of the sea in the four cardinal directions, and plants swirled on the ocean floor along the hem. Zhaohuan's black silk floss cap had a two-tiered gold peak decorated with eastern pearls and crested with a ruby. Four square plaques, each with a jade piece at each corner and a small ruby at its center, decorated his belt.

Music began as the supplicant left the courtyard through the main gate. In quick succession a small hammer struck a wooden box three times, then a large bronze bell was sounded, followed by a smaller one hanging on a rack of sixteen bells of different sizes. Then a symphony of ten zithers, sixteen flutes of three types, six mouth organs, and two pear-shaped ceramic flutes played the hymn. The musicians played each note in full, even pitches; four notes to a measure, punctuated by the soft patter of four raps on a small hand drum between every two notes. The sound of a jade chime hanging on a rack of sixteen—corresponding to the rack of sixteen bells—concluded each measure. Eight measures composed a hymn, after which a large hanging-jade chime, corresponding to the large bell at the beginning, was sounded, followed by the grating rustle of a bamboo switch rubbed across the ridged spine of a wooden tiger. A drum in the Apricot Pavilion was sounded as the celebrants stepped back from the walkway to make way for the spirit, led by the supplicant.

The Master of Ceremony (*tongzan* 通贊) stood at the front of

the platform to announce each phase of the rite. Now he intoned in a slow, even voice: "Offer the silk. Perform the first offering." The liturgist (*yinzan* 引贊), who stood beside the duke to instruct him throughout the ceremony, said, "Go to the washbasin." Just as the duke stepped toward the basin, the courtyard erupted into instrumental music, song, and dance. The musicians played and the chorus sang the Proclamation Hymn:

> We cherish his brilliant virtue [yu huai ming de 予懷明德]. . . .

Each of the dancers in red robes had faced the altar holding his flute horizontally across his pheasant feather, which he held upright in a clasped hand at his chest. As the first word of the hymn was slowly intoned, they uncrossed flutes and feathers and held both vertically at their waists. With the second word, the dancers turned inward toward the center of the platform, shifting their weight to the inner foot and turning their heads in the other direction, away from the center of the platform, while holding their flutes out horizontally in their left hands across their feathers, held vertically in their right. As the third word was sung, they turned back toward the altar, standing squarely upright again with feathers and flutes remaining crossed. With the fourth word they held their flutes upright close to their shoulders, and lowered their feathers horizontally across the bottom of their flutes. These early transitions were subtle, but required concentration and discipline. For the younger boys participating in this rite for the first time, this was the beginning of a life of ritual mastery. The movements of the ninety-six postures would become increasingly demanding during three dances (or "sequences") performed during the three offerings—almost invariably, a boy fainted—but withstanding the physical stress of performing the rites was neither a goal nor a mark of virtue. It was simply to be mastered.

While the dancers executed this sequence of steps, an acolyte poured water on the duke's hands over the basin, then another acolyte handed him a towel to dry them. The duke then washed and dried the tripods, which were borne by three wine bearers. He ladled wine from a libation urn into each of the three tripods, one for the Supreme Sage and two for the Correlates, Yan Hui and Kong Ji, who sat in the *zhao* position on the Sage's left, and Zengzi and Mencius, in the *mu* position on the Sage's right. The hymn continued:

> *Jadestones chime, bells respond.*
> *Incomparable is He since the birth of the people . . . .*

As the hymn continued, the Master of Ceremony announced, "Proceed to the spirit tablet of the Founding Ancestor, Supreme Sage, First Teacher." The silk and three tripods of wine were held high by their bearers, who ascended the steps and entered Great Completion through the middle door. The silk bearer stood in front of the altar on the left, and the vessel-bearers stood off to the left side. As the duke ascended the stone steps on the right side he saw the platform; it was brightly lit by oil torches. Dancers stood in rows at the front of the platform, and the musicians stood near the large open doors of the hall. The duke stepped over the door well into the hall, past the Correlates' and Savants' niches, past the ox, goat, and pig prepared in the kitchen hours earlier and splayed on racks, and stopped in front of the high altar devoted to Confucius. It was laden with three pots of unsalted broth and soups, ten baskets of grains, dried fish and venison, dates, nuts, honey cakes, and ten wooden bowls of sauces, leeks, celery, edible grasses, and bamboo shoots. This was a simple repast with no strong flavors, meant to honor the spirits, who did not care for rich foods and full-bodied wines.

Now Kong Zhaohuan gazed up past the feast and looked upon the regal figure of his Founding Ancestor and pondered the Supreme Sage. The bearded figure of a man sat in the altar niche wearing the robes of an ancient king. Twelve strings of green jade hung from the front of the mortarboard atop his high cap, and the twelve insignia of the sovereign adorned his dark blue robes. A sun, moon, and astral constellation were embroidered on the robe's two shoulders; a mountain, a five-clawed dragon, and a feathered creature adorned its long sweeping sleeves; and ancestral vessels, a water plant, fire, rice meal, an axe, and the *fu* sign completed the lower garment.[22] His royal scepter of lustrous green jade inscribed with stars and the sacred mountains that hold up the sky announced the sovereign's pacification of the realm. A gilded red tablet proclaimed the bearded figure to be Master Kong, Supreme Sage and First Teacher.

The hymn continued:

Expansive, his Great Completion.
Altars and vessels throughout the ages. . . .

An acolyte knelt and held up a round, red-lacquered incense box to the duke, who took a stick from the box, lit it in a small brazier, turned to the altar and knelt, then stood to place the burning incense in a censer on the altar. The silk bearer knelt and held up a rectangular box of carefully folded silk damask, which in the time before coinage had been the standard of exchange among the living as well as the spirits. Now it was presented to the spirits as precious currency for use in the netherworld. The duke took the silk and respectfully held it up to the spirit, then placed it in the middle of the altar. A wine bearer knelt and held up a tripod, which the duke took, held up to the spirit, then placed on its stand on the altar. He knelt to perform a single *koutou* and stood.

The rites of Spring and Autumn.
The pure wine arrayed. . . .

As the hymn continued, the dancers, who ended the last measure facing forward with feather held at forehead level across an upright flute, turned inward while holding the feather upright and crossing it with the flute. They then turned outward and bent forward with the outer foot raised and pointing upward while lowering flute and feather, crossed at an oblique angle, to waist level. The duke went to the prayer station, where he knelt as the Master of Ceremony intoned, "All kneel," just as the last words of the hymn were completed:

Incense wafts aloft.

The music stopped, and the dancers ended their sequence with the flute held horizontally high above the head across the upright feather. All present, including the musicians and dancers, then knelt to perform a single prostration. The courtyard was utterly quiet as the singular voice of a liturgist instructed, "Read the prayer." The supplicant went to the prayer station, knelt to perform three prostrations, held up the prayer board, and declaimed:

Let it be said that on this, the seventh day of the second month of the twelfth year of the Qianlong emperor's reign, Zhaohuan, the seventy-first-generation descendant who inherited the title Duke for Fulfilling the Sage, humbly announces before the Supreme Sage, First Teacher . . .

The supplicant's voice shifted from even formality to song:

Our ancestor's virtue matches Heaven and Earth; his Dao surpasses all for eternity; he compiled the Six Canons and bequeathed the regulations for all time. On this second month of spring, we solemnly present these victims, silk, libation, grains, and other items all arranged perfectly on the altar as offerings to you and your Correlates: the Returning Sage, Master Yan; the Ancestral Sage, Master Zeng; the Following Sage, third-generation ancestor, Master Si [Kong Ji]; and the Second Sage, Master Meng. We do hereby offer up this feast.

Completing the prayer, the supplicant held up the prayer board again, then rose to place it in a box on the altar. Standing to the right of the altar, he knelt again, to perform three prostrations, then withdrew to the front of the platform as all celebrants rose.

The duke led all present through another set of three kneelings and nine prostrations, then went to the altars of the Four Correlates. Their statues held the earl's scepter, their caps had nine strings of jade pendants, and their robes bore nine embroidered insignia (sans sun, moon, and astral constellation). He offered up incense, silk damask, and wine to each of the Four Correlates according to the same ritual procedures as those used in the primary rites to Confucius. While the duke performed these offerings, two consecrators offered sacrifices to the twelve Savants in the main hall and six more to the seventy-seven worthies and forty-six scholars housed in the two cloisters.

The 140 figures housed in the Kong Temple played a major role in promoting the Confucian Dao that lay at the heart of the imperial cult of Confucius. The Supreme Sage was the "teacher and paragon of the ten thousand generations," his disciples advanced his teachings, early exegetes of the Five Canons transcribed and expounded upon the wisdom of the ancient sages, and later scholars received the Dao that had not been transmitted for more than a thousand years, and illuminated it in the world again. Had this ceremony held in Qufu's Great Completion Hall honored these men alone, then it could be regarded as simply venerating the philosophers who propounded imperial orthodoxy. Although it certainly did so, it accomplished much more. Just when the duke served the Correlates and the worthies and scholars received offerings, five retinues left the temple yard and dispersed to shrines adjacent to the Great Completion courtyard. Ten assistants accompanied a consecrator to the Hall of Repose behind Great Completion to offer feast to the spirit of Kongzi's wife, surnamed Qiguan. A large entourage of fifty-one assistants and acolytes accompanied three consecration officers to the Adoration of the Sage Shrine, located in a walled complex east of Great Completion, to serve the spirits of five generations of Kongzi's ancestors.[23] Two more went to the Giving Birth to the Sage Shrine, in an adjacent walled complex to the west, to offer feast to Kongzi's father, Shuliang He, and mother, Yan Zhengzai, in the Hall of Repose. Another consecrator performed rites in the Kong Ancestral Temple. Finally, another went to a small shrine behind the walled complex, where Houtu, the tutelary Spirit of the Land, received offerings. In these various ritual sites, the consecrators severally presented feasts of libation, a goat and pig, soups, eight baskets of grains, dates, and cakes, and eight bowls of sauces and celeries.[24]

CONCLUSION

The complement of rites performed on this day situated the cult of Kongzi in a nexus of imperial, ancestral, and local cults. The men enshrined at the most exalted level of the temple hierarchy produced the teachings that constituted the basic tenets of imperial orthodoxy, which candidates sitting for civil examinations were expected to master. As the object of a middle-level imperial cult, the Confucius of the Kong Temple occupied a place among other deities and spirits of a pantheon also patronized by the imperial bureaucracy elsewhere in China and by the royal courts throughout East Asia. As a temple literally surrounded by ancestral shrines where imperial officials also conducted services, this Confucius remained a son, husband, and ancestor. The rites to Houtu, a tutelary spirit who nourished and protected the soils of the surrounding fields, located this cult in this particular place. The liturgy of the imperial cult of Confucius thus confounded clearly drawn boundaries between public and private or between imperial and ancestral domains.

What can we learn from the rites to Confucius? They instilled a profound devotion to one's ancestors. Through pious feasting of ancestors, one gained an abiding mindfulness of them as the source of one's being, which paralleled Heaven as the source of all things in the world. This same pietism extended to one's parents. Some have said that an innate love of one's parents provided the foundation for one's reverence toward the ancestors. The rites also inculcated a conception of the self as part of a continuous lineage of ancestors extending back through time, which, if properly provided for through sacrifice, could affect some small part of the cosmos—a cosmos governed by other spirits and powers such as yin and yang. This self-conception grounded in lineage taught a profoundly personal sense of history, because the past in which one's ancestors had lived influenced one's place in the present. The pious celebrant entered history through remembrance of what the ancestors did—their accomplishments and hardships. This historically grounded self also located one geographically in a particular place: the land where one's ancestors dwelled. Ancestral cults were not readily transportable, in part because the tablets ideally belonged where the ancestors had dwelled while alive. Even

merchants and migrant workers whose families had left home generations earlier still identified themselves as natives of the town or village
of their ancestors.

Participation in these rites trained one to integrate an awareness of
spirit presences with physical sensation, such as the feel of the carved
surface of an old wine tripod used only for such occasions, the taste of
a simple libation accepted by the spirits, and especially the smell of
burning incense filling the hall to bring the spirits to the altar to receive
cult feast. Modulated by ritual orchestration of musical pitch and colored tones, yin and yang flooded the ears with harmonious sounds that
facilitated human interaction with the gods and spirits. As ethereal beings, gods and spirits could not be seen, except fleetingly by the filial
son who, once purified, "catches faint glimpses of the spirits when he
enters the shrine and a gentle sense of their murmuring at every point
during the rite." By the sheer force of the sacrificer's filiality, gods and
spirits received the feast through its aroma and formed one body with
their living patrons. Even the most philosophically *dis*inclined could
not help but appreciate the workings of esoteric principles in such
richly textured ritual experiences.

On another level, we have seen that the permeability of cults dis-
rupts modern expectations of distinct boundaries between public ceremonies and private, familial religious life. As we saw in chapter 5,
the participation of the court and bureaucracy in religious activities
such as public worship of gods sheds light on the very nature of the
imperial Chinese government. That imperial and ancestral cults inter-
sected at key moments during the rites should alert us to the infelicity
of distinctions between public and private, state and religion, which
people today have come to expect.

SUGGESTED READINGS

Descriptions of the temple rites are based on Kong Jifen, *Queli
    wenxian kao* (1762) and *Kongshi jiayi* (1765); Pan Xiang, *Qufu
    xianzhi* (1774). For a social history of the Kong family of Qufu,
    see Christopher Agnew, "Culture and Power in the Making of the
    Descendants of Confucius, 1300–1800" (Ph.D. dissertation, Uni-

versity of Washington, 2006); for the use of images in official rites, see Deborah Sommer, "Images into Words: Ming Confucian Iconoclasm," *National Palace Museum Bulletin* 14 (1994): 1–24; for ritual music, see Joseph S. C. Lam, *State Sacrifices and Music in Ming China: Orthodoxy, Creativity, and Expressiveness* (Albany, NY: SUNY Press, 1998).

For Qing ritual robes, see Gary Dickenson and Linda Wrigglesworth, *Imperial Wardrobe*, revised edition (Berkeley: Ten Speed Press, 2000); John E. Vollmer, *Ruling from the Dragon Throne: Costume of the Qing Dynasty (1644–1911)* (Berkeley: Ten Speed Press, 2002). See also *Qing huidian tu* (Beijing: Zhonghua shuju, 1991).

On Chinese religion, see Emily Ahern, *The Cult of the Dead in a Chinese Village* (Palo Alto, CA: Stanford University Press, 1973); Kenneth Brashier, "Han Thanatology and the Division of Souls," *Early China* 21 (1996): 125–58; Michael Loewe, *Ways to Paradise: The Chinese Quest for Immortality* (London: George Allen & Unwin, 1979); Mu-chou Poo, *In Search of Personal Welfare: A View of Ancient Chinese Religion* (Albany, NY: SUNY Press, 1998); Stephen Teiser, *The Scripture of the Ten Kings and the Making of Purgatory in Medieval Chinese Buddhism* (Honolulu: University of Hawaii Press, 1994); Yü Ying-shih, "'O Soul, Come Back!': A Study of the Changing Conceptions of the Soul and Afterlife in Pre-Buddhist China," *Harvard Journal of Asiatic Studies* 47, no. 2 (December 1987): 363–95.

A Confusion of Confuciuses:
Invoking Kongzi in the
Modern World

They [the Chinese] are a harmless race when white men either let them alone or treat them no worse than dogs.
— MARK TWAIN, *Roughing It*

The notion of a national religious community . . . is difficult to invent ex nihilo.
— VINCENT GOOSSAERT, *La Pensée en Chine aujourd'hui*

For many scholars it is now an article of faith that ruxue *[Ru Learning],* rujia *[classicist, Confucian] culture, and* rujia *thought commanded a unique and historically privileged position in China's traditional cultural identity.*
— MAKEHAM, *Lost Soul*

I N CHINA, THE TWENTIETH CENTURY STARTED IN 1898, WITH the short-lived Hundred Days Reforms launched by Kang Youwei (1858–1927). (In that same year, 1898, halfway around the world, in England, the prestigious Clarendon Press issued a luxury edition of English translations of the Chinese Classics by the Nonconformist Protestant missionary James Legge, heralding the new discipline of "comparative religions" in the West.) Essentially an attempt to resist the twin evils of Western colonialism and Christianity, Kang's Reforms—supported by the young Manchu emperor—included a number of provisions bound to rile conservatives at court. The Reforms are now chiefly remembered as an attempt to turn the absolutist Manchu government into a constitutional monarchy on the model of England or Germany, the leading imperialist powers in Europe at the time. One important part of the plan (generally forgotten) entailed converting all Buddhist and Daoist temples, as well as local shrines erected to local gods, into primary and secondary schools on the Western model. A second plan aimed to make Kongzi the center of a "national religion" (*guojiao*) modeled on Christian sects and equipped with its own churches and a unifying ideology combining the best features (the "essence") of Chinese culture.[1] Through such radical innovations, Kang Youwei hoped to counter the growing threat posed to the national culture and national sovereignty by the allied forces of Christianity and Western imperialism. To justify such controversial changes, Kang asserted—contrary to all previous traditions—that Kongzi was the single author of all parts of the Six Classics, whose texts, being invested with his "subtle words," would reveal, after suitable decoding under Kang's guidance, Kongzi's master plan for major institutional reforms. Not for the first time in Chinese history was Kongzi shown to be remarkably prescient with respect to momentous political changes (see chapter 3).

Representatives of the Christian churches and states had little opportunity to consider, let alone formulate a response to, the sweeping implications of Kang's reforms to Protestant and Catholic missions in China before the abrupt collapse of the Reforms. In October 1898, only three months after the first promulgation of the Reforms, the dowager empress Cixi seized power from the young emperor and placed him under house arrest within the Forbidden City.[2] It took Cixi, an empress who certainly understood power, remarkably little time to see that the main thrust of the so-called Hundred Days reforms would be to sharply reduce Manchu hegemony within China. Prices were put on the heads of Kang and many of his closest disciples, who were immediately forced into exile (mostly in Japan and Indonesia). Kang himself never returned to China. The outline of this dramatic sequence of events is well known to China watchers, at home and abroad. However, very few realize that part of Kang's most ambitious plans were, in fact, executed in his absence, long before the downfall of the Manchu-Qing empire in 1911. True, Confucianism never became the state religion (*guojiao* 國教) of China, but in the years 1900–1904, following the debacle of the Hundred Days, daring reformers safely outside of the capital of Beijing—reformers such as Cai Yuanpei (then in Shaoxing)[3]—oversaw the conversion of an estimated half-million temples in China into primary and secondary schools or local governmental offices.

These events, commingling patriotic and religious fervor, set the stage for the virulent campaigns for and against Confucius during the rest of the twentieth century and into the twenty-first. Up to Kang's time, as earlier chapters in the book have shown, Kongzi was credited with either founding the Ru 儒 or serving as the chief moral exemplar for these professionals qualified by classical learning for officeholding or teaching; in those two capacities, Confucius received cult offerings, along with other deities in the state, local, and Kong family pantheons. When Kang Youwei advanced his highly eccentric reading of Confucian tradition as the basis for a new "state religion" in China, he expected his state religion, modeled after Christianity, to (a) receive state sponsorship; (b) require absolute adherence from all Qing subjects; (c) suppress rival religions such as Daoism, Buddhism, and Christianity; and (d) successfully merge religion and politics.[4] Thereafter, traditionalists who were repulsed by Kang's ahistorical creation sought to counter it with their own equally ahistorical invention of Kongzi, by which the Master became a "secular humanist" whose main contribution to Chinese civilization supposedly consisted of the principled rejection of every single manifestation of "superstition" (i.e., religion). Not coincidentally, this version of Kongzi as "secular humanist" cast Chinese "tradition" as thoroughly compatible with modern political systems and therefore "acceptable" to foreign, especially European and Japanese, interests (religious and not), without alienating large segments of the Chinese population committed to modernizing efforts.

Thus began what were essentially a series of oscillating culture wars, with some groups of reformers attributing the ruling elite's adamant refusal to embrace necessary political changes to the heavy weight of tradition, especially organized religion, and others insisting that only a "national religion" was likely to unify China to withstand the "barbarians." Kang Youwei's conflation of "Confucian" teachings with religion provoked the anti-superstition crowd to tar the Daoist, Buddhist, and Confucian religions with the same brush, on the grounds that all rituals sapped time, money, and energy while diverting talent desperately needed for more pressing national projects. Accordingly, such groups of reformers saw themselves as "secular clerics" engaged in a holy war to "save China" from the corrupt power brokers of the old order who were cynically manipulating religion as the opiate of the masses. To counter these charges against hallowed tradition, other equally fervent groups, loosely organized around the National Essence movement and desperate to salvage *something* of the past, projected a different identity for Kongzi. Members of this second group of reformers made it clear that the Confucius cult they envisioned would not challenge in any way the main theological tenets of monotheistic religions by establishing a devotional community intent upon tapping the full powers of Heaven-and-Earth. This newfangled brand of secular humanism could embolden "anti-superstition" campaigns, ostensibly to foster universal education and New Culture, but more crucially to make patriotism the primary focus of every religious impulse.

From the collapse of the 1898 Reforms up to the time a century later when Deng Xiaoping was fully at the helm, these culture wars flared up with depressing regularity. By turns, the Sage was to be dumped unceremoniously in the trash bin of history or "restored" as some kind of "comeback kid" newly in vogue. The same old ideas were often recycled again and again, even when they were placed in new configurations and contexts, without ever resolving such fundamental questions as how much of the past was needed to provide a stable foundation for the future and how much of the past must be jettisoned if China was to stride comfortably into a brave new world. Did "modernity" itself mean a growth in secularism (as Marx had assumed), or did the state need to drum up a kind of religious fervor in order to unify and industrialize the nation? With many such questions unresolved, Confucius gradually became what one scholar has called "a free-floating signifier" (i.e., a pseudo-historical figure on which propaganda points were inscribed in the name of the Sage). Just as Kang Youwei had once called for the state's backing for a religious version of "Confucianism" designed to bolster, rather than distract from, patriotic fervor, so, too, did the leaders of the Chinese Communist Party (CCP), a century later, look to an invented figure of Confucius to shore up their tattered claims as "vanguard of the proletariat."[5] More than a century of dizzying political change witnessed the astounding transformation of former revolutionaries into entrenched politicos seeking ways to preserve the status quo. The leadership of the CCP then simply borrowed a leaf from the emperor's book. Thus, in November 1986 the PRC government decided to fund an experiment, paying nearly fifty scholars to devote themselves full-time to the study of the "New Confucianism" movement—a movement that had already surfaced in Taiwan, Korea, Japan, and Singapore (see below)—in the hopes that the publication of thousands of books and essays devoted to the subject would help foster a more "aesthetic and harmonious" (*youmei hexie* 優美和諧) society whose traditional roots could plausibly be traced back to imperial teachings and institutions.

Throughout the twentieth and twenty-first centuries, the dominant analysis of the crux of the Chinese problem has remained the same, regardless of the particular political orientations of specific would-be Chinese reformers at any given time:

> The difficulty of reform lies perhaps in the fact that we [the Chinese in Chinese-speaking lands] are constantly worrying over "whether the Chinese will remain Chinese" enough.[6]

Or, as another put it,

> The larger problem is: How can we Chinese feel at ease in this new world which at first sight appears to be so much at variance with what we have long regarded as our own civilization? For it is perfectly natural and justifiable that a nation with a glorious past and a distinctive civilization of its own making should never feel quite at home in a new civilization, if that new civilization is looked upon as . . . alien . . . and forced upon it by external necessities.

That Chinese thinkers could so incisively identify their dilemma may well have been due to China's unusual status within Asia as one of the few countries—and the only empire—never to be colonized outright;[7] also as the only Asian empire where members of a semiautonomous literati group—recruited, legitimized, and organized by meritocratic criteria ultimately derived from the Classics associated with Kongzi— succeeded in monopolizing access to the imperial throne via their high status as scholar-officials.[8] (These literati have often been dubbed "Confucian" by those who cannot decide whether Confucianism is primarily an ethical or a professional orientation. It would be more accurate to say that the examination system in Ming and Qing encouraged the growth of a large group of classically educated men who were trained to apply a wide range of technical skills in governance, including the complex liturgies employed by the consecration officers at the imperial altars and ancestral temples.) Over succeeding generations, the fervent desire by outspoken claimants to new-literati status to sustain at all costs a comparable if not heightened degree of independence, social significance, moral authority, and political capital in the modern world seems to have propelled every movement for and against Confucius during the twentieth and twenty-first centuries. In other words, ever since 1898, members of the intelligentsia—at times allied with groups of workers, peasants, students, and army men and at other times opposed to these groups—have sought to ascertain whether and to what degree the monumental figure of Confucius (suitably modified) could serve their political and cultural agendas.

Lu Xun (1881–1936), China's most famous modern writer, once observed wryly that "Confucius has not been treated kindly in the twentieth century." And it is true that in between these two spikes in "Confucius-fever"—1898, when Kang Youwei made Kongzi the divine precursor of modern constitutional reformers, and 1986, when Chinese Communist leaders, anxious to inject new life into the Party, looked to Confucius as a long-lost savior, making "traditional values" their new slogan—the figure of Confucius often fared poorly in the popular press, in party propaganda, and in academic journals. But the remarkable importance attributed to Kongzi by the Chinese intelligentsia, no matter whether he was viewed as outright impediment or as sublime role model for reform, ensured that images of Confucius would never be relegated to the dustbin of history so long as China was burnishing its image for the world stage. Witness the decision at the end of 2007 by the official Xinhua News Agency in the People's Republic to unveil an official portrait of Confucius—even if that image brings to mind the laughing Buddha.

With the benefit of hindsight, it is clear that most if not all of the bizarre twists that Kongzi's reputation took before, during, and after Deng Xiaoping's (1904–97) triumphant return to power in the years 1978–80 have faithfully mirrored the highs and lows of China's self-confidence about its own place within modernity, in relation to the su-perpowers of the day. Recently this tight link between Chinese intellectuals and Chinese foreign policy has been forged through the experience of thousands of intellectuals and party members who have spent time in the United States since the 1980s, many of whom came away with mixed impressions of American policies. As a result, not merely the status, vanities, and incomes of the intelligentsia but also perceptions of national honor itself have come to be tied to the place of Confucius.

This last chapter introduces a wild array of Confuciuses and Chinas enlisted in the service of the modern and modernizing world, many created within the context of the concerted Enlightenment attacks on "Asiatic theurgy" that survive in the crazed narratives of Lyndon LaRouche and in Samuel Huntington's apocalyptic prophecies about the coming "clash of civilizations." Naturally enough, Kang's com-pelling (if false) portrait of Confucius as Chinese counterpart to Jesus Christ has prompted competing versions of Confucius. There are Confuciuses-in-Asia as self-help gurus and as "Asian values" poster boys. In the United States, Confucius appears as a cookie-cutter law-and-order man, a prototype of the capitalist CEO with a dash of Sunzi's *Art of War* thrown in for good measure, and a sublime thinker offering intriguing alternatives to the dominant discourse of individu-alism and the nation-state. (No one has yet had the temerity to con-ceive of Confucius as a proto-feminist, but that day may yet arrive!) The popular and academic presses have made Confucius the secular-humanist jog alongside Confucius the running-dog of the idle rich and Confucius the early champion of democracy and human rights. This proliferation of latter-day Confuciuses has domesticated—and therefore trivialized—the teachings once ascribed to this monumental figure. Not coincidentally, surprisingly few of the new Confuciuses conceived in China or in the United States pose a stark challenge to the status quo.

PART 1. BACKGROUND: CHINA FIGHTS BACK! (1900–1989)

Suddenly, at the dawn of the twentieth century, to be Chinese was no longer to be superior automatically. Better-educated men and women of Chinese ethnicity needed to find ways to defend China's interests against the twin predations of a moribund Manchu Qing court and aggression by the imperialist powers. In 1905, when the Qing court decided to jettison the classical examination system based on the "Confucian" Classics without making new provisions for selecting capable men by another meritocratic method, the dynasty unwittingly severed the most important ties binding educated Chinese to its rule, and, in the process, forfeited their allegiance. Henceforth the classical learning associated with Kongzi would not even operate on a level playing field with social, intellectual, and political models imported from Japan, Europe, and the United States, given reduced state support and its ties to the "old order."

The Qing collapse came barely six years later, in 1911. At that point, those trained in the Classics could still hope to persuade their compatriots that the crisis engendered by Manchu ineptitude hardly called for a total rejection of the "Confucian" past. Equating the Chinese National Essence with the "old virtues" espoused in those Classics, passionate voices sought to defeat the "antiquity doubters" in their midst. The "doubters" openly scoffed at the idea that the Classics accurately described historical events before unification in 221 BCE, so the National Essence proponents accused the "doubters" of the "worship of . . . other countries," even as they made the foreign discipline of archaeology their own handmaiden. Touted by proponents as incomparably more "scientific" than history or literature, archaeology was used and abused to shore up assertions that China was the "oldest continuous civilization"—and thus morally superior to that of the ancient Near East and Egypt, or classical Greece and Rome. Of course, the rhetoric of National Essence ignored such challenging historical questions as "Was China a single and continuous entity during the long centuries of disunion, some of them under foreign rule?" or, "If we grant that China was often a single political entity, which specific features of its culture and society besides the writing system were actually continuous?" Even the most ardent defenders of the Chinese Classics could no longer celebrate them as sacred canons applicable to every time and place, culture and society. Rather, they accepted the Classics as windows onto a Chinese past that could successfully compete with Western civilizations on either one of two contradictory grounds: that China was older and hence superior or that it was unique and so comparably great. Social Darwinism succumbed to the Lamarckian vision, the better to turn heritage from a weakness into a strength.

"Every policy shift in recent Chinese history has involved the rehabilitation, reevaluation and revision of . . . historic figures,"[9] with successive governments pitching "history" as the "prime vehicle" for propaganda. The consequent desire to fix a definitive narrative about Confucian traditions within the larger context of Chinese history expressed itself in four major twentieth-century movements: the May Fourth Movement (1919–26); the New Life Movement under Chiang Kai-shek (1934–37); the "anti-feudal" mass movements directed by Mao Zedong, which culminated in the "Criticize Confucius" campaigns of the early 1970s; and the New Confucian Revival of the 1980s–1990s. Quite significantly, in each of these movements the governing elite sought dramatic changes within society to restore cultural integrity and civilizational grandeur to China, so that it might resume its "rightful place" on the world stage. Each movement redefined tradition in highly idiosyncratic ways, essentially reinventing the past to facilitate China's struggles with the Western (and later Japanese) powers. Participants in these four movements typically expressed a mixture of pride and hostility toward their own heritage. In one breath they championed the unparalleled antiquity of the Chinese past and denounced the disabling weight of tradition. Such extraordinary ambivalence aptly reflected the complexity of real historical truths: on the one hand, for millennia classical learning had played a crucial role in establishing Chinese cultural and political hegemony well beyond China's borders, but during the last three dynasties in China, classical learning had justified upholding the narrow interests of the ruling classes at the expense of internal cohesion. Reformers looking to the future in the twentieth century (as in the twenty-first) therefore confronted an impossible choice: Should they place a high priority on preserving the literary and artistic masterworks of the past, or should they work instead to ensure the survival and security of the majority Han "race"? In other words, as the writer Lu Xun (d. 1936) put it to his readers, the leadership would have to decide whether it was "more expedient to save their own skins" or to "worship Confucius and perish."

Members of the May Fourth generation never settled on the best program by which to "save China," but they were unified in their opposition to anything they felt smacked of Confucianism. To be fair, the incredible turmoil and treachery of Republican-era politics left the younger generation little time to appreciate the finer points of the old imperial system, which somehow had brought pre-modern China high rates of social mobility and capitalization, along with no more repression than that of pre-modern Europe. And unlike their elders, the May Fourth student leaders could not be expected to appreciate the attractions of classical learning, since they knew almost nothing about it. Steeped in the Western-style learning of their own era, with its almost mystical faith in progress, nationalism, and "survival of the fittest," students at China's most prestigious universities blithely proclaimed the "natural law" that the old must give way to the new, since that would leave them in charge. Therefore, in the heady first decade of the new Republic (1911–49), the "New Youth" gleefully watched as interest in Confucius and classical learning plummeted in direct proportion to government shortfalls in funding for the old-style educational programs. Oriental despotism was indisputably bad, and if Confucian teachings had stifled the natural human functions of innovation and self-renewal (except, quite inexplicably, in Japan),[10] then the "Old Confucian Curiosity Shop" had better be shuttered to make way for those brash newcomers, Mr. Science and Mr. Democracy. The students feared that any tradition aiming to instill a Middle Way could well undermine China's ongoing efforts against the imperialists. As Chen Duxiu and Hu Shih, leading the Communist Party and liberal left, respectively, warned in *New Youth* magazine in 1918, "It is Oriental [i.e., backward] to compromise and only go halfway . . . for fear of opposition." Cultural holdovers became anathema. Given the spirit of the times, even Fu Sinian, perhaps the most prominent classical scholar of the time, was persuaded as a student at Peking University to condemn the "Confucian" family as "the source of all evil," insofar as it induced a "slavish" mentality of "blind obedience" that constituted *the* major impediment to rapid modernization of industry and sociopolitical structures.

Such May Fourth narratives conveniently blamed China's sorry plight as much on the corrupt and corrupting Manchus as on their state-sponsored ideology. The racial overtones became more insistent after 1931, when Japan's swift invasion of north China and Manchuria propelled many thoughtful Chinese to propose that national unity be based in a single common ethnic origin. Initially, at least, in the mid- to late 1930s this heightened racial awareness on the part of Chinese intellectuals worked in favor of Confucius-as-Chinese. For instance, the social critic Lin Yutang, always just ahead of the curve when it came to anticipating new trends, boldly mocked the Sage as a vulgar hypocrite and social climber in his 1922 satire titled "Confucius Meets Duchess Nanzi," but by 1938 Lin had grown quite fulsome in his praise of the Master. His book *The Wisdom of Confucius* began with these ruminations:

> Can one be enthusiastic about Confucianism nowadays? I wonder. The answer seems to depend on whether one can be enthusiastic about sheer good sense, a thing which people usually cannot work up very much enthusiasm for. The more important question seems to be whether one can *believe in* Confucianism nowadays [emphasis added]. This is a question especially important to the modern Chinese of today, a question that . . . cannot be brushed aside. For there is a centrality, or shall I say, universality about the Confucian

attitude and point of view, reflected in a joy in Confucian belief
that I see even among maturing modern Chinese who have received a Western education.

> During the political chaos ... Confucianism won the victory
> over Taoism, Motianism [Mohism], Naturalism, Legalism, Com-
> munism and a host of other philosophies. It maintained this su-
> premacy of the Chinese people for the length of two thousand five
> hundred years ... and it always came back ... stronger than
> ever. . . . Confucianism, as a live force in the Chinese people, is still
> going to shape our national conduct of affairs and modify Commu-
> nism in China.

The idea that Confucianism was the only belief system and code of
behavior vigorous enough to "modify" (i.e., defeat) Communism
gained great currency in Chinese society and abroad. It became the
common ground for both the ill-starred "New Life" Movement under
Chiang Kai-shek before 1949 and Mao Zedong's attacks on the "rem-
nants" of Confucianism after 1949.

The failure of the May Fourth Movement to achieve any of its four
ambitious goals (national independence, modernization, emancipation
of the individual, and justice for all) naturally shaped the rhetoric of the
succeeding New Life Movement organized by Chiang Kai-shek as head
of the Nationalists (better known as the Kuomingtang or KMT, or
Guomindang). The KMT welcomed Chinese who looked to "culture
construction" to root out debilitating "old" tendencies. The party saw
this process as the first step on the long path leading Chinese citizens to
rededicate themselves to the "greater good" of the Chinese republic, as
defined by the party. Meanwhile, to Chiang Kai-shek's way of thinking,
the party dictatorship and the total abnegation of the individual would
serve to "nationalize, militarize, productivize" the Chinese people, restoring them to their former preeminence. In Chiang's logic, Chinese society
could be reinvigorated "by adapting existing institutions or businesses to
new needs." The party merely had to imbue the masses with a carefully
syncretized ideology embodying the best elements of Western and Chinese cultures for the resultant burst of "self-confidence" to promote full
national integration via "exaltation of the nation."

Chiang Kai-shek, an incoherent thinker at the best of times, understood well enough that the specter of modernization frightened vast numbers of ordinary people facing economic decline, political fragmentation, and forced entry into international markets and global wars. To counter the masses' panic, Chiang reasoned, one could demonize the May Fourth reformers' supposed propensity for "smearing and slandering" Chinese culture and announce a backward-looking "revolution" that laid claim to being "heir to an ancient tradition." After all, if the May Fourth stereotypes were accurate, and Confucianism truly was anti-individualistic, hierarchical, and undemocratic, it was precisely this constellation of virtues that Chiang Kai-shek intended to harness in the service of his government. Accordingly, New Life Promotion Associations sprang up everywhere under government prodding after Chiang Kai-shek delivered a series of five speeches in mid-February 1934, explaining New Life methods and goals. These methods and goals were encapsulated in ninety-six short rules designed to make life more "militarized, productive, and aesthetic," more hygienic and more orderly:

> Look straight ahead!
> Keep your buttons buttoned!
> Sit up straight!
> Be prompt! . . .

The gap between Confucius's gentle maxims and those of Chiang Kai-shek, which advocated "healthy violence"—not to mention the KMT's unseemly drive to line the pockets of its officials with ill-gotten gains—made the New Life Movement seem little more than a "distorted echo of Confucianism," irrelevant at best, regressive at worst. Still, Chiang's promotion of New Life values from 1935 to 1949 meant that Mao Zedong would remain deeply suspicious of any remnant Confucian "taint" in China's culture and society after his victory over Chiang. Mao's sense of unease first flared up in the 1960s, in the lead-up to the Cultural Revolution. But his vague unease blossomed into full-scale paranoia when two of Mao's most trusted supporters, Liu Shaoqi and Lin Biao, queried the wisdom of the Supreme Helmsman's radical policies, preferring gradualist solutions for China's assorted ills.

By 1967, the start of the Great Proletarian Cultural Revolution, Red Guards under directions from Mao and his faction identified "Lauding and Glorifying Confucius's Thought" with "Maliciously Attacking Mao Zedong Thought" and "Maliciously Attacking Proletarian Dictatorship." Followers of Mao Zedong openly attacked the "four olds" (old culture, old ideology, old customs, and old habits), using the opportunities afforded by the chaos to exact vengeance upon old enemies. By 1968, Liu Shaoqi was expelled from the Chinese Communist Party; he died a year later in prison. In 1971 General Lin Biao's plane was shot down, reportedly as Lin was trying to defect to the Soviet Union. Immediately following, a "Criticize Lin Biao/Criticize Confucius" mass propaganda campaign began in which Party organs made much of a 1969 decision by Lin and his wife to hang two calligraphy scrolls in their bedroom that quoted the *Analects* maxim: "Of all things, this is the most important: Conquer thyself and restore the rites." All counterrevolutionary activities were deemed desperate acts "made in imitation of Confucius." By September 1973, Jiang Qing, her Gang of Four, and working-class activists made Confucius and the Kong family bywords for the worst excesses of the reactionary slaveholding class. The "subtle words" (*weiyan*) said to be inserted into the "Confucian" Classics were nothing more than cheap rhetoric exploited to provide cover for Confucius's backward-looking anti-egalitarianism. Even Confucius's pedagogical approach deserved condemnation for "chaining the minds of many people" and "hampering the in-depth development of the proletarian educational revolution."

With Mao's death in 1976 and the ascendancy of Deng Xiaoping in the early 1980s, orchestrated attacks on Confucius gradually died down.[11] Ironically, the very bellicosity of Jiang Qing's anti-Confucian harangues lent Confucianism a certain cachet with many in Deng's inner circle who had been tarred as "rightist" and "Confucianist" during the Cultural Revolution. Assertions that Confucianism had lulled the masses into accepting stability seemed ample "proof" of Confucianism's potential to temper the dangerous political and economic extremism associated with Mao, his wife, and her henchmen. In the minds of Mao loyalists and critics alike, then, Confucianism—by any definition—came to seem quintessentially "traditional" and "Chinese." Deng himself could see few if any obvious disadvantages in a Confucian revival, so long as it did not impede the privileged access enjoyed by those in Deng's inner circle to the fruits that globalization could offer. After all, such a revival could provide safe ground on which "deculturalized" Chinese in the PRC could meet their Chinese compatriots in the diaspora, since both sides equally welcomed the idea of a unique sociopolitical creation of Chinese intellectuals becoming a universally admired ideology propagated throughout the world. Thus Deng's reintroduction of state-sponsored Confucianism—the first major reversal of policy directed at Kongzi since the early Republican era—became part and parcel of Deng's well-coordinated "greater China" discourse. Deng's "socialism with Chinese characteristics" portrayed Confucianism as an indigenous alternative superior to the Protestant ethic that would inoculate true believers against "spiritual pollution" imported from the West. Older intellectuals, in particular, looked to a Confucian revival to safeguard them from the perceived ills of postmodern life accompanying China's latest "opening to the West" (e.g., irrationality, nihilism, self-centeredness, hyperactive libidos, absurdity, and gross consumerism). Thrift, education, and self-sacrifice—what could be wrong with these age-old prescriptions? A revival would at the very least provide intellectuals with psychic compensation for the abrupt loss of Mao's "iron rice bowl" guarantees for education, work, health, and retirement. Respectable Chinese could at least savor the glories of Chinese civilization.

But with Confucius deemed the pragmatic "solution" for such a wide array of modern ills, would-be salesmen pitched a profusion of Confuciuses in the marketplace of ideas. One prominent "New Confucian," Zheng Jiadong, a member of the Chinese Academy of Social Sciences, tried to see the big picture in 1995:

> Against the broad canvas of saving the nation from extinction . . . it has been perhaps even more important to carry on the flame of national culture than to address the question of where the ultimate meaning of life was to be grounded.[12]

Zheng's statement is highly suggestive: apparently the New Confucian revival of the 1980s and 1990s did not grow out of a perceived need for a more coherent and well-defined cultural identity, let alone a secure presumption of cultural superiority. Rather, educated elites pressed an agenda premised on the Chinese community's "primordial collective personality of unique origins"[13] as prelude to moral regeneration and eventual self-strengthening, promoting a type of "cultural nationalism" well suited to serve Chinese interests in the global arena.

PART 2. THREE SNAPSHOTS OF ASIA TODAY

These three snapshots from Asia illustrate merely a few of the many contemporary approaches to rethinking the role of institutional Confucianism (and less so Kongzi) that have prevailed within Asian elite circles since the 1990s. As the dominant approaches have been geared mainly to corporate types, academic elites, and leading politicians, the three snapshots taken together constitute a sampling of major figures in the media, politics, and academia across Asia. There are the so-called Third and Fourth Wave New Confucians based in the academic strongholds of Hong Kong, Taiwan, South Korea, and (increasingly) the People's Republic, who likewise seek to adapt Kongzi's message to the intellectual demands of the world today. There are two ministers in the Singaporean government who routinely invoke the name of Confucius to sanction one-party rule over a multiethnic community. And there is Yu Dan, a popular TV personality and self-styled self-help guru who cheerfully appropriates the *Analects* as grist for her media mill.

Although the phrase "creative transformation" is continually on the lips of nearly all self-professed Confucian Revivalists in Asia, the rhetoric of the contemporary Asian "New Confucianists" has paid shockingly little attention to ethical, social, or political issues.[14] As the Hong Kong scholar Zheng Zhongyi complains, the New Confucians have been overly preoccupied instead with "intellectual Ru learning"—with metaphysics and ontology. In the People's Republic, for example, two consecutive Five-Year Plans for the social sciences (1986–1990, 1991–1995) subsidized large cooperative research projects devoted to ostensibly "Confucian" topics, producing thousands of scholarly books and articles in the process. Notwithstanding the flurry of activity, the Chinese intelligentsia or *zhishi fenzi*, with rare exceptions, has done little to try to stimulate grassroots interest in the values they label glibly as "Confucian." Advocates of a "return to tradition" (singular) tend to be cultural nationalists more interested in preserving the status quo via identity politics than in engaging in the sorts of serious and sustained efforts that would be required to devise Confucian norms and practices for the modern world. As Yu Ying-shih, a prominent American academic, has put it,

> The sort of practiced skill or technique that a true "Confucian" (*rujia*) concerns himself with is putting into practice what he stands for. What is being developed right now [in New Confucian circles] is nothing more than a skill for clever talking. . . . Mere clever talk cannot "summon the soul" [i.e., recapture the old spirit]. To summon the soul requires individual practice.[15]

The sacred character ascribed to classical learning perhaps ceases to exist as soon as classical learning becomes an object for scholarly analysis and criticism, rather than a guide for daily spiritual praxis. So it is fair to ask the following questions: Can the academic study of late imperial Confucian ideology or theology ever really spawn a mass movement with the potential to shape China's entry into the global marketplace of ideas and goods? How much can a national or global movement rely upon a rarefied moral idealism composed of "soulful exchanges" and "intellectual dialogue" among academics of similar persuasions?[16] What are we to make of the pious references to the "enduring Chinese spirit" or to "humaneness, rightness, ritual propriety, wisdom, good faith, doing one's best for others"? Is there anything specifically Chinese or Confucian in this list of virtues? And why has the current scholarly preoccupation with the role of Confucianism in Chinese history not spurred major revisions to the standard portraits of Kongzi that draw upon the disparate roles attributed to him through the ages? As one Western expert sniffs, the New Confucians have given a "perfunctory genuflection" to "vague, contextless cosmological notions" (e.g., harmony; the unity of Heaven and humans), plus a nod toward some "traditional virtues" deemed "central to the Chinese cultural tradition" (usually obedience and filial duty), but this "hardly adds up to a compelling vision for the rapidly evolving future."[17] One may press further to ask why elites in China, Taiwan, South Korea, and Hong Kong have each chosen to assert proprietary claims over the one "true" line of transmission for the *Daotong,* or Confucian Way, in the face of broader trends—international investments, academic conferences, flows of legal visitors, and traffic in workers (some of it illegal)—that have tended to reduce cross-straits tensions.

Snapshot 1. "New Confucians" and the Neo-Cons in Taiwan and Hong Kong

Modernists and postmodernists alike identify interconnectedness as *the* most seminal feature of the last century, thanks to such inventions as the telegraph, the fax machine, the Internet, the satellite broadcast, and the cell phone. Of course, the ongoing circulation of ideas, peoples, and things has been a feature of human life since time immemorial, as the many Silk Roads attest. But during the first half of the twentieth century, thinkers promoting a Confucian revival left the mainland for Taiwan, Hong Kong, and the United States, where they trained new generations of intellectuals in the fine art of splicing Western culture onto Confucian traditions. In the mid–twentieth century, members of the so-called Third Wave Confucian movement knew that they, as the chief proponents of Kongzi in the modern world, would have to assist the cause of Western science and democracy in Asia, if any form of Confucian teaching was to survive.[18] They also believed that political equality was as vital to the full realization of Kongzi's virtue of "humaneness" in the twentieth century as self-abnegation and moral purity had been in earlier eras. Equality was not such a big stretch after all, since Kongzi's Middle Way invested exemplary figures with a powerful charisma that stemmed not from hereditary privilege but from a combination of learning and humane action.

The most impressive of these Third Wave New Confucians, the

historian Hsu Fu-kuan (Xu Fuguan, 1903–82) and the statesman Car-
sun Chang (1887–1969), were strong voices calling for full equality in
politics, law, and society, despite the repressive conditions in Asia during World War II and the cold war. Angry at Chiang Kai-shek's sus-
pension of the Chinese constitution before and after 1949, Hsu and
Chang, in defiance of martial law, continually agitated for the greater
separation of governmental powers, for greater freedom of expression
and assembly, and for other individual human rights. Chang, one of
the authors of the UN Universal Declaration of Human Rights, saw to
it that Articles 22–27, devoted to social, economic, and cultural
rights, were included in the final Declaration. Hsu, a prominent academic in Taiwan, produced massive compilations on the history of
early thought in China (some fifty works in all), each acquainting
readers of modern Chinese with the relative strengths and, yes, weak-
nesses of their traditions. Outside academic circles, Hsu and Chang
are mainly remembered for their courageous decision to publish "A
Manifesto for a Reappraisal of Sinology" (1958), a plan for a Confucian revival in Asia that remains a touchstone for some Confucians in
Taiwan and Hong Kong to this day.

Meanwhile, the more conservative among their New Confucian
contemporaries (the neo-Cons),[19] along with their successors in
today's Fourth Wave, have consistently sought to restore the old
power structures through a neotraditional ideology shot through with
religious inflections, in the belief that only this sort of powerful ideology can simultaneously ensure social stability, cure China's ills, and
co-opt useful Western techniques, so as to pave the way for Chinese
communities to stride confidently into an uncertain future. For the
neo-Cons, the patriarchal family remains the basic unit for moral education. The Doctrine of Mind and Nature, first read into the *Constant
Mean* and the *Mencius* by the Cheng brothers and Zhu Xi and later
elaborated by Wang Yangming (1472–1529), explains the process
whereby these moral patterns generated within the family can and do
multiply themselves throughout society and the cosmos. According to
that doctrine, nature, mind, and Heaven are manifestations of the
same unitary Principle, which finds supreme expression in cosmic harmony, personal purity, and social unity. In humans, the desired state of

"integrity" and "wholeness" (both signified by *cheng* 誠) is attainable only via a settled mind (*jing* 靜) that is both a precondition for and a final realization of the numinous (*ling* 靈) and godlike (*shen* 神) nature endowed by Heaven. The neo-Cons' corollary to the Doctrine of Mind and Nature posits a "transmission of the Way" (*Daotong*) that relies less on historical institutions or philosophical proofs than on the intuitions, even mystical revelations, granted a chosen few "Scholars Poised between Heaven and Earth." The neo-Cons' portrait of the "authentic" moral self[20] whose "solitary mind" operates amidst loneliness and isolation owes much to Weber's Protestant Ethic theory, in which the successful mercantile spirit reflects an inward-looking, agonizing drive for moral purity. Perhaps this gives the neo-Con spokesmen (there are no spokeswomen as yet) the confidence that this rarefied interior condition of the select few can yet serve as the single most widely accepted marker of Chinese identity, the basis of a national ideology, and a major force in global economic progress.

Adopting a sectarian model more typical of Catholic-Protestant disputes than of imperial Chinese traditions, the neo-Cons adamantly deny Daoism and Buddhism any role in shaping "mainstream" cultural expressions in Chinese culture. The neo-Cons nonetheless have been forced to address Enlightenment and post-Enlightenment notions of personal autonomy and liberty, if only to expose their limitations. Less doctrinaire than their predecessors—or at least less anti-Communist, since the PRC is a force to be cozened, if possible—the Third and Fourth Wave neo-Cons freely cite Marx and Kant and Freud in order to "set up a dialogue" between Confucianism, Christianity, Marxism, and Freudian analysis. Since the result tends to be unwieldy abstractions that reference several traditions simultaneously, these would-be defenders of Asian values and Confucian learning are in danger of leaving hardly anything in place that is genuinely Confucian or Chinese. Their subtext is more easily understandable: an Asian cultural pride that resists sloppy equations of modernization and Westernization:

Today we have left behind the days of the May Fourth Movement (1919–25, in the early Republican era). We no longer approve of talking about total Westernization. What we want is to harmonize traditional and contemporary values, to accomplish the modernization process, in order to advance toward the postmodern new world.[21]

In other words, only the pursuit of Confucian ethical urges can ever truly satisfy Chinese people experiencing late-stage consumer capitalism.

Doubtless, the most important philosopher providing inspiration to this neoconservative branch of the Third Wave was Mou Zongsan (1909–94), who tried to devise a rigorously logical defense of Kongzi and the "moral conscience" by engaging with—critics call it "rummaging through"—modern Western philosophy, from Descartes to Kant to Whitehead, plus Tiantai Buddhism. Mou began with the same premise that informs all of Zhu Xi's writings: that after Mencius nearly all the Confucians substantially misconceived the "true" transmission of the Way, which accounts for their failure to produce perfected teachings. At the same time, Mou faulted Zhu Xi for a formal rationalism and an emphasis upon intelligible cosmic principles that Mou deemed too "intellectualistic" and alien to the emotions. In Mou's construction of the "praxis of moral intuition," true sages define correct values through the propagation and strengthening of four Heavenly[22] patterns: *Tianming* or the Mandate of Heaven; humane acts within society; the *xin* 心 (the heart, credited with intellectual and emotional capacities); and human nature, most specifically, inborn inclinations to do good. To fully apprehend the fundamental patterns inherent in these preordained moral orders, Mou argued, the hearts and minds of good persons must operate on two levels simultaneously: at the level of a penetrating moral awareness and at the level of everyday consciousness of the experiential world. The requisite knowledge of this experiential world is to be gained through the study of science and of human cultures, past and present; the use of ritual as a profound tool for communication; learning how to direct the *qi*, or configured energy; and striving for the highest good in every situation. Thus Mou's teachings urge his students to "explore to the utmost the wisdom of the ancients" while sharply reducing the burden of the past when it interferes with efficient functioning in the modern world.

Increasingly, the neo-Cons in the Third and Fourth Waves have portrayed themselves as a fearless vanguard spearheading international ethical projects, first and foremost in the East Asian countries that once looked to China for models and institutions, but secondarily in any countries open to the Chinese diaspora (i.e., anywhere in the world). Since most neo-Cons contend that an authentic embrace of Confucius must be grounded in reverence for a continuous tradition passed down through small groups of highly trained intellectuals, some views of Yu Ying-shih, recent recipient of a million-dollar prize from the Kluge Center at the Library of Congress, have found particular favor to the degree that Yu, a highly respected historian, blurs the distinctions between pre-modern and modern Chinese forms of learning and praxis:

> As much as I would like to distinguish the *shi* ("scholar-official" of imperial China) from the *zhishi fenzi* (modern "intellectual"), I must point out that spiritually the latter has continued much of what had been cultivated by the former. For example, the idea that the intellectual must always be identified with public-mindedness is not a cultural borrowing from the modern West, but from Confucian heritage traceable ultimately to the sage himself.[23]

Though Yu, to do him justice, quite often emphasizes *jian*/remonstrance over *zhong*/loyalty, such statements encourage more conservative intellectuals rooted in and rooting for backward-looking politics to maintain their sense of time-hallowed legitimate privilege.

Lately the ranks of the Third and Fourth Wave neo-Cons have witnessed acrimonious disputes over who is worthy of inclusion in their select group. A leading concern of researchers throughout Asia has always been to clarify who does and does not qualify for the prestigious title of "New Confucian," given Asia's tumultuous political history during the last century. After all, for hundreds of years, moralists in imperial China busied themselves with the task of constructing genealogies of the Way (see Suggested Readings).[24] Such an intense competition for "proprietary rights" over the New Confucian identity reflects the urge to exert an interpretive monopoly (*jieshiquan* 解釋權) over Confucian discourse in the twenty-first century. While "heretics" like Jiang Guobao (Suzhou University) blame Mou Zongsan and his disciples for an infatuation with "scholastic rationality" and "theoretical systems" that have contributed more to the demise of *Ru* Learning than to its reinvigoration, most outlines of sagely transmissions choose one of the following definitions for the New Confucians:

1. the disciples of Mou Zongsan and Tang Junyi (i.e., a genealogical line that generally omits liberal democrats even as it exalts visions of unending humane creativity),
2. the adherents of Wang Yangming, the Ming thinker and critic of Zhu Xi, or, more inclusively,
3. any persons who "strive for a renaissance of Confucianism," "believe that Confucianism is the 'core belief' and 'dominant force' underlying all of Chinese culture," and accept the need to "absorb and amalgamate Western philosophies, so as to bring about the modernization of Confucianism."[25]

The more elitist of the neo-Cons evidently do not believe that all peoples—or even all Chinese—have inherited from Confucius the same patrimony, since the transmission of a Confucian way of life was interrupted for decades in the People's Republic (by Maoism), in Singapore (by British colonialism), and in other areas (by other factors).

Views of the Chinese past and of modern China will continue to evolve, if they do not founder once again on two self-congratulatory myths that have been pushed aggressively in China and in the United States for a century or so: the Chinese myth of a unitary and unique "Han [majority] identity" with remarkable powers of ethnic assimilation, and the American myth of the Western origins of Enlightenment, modernity, and modernization, which makes these three phenomena irretrievably "foreign" to China. As recent Sinological work has shown, the words now used to convey "Han identity" were not much in favor before the (foreign) Liang dynasty in the sixth century CE, when the same words did not connote today's belief in a superior Chinese culture that absorbs the inferior cultures of its neighbors. (The Han powers of assimilation were first systematically touted by Republican-era intellectuals intent upon justifying their anti-Manchu revolution and defending their culture against diffusionist theories claiming that major features of Chinese civilization came from outside its borders.) Research into Western history and Chinese science demonstrates that the presumed pillars of Enlightenment tradition—science and equality before the law—are not so much Western as modern in origin, given that they can be found nowhere in their present forms before the late eighteenth century. Furthermore, important features of modern life have relied heavily on a series of Chinese inventions, including mass printing, sail-rigging techniques, the compass, paper, and rudders for oceangoing vessels.

Why have these two myths proven to be so powerful, even in the face of repeated academic studies proving them false? Quite possibly some ideas are just too bad to die. But one recognizable pattern throughout human history is that myths of autochthony (i.e., miraculous self-generation) usually exert maximum pull on human societies when a given population fears the wholesale importation of new ideas and institutions into areas of life that it prefers to take for granted. This pattern does not augur well for an increasingly globalized future tossed this way and that by invented traditions.

Snapshot 2. Ministering to the Majority: One-Party Rule in Singapore, under Deputy Prime Minister Goh Keng Swee (1968–86) and Prime Minister Goh Chong Tong (November 1990–August 2004)[26]

Lee Kuan Yew (b. 1923), the grand old man of Singaporean politics, reckons that his city-state is situated "at the confluence of three great civilizations from Asia, the Confucianist, the Hindu, and the Muslim." That assertion provided the ostensible rationale for Singapore's decision in the mid-1980s to establish an Institute of East Asian Philosophies, to spearhead efforts to reintroduce the study of Confucianism to Asia while researching its potential to promote social harmony within pluralistic communities of diverse ethnic identities. In reality, Lee fashioned Singapore as a bastion of "Asian values" because he hoped to kill two birds with one stone: Asian values, if crafted with sufficient care, could provide a sound ideological justification for the "soft authoritarian" policies mandated by Singapore's ruling party, while supplying a plausible way to edge closer to Deng's China after the United States, Singapore's staunchest ally during the Vietnam War (1954–75), abruptly lost interest in Southeast Asia. (Recent PAP party platforms explicitly link Singapore's economic future to the "transformation of contemporary China's economic institutions" under the direction of the Chinese Communist Party.) So, in 1991, the Singaporean government, under Lee's direction, produced a government position paper devoted to the topic of "Shared Values," code words for Lee's frontal attack on individualism and "permissiveness." This white paper broadly defined the "Confucian heritage" in terms of four attitudes that supposedly underpinned all East Asian cultures: (1) a willingness to place nation and society above self, and a willingness to embrace the "transcendent whole"—the state sanctioned by the cosmic order—over the countervailing draw of the individual and the nuclear family; (2) an allied belief that the family rather than the individual constitutes the basic building block of society; (3) a decided preference for conflict resolution through consensus-building; and (4) an emphasis—conscious and unconscious—on harmony and "blending" (i.e., conformity) as opposed to individuality and legal rights. To this list of four shared values, a fifth was soon added: dedication to a "Confucian" work ethic in pursuit of national economic progress.[27] As Mark Hong, Singapore's former ambassador to Russia and the Ukraine, phrased it when talking to the domestic media,

> The challenge is to modernize while remaining Asian. . . . We fear that our populations [in Singapore] may begin to believe that the existing patterns of families in developed societies [with their high rates of divorce, mental illness, and crime] represent the wave of the future. . . . A new Darwinian contest for the best social values and practices has already begun [in the global arena].[28]

With Singapore taking the lead, a group of Asian leaders hastened to adopt similar language while preparing to resist "any attempts to use human rights as a condition . . . for extending development assistance." (The Bangkok Declaration of 1993 formally denounced such attempts on behalf of forty-plus Asian and Pacific states.) For these

Asian states, political stability is the sine qua non for economic growth, national pride, and the future health of the body politic; the introduction of "Western science and technology" is welcome so long as it does not interfere with the ongoing "values conversation."

How had the Singaporean leaders forged such a strong identification between traditional Asian values and conservative policies so quickly and effectively? After all, Singapore never hid the fact that it had escaped what earlier generations perceived as "corrupt" and corrupting Confucian influences during its long colonial period (1867– 1942) under the British. As Singapore's Director of Curriculum Development Institute confessed, Singaporeans had little real familiarity with Confucian ethics. Yet Singapore knew how to turn this potential disadvantage to its advantage: because Singapore was a virtual tabula rasa beholden neither to Taiwan nor to the PRC, Singapore boasted that it was the optimal environment for the creation of a new multiracial "Confucian Third Way experiment" that would be capable of brokering compromises acceptable to all the regional powers. Adopting a business model, Singapore invited outside consultants to "draw up a conceptual framework" for teaching Confucianism as a new academic subject. The most influential of these overseas experts, Professor Tu Wei-ming (Harvard University) and six other self-identified "Confucian" scholars from the United States (all but one a Chinese-American), concurred with Lee's vision. They further argued that a prudent selection of "Confucian" values from the pre-modern era could easily be accommodated within a rapidly modernizing society. Ignoring the profound religious dimensions of the Confucius cult, underscored since Kang Yuwei's Reforms in 1898, Minister Goh Keng Swee proclaimed that Confucian ethics had always been "completely secular," and hence could serve as an ideal type of "cultural ballast against the less desirable aspects of Western culture."[29] Goh blandly continued, "Now, *that* is the sort of ethic we should teach in Singapore. It is up to the scholars to find it somewhere in Confucian literature."

Despite all the hoopla surrounding the development of those "Religious Knowledge" courses, in which "Confucian ethics" featured prominently, Singapore decided to quietly phase out the courses after only a few years. As Lee Kwan Yew noted in a 1994 speech, the new Religious Knowledge curriculum, contrary to expectations, threatened to destroy the delicate balance of power in multiethnic and multireligious Singapore. Evidently all that media attention had contributed to an upsurge of interest in the more organized but less "Chinese" religions of Buddhism, Islam, and Christianity. And the very existence of the Confucian Ethics option enraged leading critics of the government, who saw the option as yet another concerted attempt by the PAP to reinforce authoritarian rule over Singapore. No matter. By 1997 the Singaporean ministers stated that "Confucius had already taken up permanent residence in Singapore." The second Goh-in-high-office confirmed his determination to "pragmatically adopt only those aspects of Confucianism which were relevant to Singapore." "If necessary," Goh said, he "would turn Confucius on his head to make him appropriate for Singapore."

Since the legendary figure of Confucius had long been thought, under Lee's tutelage, "the most enduring, broadest, and uncontroversial representation of Chinese culture" available to the Singaporean state propagandists, it was not long before other "Confucian" activities supplanted the Confucian ethics course in the hearts of local bureaucrats. A national Filial Piety holiday was duly instituted, and a new "life skills" curriculum that highlighted intensive "family etiquette" courses was organized around "Confucius' Hometown Cultural Tours." The Ministry of Education also offered to sponsor the "professional development" of citizens of Chinese origin so long as they demonstrated a willingness to participate in the "propagation of Chinese culture." On the campus of Nanyang Technological University (NTU), a new Confucius Institute sprang up, with the explicit mission of "branding" Confucius's name and story. According to the institute's literature, the supposed benefits to be derived from the Primary One Enrichment Course include the inculcation of "important values, such as filial piety and respect for elders," along with learning a "fun" way to absorb basic information and business strategies while "managing human capital." The purely instrumental resurrection of "traditional values" to foster economic growth and political stability meant that quotations from the *Analects* jostle against lines from Sunzi's *Art of*

War in the institute's textbooks. As the cynics have observed, a stock version of "Confucian paternalism" now props up the PAP's joint "disciplinarian and custodial roles" in maintaining its Chinese majority.[30]

Singapore's ruling party aspires to re-create the ideal of late imperial China, whereby a Confucian male elite educates the family in ritual, directs scholarship through education, and controls access to state power through a meritocratic civil service examination. But a backward-looking "creative transformation" of Confucian values runs counter to those Confucian teachings that encourage those with access to power to maintain an independent (and occasionally critical) voice in politics and society. Kongzi in the *Analects* despised the "village goody-goodies" who made conformity to local mores the supreme value in their lives.[31] Besides, it is not altogether clear that invented "Confucian" rituals will prove popular enough in a city-state like Singapore, where the extended family is an anomaly and the Web rules. Only time will tell.

Snapshot 3. Yu Dan, the PRC's Self-Help Queen

Yu Dan, China's home-grown Oprah, manages her own book club and publishing industry, thanks in large part to her role as hostess of *Lecture Room,* a popular afternoon TV talk show broadcast in Mandarin on the state-run Channel 10. Once a university teacher in Media Studies in Beijing, the irrepressibly perky Yu Dan, at the age of forty-one, left the chorus of talking heads to become a virtual pop star after she devoted, in 2006, an entire series of programs to the teachings of the Confucian *Analects.* Yu Dan's fans accept her as a devout "defender of traditional culture" and a significant "force for harmony" within Chinese society. Certainly the TV series proved to be such a hit that it spawned a bestseller, Yu Dan's *The Analects: Insights,* which sold three million copies in its first *four months* of publication in China—*before* Yu Dan launched a record-breaking tour of Taiwan in April 2007. (Some bureaucratic units of the People's Republic reportedly purchased hundreds of thousands of copies, sending them to schools and prisons for use in political training and reeducation.) Yu

Dan's vision battens upon nativist impulses positing a particular "Chinese people's view of history" as well as a "singular and unique" cultural trajectory. But presumably Yu Dan's hordes of fans also share a common perception with those teachers and guards regarding CCP policies under Deng and his successors: those policies left a majority of China's 1.3 billion people with more disposable income than under Mao, but without a clear moral compass.[32]

The condescending premise of Yu Dan's TV show and her bestseller is much the same: since "Kongzi is what the masses need," the "colorless pedant" of the Chinese imagination can and will be jazzed up to induce greater mass consumption. The genius of Yu Dan's enterprise was this fresh rebranding and multimedia marketing of a familiar name that had already become more or less emptied of actual content. To this end, Yu Dan's Confucius becomes a dynamic go-getting pragmatist in the John Dewey mold (building on Dewey's current vogue in China)—except when he's being morphed into a dreamy recluse in the style of Tao Yuanming (365–427) or a Zhuangzi-clone who regards the world with cool detachment. In general, Yu Dan's Confucius avoids conflict, reduces his dependence upon others, and "tends his own garden" (*pace* Voltaire). Unique among the many Confuciuses on offer in the modern world, Yu Dan's Kongzi comes perilously close to making the Sage an eerie double for Chauncy Gardiner, the vacuous cipher at the center of the Peter Sellers movie *Being There*. Confucius, Yu Dan seems to think (contrary to all early traditions), got ahead in the fame game through his enviable pliability and his willingness to kowtow to those in power.

Celebrity and wealth are easily mistaken for shrewdness and profundity. Yu Dan's detractors—and they are legion in the PRC, especially in academic circles—accuse her of seriously distorting the original teachings of Confucius, although they concede with a sneer that most of her errors may be unintentional. After all, her reading level in classical Chinese is so inadequate that she regularly mistranslates the phrase "petty person" as "little person" or "child." As Confucius, in no fewer than twenty-four *Analects* passages, reserved his disdain for "petty" adults of weak morality in high positions at court, Yu Dan's "insights" are as likely to mislead as to illuminate. Critics blame Yu Dan's avidity for monetary gain for leading her to "amuse the masses with idiocy all day." She strikes them as more of a crass hawker of cheap second-rate goods than as the versatile and accomplished academic she pretends to be. The harshest of her critics in the PRC compare her unfavorably to the "scholar-officials from the feudal society" who were simply determined to uphold "the vestiges of the old society." Of course, Yu Dan may well be laughing all the way to the bank. What is unfortunate is that the controversies over her book provide additional opportunities for the uninformed to recycle old slanders against the Sage. To take but one example, Yu Dan repeats the old canard, advanced for the first time during the Ming dynasty (1366–1468), that Kongzi "famously considered a good woman to be an illiterate woman." No matter that no credibly early tradition has Confucius weighing in on gender issues at all—not surprising, given that he lived in an aristocratic age when birth trumped gender.

Yu Dan's "insights" frequently appear to contradict one another. (Her preface intends to forestall potential objections with a comment that Confucius himself was not much good at logic anyway.) The 2006 PRC annual state report speaks of 87,000 violent incidents involving one hundred people or more. Yu Dan nonetheless insists that the "harmony" advocated in the *Analects* can already be found in today's blessed PRC, where people "exercise tolerance of others" and ethnic groups "blend together,"[33] giving due deference to the latest CCP injunctions against ethnic and class tensions. In the same breath, however, Yu Dan proclaims that the material improvements of the post-Mao era demonstrate the wisdom of allowing "different voices and differences of opinion" to contend. The consequent social dislocation, she predicts, cannot really last for very long, given the political and biological perfections that happily come together in the persons of PRC citizens. As Yu Dan's Confucius reminds the Chinese people, a thoughtful citizenry with "settled hearts" makes for a more secure society that *eventually* will achieve the greatest good for the greatest number. Yu Dan makes Kongzi into a marvelous birthright, if you're biologically Chinese and lucky enough to be residing in the People's Republic of China. Citing PRC polls that claim the Chinese are happier than EuroAmericans—polls that contradict other polls conducted elsewhere—Yu Dan believes that the Sage wanted the Chinese people to learn how to "make friends and influence people," while shielding themselves from the worst excesses of capitalism. (Apparently, Yu Dan has been too busy to visit shopping malls in today's China.) In Yu Dan's parallel universe, China is vastly superior to the West, for China alone recognizes the power of morality and civility, engages in the search to balance creativity with harmony, and maintains an enviable "oneness with Heaven" or the cosmic order—and all this despite near-lethal levels of air, water, and noise pollution. Still, it is not enough for the Chinese to hearken to the *Analects'* injunctions; they should buy her book, if they mean to be happy, orderly, and content to "stay in their places"! Even Kongzi benefits from this latter-day interpreter who has helped him "adjust" his ethical prescriptions to a new age.

What is lost and what is gained in all this? Yu Dan reads the *Analects'* emphasis on practical wisdom (learning to reliably act in humane ways) as references to "talent," which Yu Dan equates with the ability to get ahead. Since Yu Dan reads "good learning" as "learning that guides thoughts" so that they are "in compliance with [present-day] societal needs," she blithely ignores the connection that Kongzi made between self-improvement and serious study of the past. Even more stunning, Yu Dan's work offers nary a hint that roughly a third of the *Analects* deals with social justice and economic redistribution. In the end, Yu Dan deems Confucius to be extraordinary solely because of the *strength* of his commitments. She seems to think it matters very little what the *objects* of those commitments were, nor does she fathom the subtle role those commitments play in shaping a person's character and fate. Typically, great teachers promote a radically new set of intuitions about the world and its operations, and it is up to their followers to explain away the most unconventional aspects of their masters' often inchoate visions in order to render them more palatable to the ordinary public. In one sense, however, Kongzi may have met his best disciple yet in Yu Dan, for Yu tells us that no sacrifices are required if we would make ourselves into happier, more productive, and more mindless human beings.

Understandably, responses to Yu Dan run the gamut from adulation to excoriation. A popular website devoted to her in China recorded the following blogs on two days, May 8–9, 2007:

> It is *so* great that someone talking about Kongzi's teachings has become famous. It is a sign that China will be a great nation. If only a man were to come to lecture about *Lunyu* (just as the lady did), it would be perfect!

> Include me among those who are outraged—OUTRAGED—by this book. To those who ask "What's the harm?" since one Eastern Han book compiled by members of the Kong Family urged people to "recite the Classics to help oneself" (言經以自輔)," we might reply: "Because it misses the point."

As John Dewey once observed, "Apparent contradictions always demand attention." Up to now, nearly all the players dominating the Asian scene have accepted the inevitability of particular patterns of political, economic, and cultural development introduced to Asia by the Western powers and Western missionaries, even while casting China as the rising star of the twenty-first century. China's unprecedented leap to global influence since the 1990s means that some Yanks have finally decided to take Confucius as seriously as the Europeans (especially the French) take the eighteenth-century *philosophes*. But lest those in the United States absolve themselves of parading their own brands of incongruity, this chapter turns to examine Sino-American relations in recent times.

PART 3. AMERICA IN THE MIRROR (1900–1989)

In his provocative 1993 essay, Milan Kundera characterized the mentality of "small nations" by measuring the "intensity of their cultural life" and their profoundly "human scale," while noting that the tight-knit cultures built within small nations tend to feel confining: "Within that warm intimacy, each envies each, everyone watches everyone." Kundera's thesis sounds plausible, and students of Chinese history can quickly relate his thesis to the life of Kongzi in his small home state of

Lu, where envy and fear supposedly prevented any of the governing elite from making use of Kongzi or his teachings. But one obvious objection may be raised to Kundera's observation: the United States and China—among the very biggest of the continental powers—have been watching each other with that same degree of obsessiveness since the dawn of the twentieth century.

This phenomenon was first explored in Harold Isaacs's now classic work, *Scratches on Our Minds* (1958; revised in 1980), which charts a series of crazed reversals in American images of China, by which eras of profound admiration for China alternate with eras of extreme loathing and contempt. In the chart on pages 266–267, I follow Isaacs's lead in characterizing American attitudes toward events in China in terms of stark despotism or sunny social harmony, implying that such contradictions have contributed to political instability within both China and the United States at least as often as they have provoked reasoned responses. A perceived capacity to "understand China" relies on the coherence of the stories told about it by "authoritative sources." Unfortunately, study after study documents the ignorance and prejudice within government circles in the United States that have inspired these popular images.[34] For more than 150 years, Isaacs notes, Sino-American relations have been "heavily marked" by the continuing impact of the American missionary enterprise in China.[35] The warring moralizing stereotypes derive, in no small part, from self-righteous sentimental imperialists on both sides of the Pacific claiming God, history, or empire on their side. Remember, from 1949 to 1971 (officially) and 1980 (in actuality), nearly all contact between China and the United States was abruptly severed, after which the bilateral exchanges swiftly resumed their old pattern of swinging between adulation and excoriation.

Larger shifts in the American psyche have also colored views of China, the Chinese, and Confucius over the last hundred years or so. As a result, American engagements with China can be divided into eight separate eras—each characterized by different "moods"—eras ending with the Ages of Re-enchantment (1980–June 1989, i.e., Tian'anmen) and Revulsion (June 4, 1989, to the present). Notably, the only three points of continuity within these contradictory portraits of China are the American emphases on the teeming masses (the "human sea") making up the Peoples' Republic of China; the image of

the Chinese as hardworking;[36] and the expectation that such coolies—
"bitter laborers" to the end—invariably will uphold customs that are
anathema to red-blooded, freedom-loving Americans. The notion that
clashes between the United States and China are inevitable has grown
ever more insistent since 1989, the date of the government crackdown
on the Chinese democracy protestors in Tian'anmen Square. Reports
that China's environmental devastation is on a scale sufficient to damage the United States adds fuel to the fire. (While an estimated one-
third of the pollution in Los Angeles comes from China, only in 2006
did China surpass the United States in polluting.) Reports of sweat-
shops in China, inferior quality control over Chinese exports, and
widespread official corruption merely underscore the perceived nega-
tives, even as China is what Isaacs calls "a central and often even a
dominating factor in the host of decisions forced on the United States
by its . . . place in world affairs." Think of the United States' role in reconstruction efforts in Asia after World War II; its struggle for dominance during the cold war; its eagerness to fight proxy wars in Korea
and Southeast Asia aimed at weakening communism in general and
China in particular. Then consider the encouragement of U.S. investment in China, the pegging of the Chinese RMB to the American dollar, American dependence on cheap Chinese imports, and the PRC's
$288-billion investment in U.S. government bonds that subsidizes our
exploding deficit.

For better or for worse, in the United States, as elsewhere, the figure
of Confucius has come to signify the "timeless essence" of Chinese culture. Put another way, Confucius and "Confucian culture"—however
ill-defined—have come to symbolize China and the Chinese. As one
prize-winning documentary put it, "It was Confucius who through his
teachings founded the strict moral orders and political ideology that
have dominated over two thousand years of Chinese life."[37] This conflation of "Confucian" and "Chinese"—never mind which period or
which aspect of Chinese culture—crops up with equal frequency in
works by rabid China-haters and by the vaguely pro-China liberal left
(see Suggested Readings at the end of the chapter). In other words,
both the champions and the critics of Chinese culture have resurrected
the same master narrative equating "Chinese" with "Confucian" and
"National Studies" with "Confucian Learning," along with the endur-

ing "factoid" that throughout Chinese history the dominant societal relationships have always been asymmetrical and vertical (ruler to subject; parent to child; husband to wife; male to female), rather than friendly or consortial. In particular, the resurgent cold warriors in the new millennium consistently conflate China-the-nation, the Chinese people, and Chinese culture. China suffers, in their view, from three tremendous lacks: (1) the lack of a well-developed tradition of equality before the law; (2) the lack of equality within and between groups (e.g., between men and women) guaranteed both by law and by custom; and (3) the lack of that elusive quality needed to produce "good" science and art (see the film documentary *From Mao to Mozart*). These cold warriors then confidently trace China's perceived *lacks* back to Confucius's lack of prescience and his supposed elitism.

China loyalists, by contrast, are apt to characterize the quintessential Chinese self as religious or artistic, two qualities that they see as somehow "spiritual." Generally speaking, defenders of Confucius-and-China plug Kongzi into "the oldest continuous civilization," whose institutions and ideas they hope will help provide solutions for the grab-bag of assorted ills ascribed to the consumer capitalism of "the West." So that "looking toward the future" (*xiang qian kan*) might turn into something more than "looking to make money" (also *xiang qian kan* in Chinese), the defenders argue the following points:

- A stronger code of mutual and reciprocal relations (with superior and subordinate ideally equally conscious of their mutual obligations) might serve as a useful corrective for alienation and antisocial behavior.
- A reliance on more extended families and communities, in combination with more holistic views of the cosmos, might foster better care for the elderly, the infirm, and the young, not to mention the environment.
- A different and sophisticated notion of human potential fundamentally unbound to birth, inheritance, or religious institutions or ideas might provide "common ground" for multiethnic communities seeking parity.
- A revised notion of "human rights" that foregrounds economic justice as the key to citizen participation and responsibility

might give greater voice to the poor and disenfranchised currently ignored in the so-called democracies.

• A greater focus on academic achievement and hard work, and less preoccupation with personality, genius, and celebrity, might ameliorate the *fin-de-siècle* impulses of "the culture of narcissism."[38]

Curiously little has changed in American perceptions of Confucius and China from the time thirty years ago when Harold Isaacs proclaimed:

> The Chinese are seen as a superior people and an inferior people; devilishly exasperating heathens and wonderfully attractive humanists; wise sages and sadistic executioners; thrifty and honorable men and sly and devious villains; comic opera soldiers and dangerous fighters. . . . These and many other pairs . . . are often jumbled all together.

Should we be surprised that such bipolar views leave many Chinese asking for more nuanced and more dignified identities?

PART 4. AMERICAN SNAPSHOTS OF THE ETHICAL REALISTS[39]

With the exception of Yu Dan, who seems intent on constructing an ideal type of "Confucian" entrepreneur for the twenty-first century, the vast majority of East Asian political and academic leaders have gone on record urging the revival of one particular brand of late neo-Confucian teaching, the so-called Doctrine of Mind and Nature, which exalts moral purity as the tie that ideally binds the human and cosmic orders, despite the fact—or because of it?—that this doctrine flourished in late imperial China under state sponsorship. In stark contrast, Americans are noticeably less enamored of the institutions and customs of late imperial China that privileged patriline and throne. Hence the decision by many academics in the United States to focus on the early writings ascribed to Kongzi, Mencius, and Xunzi, whose core concerns were social cultivation and political justice.

A second obvious difference separating most Asian Confucians from their American neighbors is that while Asians—especially those of Chinese descent—are apt to see biological or geographical continuity as a precondition for the transmission of authentic Confucianism, insofar as it represents the "transcendent, eternal, cultural spirit" of the Chinese "soul," Kongzi's American backers credit the Sage with "important views not bounded by the calendar or the Great Wall,"[40] and therefore relevant to the human predicament in all times and places. So while the Asian factions mightily contend for possession of the mantle of the Sage, the better to appropriate his iconic authority, the Americans generally seek to portray the extraordinary capaciousness of the cloak that Kongzi and his early followers offer. Perhaps, when all is said and done, Americans are simply more used to endowing their pet theories with universal appeal.[41] Then, too, Americans are more likely to ascribe ongoing disputes between China and the United States less to the ideals or cynicism of their political leaders or academic figures, past or present, than to conflicts over trade, energy, and military prowess.[42] Consequently, disputes over the relative importance and meaning of Kongzi take on a very different significance, in part because Americans have been lucky enough to work out their views on Confucius and China without undue pressure from on high. By contrast, when Peking University professor Li Ling had the temerity to publicize a list of the most flagrant ethical lapses of some prominent Chinese neo-Cons with lofty pretensions to moral purity, he provoked smear campaigns and assassination threats in what can only be described as the first recorded Confucian fatwah. Late-stage Confucian moralism, it seems, can become a "cultural fever" no less prone to violent mood swings than evangelical Christianity in the United States.

Works by three thinkers, Herbert Fingarette (Emeritus, UC Santa Barbara), Henry Rosemont Jr. (Brown University), and Roger Ames (University of Hawaii; Wuhan University), are discussed below, for the following reasons:

1. In putting economic, political, and legal issues at the center of their analysis, these thinkers adopt a stance that is implicitly op-

posed to that of the neo-Cons, who have typically advocated backward-looking movements that celebrate a set of "traditional virtues" generally construed as "interior virtues" (usually obedience, frugality, and a craving for order).

2. Equally conversant with the American pragmatist tradition (if not equally enamored of all aspects of that tradition),[43] these three American thinkers are impatient with the idle speculations prompted by sterile hypotheticals posed in "crisis ethics" exercises (e.g., Would it be wrong to steal to feed my starving children?), and prefer hard questions about responsible actions within real-world constraints and planetary stakes.

3. All three thinkers focus their philosophical efforts upon the study of the Han and pre-Han texts associated with Confucius, in an attempt to recover what once excited the early adherents of Kongzi, the practices of everyday life that can lend charisma to those aspiring to authority.

4. All three thinkers see the Confucian texts of the classical era presenting sharper contrasts to the more questionable aspects of contemporary Western philosophy.

5. Skeptical of both the "rugged individualism" and the "competitive capitalism" that figure in many contemporary theories in the East or West, all three thinkers—but especially Rosemont—emphasize the interrelatedness and performativity of family and social life in the complex and highly ritualized socialization processes that start from birth, if not before.[44]

Distinctive concerns oblige these thinkers to sketch different trajectories for ethical thinking, although all three Americans urge a political philosophy more akin to the democratic socialism of northern Europe than to the deregulated capitalism of today's People's Republic or United States. Rosemont is hardly alone in believing that few contemporary Western philosophers would give much credence to the Song- or Ming-style metaphysics underlying much of late imperial Confucianism. By contrast, the early sources on Confucius and classical learning hold up under deeper scrutiny as well as or better than the "virtue ethics" propounded by Plato and Aristotle, due to their steadfast refusal to mandate a single set of metaphysical or scientific principles, since many aspects of human and cosmic existence are unknowable or largely irrelevant to the proper conduct of social life. Finally, because the works of Fingarette, Rosemont, and Ames are widely available in the bookstores and libraries of these United States, this chapter concludes with short summaries of their work. Of course, there are many other American philosophers doing original work today (see Suggested Readings), not to mention thinkers of equal stature to be found within today's Chinese-speaking communities. Readers of modern Chinese may enjoy the works of Li Zehou 李澤厚 (China's foremost historian of Chinese aesthetics), Lin Anwu 林安梧 (Taiwan National University), Li Ling 李零 (the eminent paleographer at Peking University), and Huang Junxing 黃進興 (Academia Sinica, Taiwan), among others, all of whom consider the rewards of refined social praxis.

FINGARETTE'S *CONFUCIUS: THE SECULAR AS SACRED* jump-started recent revisionist views of Kongzi, challenging the longstanding conventions that situated Kongzi either within the "secular humanism" envisioned by Lin Yutang and the later proponents of Christian-Confucian dialogue *or* within the quasi-religious patriotic cults favored by Kang Youwei and the CCP helmsmen of the post-Deng era. Fingarette, a highly respected philosopher whose initial training was not in Sinology but in the ethics of behavior and responsibility, began his path-breaking book on the *Analects* with this opening salvo:

When I began to read Confucius, I found him to be a prosaic and parochial moralizer; his collected sayings, the *Analects*, seemed to me an archaic irrelevance. Later, and with increasing force, I found him a thinker with profound insight and with an imaginative vision of man equal in its grandeur to any I know. I have become convinced that Confucius can be a teacher to us today—a major teacher, not one who merely gives us a slightly exotic perspective on the ideas already current. He tells us things not being said elsewhere; things needing to be said. He has a new lesson to teach.[45]

For Fingarette, the analysis of *li* 禮 (holy rite) is key to interpreting the *Analects*, in that Kongzi's emphasis on *ren* 仁 (acting in a humane fashion) flows from it. By the phrase "holy rite" Fingarette denotes more than the formal activities associated with weddings, funerals, and seasonal festivals (in China) or church services (in EuroAmerica), or the mundane formulae for greeting or leave-taking, even the customs, propriety, manners, and etiquette (in both). Rites are whatever "complex but familiar gestures are characteristic of human relationships at their most human," and holy rites are the most "emphatic, intensified, and sharply elaborated extension of everyday civilized intercourse." Hence those terms may be used of every act designed to indicate basic respect for the dignity of others and ourselves, *regardless of the particular form* that the communication of respect entails in a particular culture. A handshake or a nod of the head can be as much a "holy rite" as the most solemn ceremony, so long as 'it succeeds in helping the self and others to perceive the sacred:

> There are several dimensions of Holy Rite which culminate in its holiness. Rites bring out forcefully not only the harmony and beauty of social forms, the inherent and ultimate dignity of human intercourse; it [Holy Rite] brings out also the moral perfection implicit in achieving one's ends by dealing with others as beings of equal dignity, as co-participants in *li*. Furthermore, to act by ceremony is to be completely open to the other, for ceremony is public, shared, transparent. . . . It is in this beautiful and dignified, shared and open participation with others who are ultimately "[seen to be] like oneself" [*Analects* 12/2] that humans realize themselves.[46]

Noting that "we are least like anything else in the world when we do not treat each other like physical objects, as animals, or even as sub-human creatures to be driven, threatened, forced, maneuvered," Fingarette argues skillfully that we are conversely most sublimely human whenever we fuse personal presence to "(learned) ceremonial skill," until that point when the ceremonial act becomes "the primary, irreducible event" constituting human experience.

Fingarette's descriptions of holy rites resonate with a wistful passage from Wendell Berry, the Kentucky poet-farmer, that names "the greatest disaster of human history" the change that "happened to or within religion" leading to "the conceptual division between the holy and the world." Fingarette's *Confucius: The Secular as Sacred* would have us glimpse the rich possibilities to be had from restoring that holiness to *this* world. In Fingarette's telling, Kongzi the sage confronts us with only one significant choice in our lives: whether to deny the holy human compact and so belittle our own humanity, or to commit ourselves to finding ways to strengthen the fragile sense of connectedness that binds humans together as social beings. To act intentionally on behalf of human community—and then to keep acting the same way over and over again—is Kongzi's definition of "following the Way." In ordinary social situations it is usually far easier to ascertain the highest good than to commit ourselves to the task of attaining or preserving it, since a host of self-interested considerations can and do intervene between thought and action. Nonetheless, for Confucius, the successful inculcation of this habit of wanting to do good was "the ultimate concern," the goal that mattered more than life itself.

Therefore *ren* 仁 (reliably humane conduct) is less a quality that inheres in an inner self (its goodness, its benevolence, or its humaneness) than a dynamic, fierce, and ultimately artful dedication to acting humanely in every social situation, driven by the conscious aim to realize the human potential to become more than the sum of the animal parts with their insistent drives for food, sex, and companionship. Consistent acts of doing good build the kind of courage that can light up the person, making him or her a person of "a new and holy beauty" visible to all but the most blind. And since beauty invariably proves compelling to those prepared to perceive it, we have the explanation for the seemingly unrestricted "magical powers" possessed by the *junzi* (noble person) who accomplishes his or her will "directly and effortlessly through ritual, gesture, and incantation," "without needing to resort to coercion (mental or physical)." Once the visible performance of our lives is coherent and whole, the serene expectation is that something in the inner state will shift, mature, and ripen—in a stark reversal of the inner/outer priorities set forth in the major Christian religions.

Turning to the thorny question of how to act in the world at large, Fingarette concludes that Confucius believed the regulation of society to be too important to leave to governments and political groups that claim to know what is best for everyone. Far better to let people themselves indicate, through their actions, what actions can and will be taken to bind them one to another, economically, socially, and aesthetically. In such contexts, convention and tradition need not be deadening routines that impose a state-sponsored "regime of truth" and so impede clear articulation of our most deep-seated desires and fears. Instead, reasonable convention and tradition, as artful spoken and gestural performance, can help humans find a way to reliably notice and express their appreciation of particular human beings. Resort to conventional forms is an absolute requirement if each person is not to have to reinvent the wheel every time the desire arises to communicate something to others. (Note the absurdity of each person trying to come up with a new language each time for each exchange, and you will see how critical it is for humans to employ well-established forms.)

Clearly, Fingarette aims to shock Americans into surrendering their knee-jerk attitudes toward "sterile tradition," "empty custom," and the "force of habit." (Rosemont reinforced this point when he noted, in an early review of Fingarette, that bureaucracies, armies, and corporations oppress people more than do customs, rituals, and ceremonies.) One persuasive traditional view held that "the rites had their origins in the emotions, and in accord with what people took comfort in, codes of conduct were written down."[47] Fingarette would have us marvel, then, at Kongzi's repeated attempts—and even his occasional failures—to convey the magnitude and power of the process by which we learn ritual, for each attempt commits the person to taking responsibility within a community. But the phrase "accepting responsibility" means little unless it means taking stock of the specific social forms of life, art, and language we need to communicate the fact of our essential humanity from birth, equipping ourselves with those social forms, refusing to take comfort in manufactured images of bliss, and facing the hard reality that neither the Western legal tradition, with its peculiar definition of "responsibility," nor hard-line socialism (or hard-line capitalism, for that matter) encourages humans to make informed decisions about ways to seek moral, psychic, sociopolitical, or economic goods within their own lives.[48] So while the American ethical discourse and the legal journals blather on about "freedom," "autonomy," and "free will," Fingarette quietly redirects our attention to teaching *what* it is that must be accepted about ourselves as moral agents and the consequences of such acceptance.

Rosemont's writings complement the insights of Fingarette, implicitly posing a practical question: In a world without scriptural Confucianism, where 22 percent of the world's population live in the People's Republic of China but few Chinese intellectuals still study the Classics, what meaningful forms can a genuine interest in the works ascribed to Kongzi and his followers take? Rosemont refers us to the well-known maxim by the Song statesman Fan Zhongyan 范仲淹 (989–1052), "Literati must be the first to bear hardships [on behalf of others] and the last to take pleasure in the world's pleasures," and to Kongzi's "proper use of names" (*zheng ming*) that holds each person accountable to act responsibly within the social and political roles that she or he claims. The first practical step toward embodying Confucian ideals, then, would be for the privileged to take responsibility for what happens in their communities, demystifying the most basic aspects of the human condition while striving for that fusion of economic, social, and moral well-being that permits humans to flourish. While names-as-language are never transparent or adequate reflections of reality, so long as the names for social realities do not paradoxically obscure or controvert those realities (as when an Orwellian state or abusive parent masquerades as a nurturing "motherland" or "mother"), humans will find ways to share their experiences and enrich their personal and communal senses. Kongzi and his early followers offered three additional methods by which to cultivate the fully humane person: practical wisdom (*zhi* 智), ritual observances (*li*), and empathy and consideration (*shu* 恕). But in Rosemont's view, too many latter-day disciples of Kongzi forget the first and third methods, while misconstruing the second (as Fingarette suspected).

As Rosemont notes, the *Analects* mentions the need for practical wisdom (knowing how to act effectively in the political and social spheres in order to realize one's ideals) more often and more incisively than the final goal of reliably humane actions (*ren*). The first duty of everyone, it seems, is to learn how to translate good impulses into effective action in the larger world, a duty that will be happily carried out only by the person who learns to tap the emotions to derive and create pleasure from such acts of translation. Disembodied minds and Cartesian rationality may pervade much of Western philosophy, but the early Confucian wisdom links head to heart, the cognitive to the affective, and commitment to deed, since little practical good can be gained from either the multiplication of good intentions or the accumulation of vast stores of facts and theories.[49] To find merit in the Confucian Way is to long to perform it in a social setting—and perform it in such a way that others will admire and emulate the performance, creating a snowball effect within the community. And since Kongzi taught commonsense morality, what another calls "the impossible immediacy of the ethical,"[50] Rosemont equally deplores the real-life consequences of taking either of two theoretical positions, that humans have no independent position or value outside the social net (as some Asian politicians suggest), or that humans are substantially autonomous in their decision making (the preferred fiction of most Western philosophers).

Furthermore, Kongzi and the early Confucians believed a heightened potential for understanding the human condition could result from the constant need to juggle commitments to elders, to contemporaries, and to descendants. Armed with a passionate desire to break out of the constraints imposed by a single life span, these thinkers offered a plausible portrait of authentic spirituality premised on the insight that change, adaptation, and accommodation were not only inevitable but desirable, if we would merely respond adequately to the myriad contingencies encountered in a "seemingly random world not of our own making." As human social beings, we have urgent needs—instrumental, psychological, and social—to engage others in cooperative ventures, but effective cooperation requires us to coordinate and strike a balance among the partial viewpoints, isolated experiences, and situated judgments that we all perforce bring to the table. That explains why the ways we learn to deliberate together on the wisest course of action cannot be easily codified in a fixed set of rules.[51] Still,

Rosemont is willing to bet that collective deliberation about our fundamental needs and fears will elicit more precise commitments to future courses of action than will the fine-sounding exhortations to abstract moral perfectionism that pepper Partyspeak and the neo-Con tracts. As the *Analects* line has it, "The noble man reveres those that excel, but finds room for all."

Rosemont and Ames remind us that Chinese thinking, prior to the encounter with the Jesuits, evinced less interest in identifying entities (what is this? what kinds of things exist in the world?) than in articulating useful processes (e.g., how does one go about being an effective agent in the situation at hand?). Ergo, the Chinese refusal to see a notion of "transcendent" Western-style political rights lodged within each individual and overriding all other considerations and consequences, including those relating to economic justice. Rosemont fairly revels in how little we lose and how much we stand to gain by similarly positing "a world without substances or essences." Following his train of thought, it is obviously not enough for rights to be *theoretically* available (as the phrase "equality under the law" would suggest), if actual groups and individuals cannot afford, psychologically or economically, to exercise those rights for practical ends. Shame on the United States for its hypocrisy, then. Equally to the point, accepting the real-world limitations on "absolute" but entirely abstract freedoms demolishes one serious barrier to better understanding between Chinese and Americans, allowing full condemnation of government repression and acts of torture and terrorism, without resort to the concept of human rights, which has been the subject of endless bickering between China and the United States.[52]

Even if the two superpowers were to agree to forgo their squabbles, conceding the point that humans need kinder and gentler political and economic arrangements, Rosemont fears that unthinking cultural relativism—ironically enough, one of the few concepts shared by most well-educated Asians and Americans—may do us all in. Simply put, the sense that "impassable barriers" separate cultures, nations, and ethnic groups gives politicians the language they need to devise their own economic, energy, immigration, and environmental policies in defiance of common sense and the common good. With all we now know about global warming, what other rationale would allow the PRC to encourage its citizens to buy more cars, while the Environmental Protection Agency in Washington refuses to allow states to implement stricter emissions standards? Both decisions are defended in the name of national sovereignty and the right of a culture to choose its own tools to imperil itself. A belief in the existence of such barriers moreover forestalls such obvious but uncomfortable questions as these:

> Why is eighty percent of the world's wealth concentrated in the hands of twenty percent of its population?
> Why do one percent of American citizens command wealth equal to that of the bottom forty percent?
> Why is America's military budget still larger than the rest of the world's combined?

Particular times, places, and cultures may indeed produce specific values and standards, as Rosemont acknowledges, but surely human history, with its surging flows of peoples, things, and ideas, belies the myth of "impassable barriers," for no hallowed barrier ascribed to biology, geography, assorted ethnic claims, or a lack of information has ever lasted for very long.[53]

This emphasis on realism and cross-cultural awareness fairly cries out for a return to the political and the aesthetic, if the poet Tao Yuanming was right, and "what gives value to a person / lies within this single body's life." The sheer complexities involved in careful deliberation on reliably humane conduct calls into question the claims of some in the intelligentsia and the party to be the best judges of the "essence" of Chinese culture and the proper methods by which to "upgrade the people" until they reach "national perfection." Participation by each and every person is vital. And if the person is constituted by a complex of habits formed through successive social relations, as the Confucians would have it, rather than being the product of DNA or early childhood experiences over which the person had little or no control, then the aesthetic enjoyment imparted through rituals and ceremonies can impart zest and dignity to individual lives while supporting efforts to communicate and participate.

Aesthetic pursuits enhance that everyday "perception of the immediate good of objects" which is so crucial to the human spirit,[54] and, as Iris Murdoch once observed, "Good art reveals what we are usually too selfish and timid to realize," because it conveys a "truthful vision of the human condition in a form that can be steadily contemplated." Then, too, as Adorno contended, the aesthetic response represents one of the few avenues left for authentic subjective experience in strictly administered modern societies that give people the illusion of subjectivity and self-reflexivity even as they criminalize certain forms of personal expression.

Perhaps because Ames, along with the late David Hall, has foregrounded the "aesthetic order" of Chinese thought, he leaves readers with a grand vision of a China "able to provide cultural values and institutions sufficiently attractive to the rest of the world" to offset at least some of the disastrous human and environmental costs of further rapid and unsustainable development.[55] China's governing elite, according to Ames, is principally concerned with questions of economic equity, freedom from want, and class and ethnic conflicts within and across cultures. The very next American economic downturn may find American citizens calling for more open and frank discussions of a similar set of issues. Hence, Ames's optimistic scenario, in which there will gradually emerge more convergent or even syncretic notions of the individual, society, law, and human rights. In Ames's mind, the "good news" is that "however distinct Confucianism and American pragmatism continue to be, there is sufficient productive overlap in their core beliefs, and sufficient commonality in their sense of responsibility to their respective cultures and to the world beyond, that a real alliance is possible . . . along at least a slightly better path.[56]

Around the globe and across the ages, pragmatic traditions have asserted the utility of the Golden Rule and of leaders' reliance on the support of the people. What pragmatism never subscribes to is a tribalist belief in an unchangeable identity—"being Chinese" or "being American"—that imbues the nation-state with a metaphysical power and rectitude akin to History or Truth.

Continual cross-cultural conversations may prevent some of the mutual misunderstandings that have flared up during the last century whenever Americans, Chinese, or American-born Chinese start blaming the Other for the most hateful aspects of postmodern life, whether it be the increasing regimentation of their daily interactions, the continual indignities heaped upon working people, or the dearth of opportunities for all but a tiny elite.[57] Ordinary citizens of China and the United States lead strikingly similar lives, despite their unquestioned belief in impassable barriers and the whiff of cordite that lingers over their exchanges. Both countries have seen repeated attempts at social integration across ethnic, class, and national boundaries stifled by powerful forces integrating the economy with the state administration under the banners of "ethnic difference" and "class harmony." As Han Yuhai, a Beijing New Left historian, has observed, for all too many citizens the much vaunted "freedom" of the market economy boils down to little more than the "freedom to want to be a slave."

The New Sinology[58] aims to "engage in constant and equitable conversations with the Sinophone World." Over the last century, American views of China have influenced Chinese realities and perceptions, just as Chinese views of America have shaped present-day realities within the States. One new symptom of this burgeoning interconnectedness, as well as the Chinese deft manipulation of "soft power" diplomacy, is the proliferation of Confucius Institutes springing up like mushrooms on hundreds of American campuses and around the globe, and another, the outrageous parodies of the Confucius Institutes offered on the Net.[59] So rapid is the pace and volume of change and exchange that Chinese scholars now routinely cite American thinkers, even to the point of retranslating their English translations of classical Chinese back into modern Chinese, for ready reception within China. The recent decision by several Chinese university heads (e.g., at Peking University, Fudan University, Peking Normal University, Wuhan University, and Taiwan National University) to extend regular invitations to foreign scholars to lecture on early Chinese thought is likely to encourage even more spirited debates between Sinophone and English-speaking thinkers, as academics and politicians on both sides of the Pacific come to appreciate the gaps between and the subtleties within the Other's notions, preoccupations, and methods of critical inquiry.

KONGZI, THE PROTEAN DRAGON
RIDING THE TIMES

In the middle of the last century, Henri Maspero, one of the greatest of the French Sinologues, wrote of Kongzi in his avatar as a god—an "unseen influence effecting major change," by the Chinese definition:

> Like all the Gods of the official religion, Confucius climbed all the steps of the hierarchy one by one: he was named duke in the first year A.D., king in 739, reduced for a while to the rank of duke in 1075, emperor in 1106. . . . And on December 4, 1530, the Shizong emperor stripped him of this status, giving him simply the title "Perfect Sage and Ancient Master," which he has kept to our present day."[60]

Gods in the traditional Chinese pantheon are said to experience change and transformation effortlessly, and they are offered cult in the serene expectation that they will requite offerings by bestowals of blessings on the celebrants. What, then, are the chief blessings that Kongzi bestowed on this world, and how are we to assess the protean nature of Kongzi, Confucius, and the Classics? Certainly, Kongzi's elevation in the state-sponsored pantheon paved the way for the conversion of the Five Classics and Four Books from the common cultural coin of the realm into holy scriptures composed of separate revelations, on the model of the Buddhist sutras, Daoist canons, and (after Matteo Ricci and the Jesuits) the Bible itself. Are we then to read into "Confucianism" and what are now called the "Confucian" Classics a universal way of life, the secure foundation for a future global culture, the possession or bastion of one ethnic culture (the Chinese, in China or in diaspora), a local manifestation devoid of cultural memory, an ideology that legitimizes "soft" or "hard" authoritarian governments, or something more than what is captured by any of these characterizations? Is "Confucianism" a philosophy or a religion, an "ism" or a panoply of "isms"? And, if the latter, how may we begin to talk about the plurality of Chinese traditions in ways that are comprehensible to beginning students of Chinese culture?

A contemporary Chinese writer, Wang Xiaobo, in an irreverent essay called "My Views of National Studies" (i.e., "Confucian Learn-ing"), remarks that Confucius, Mencius, and "all that crowd" seem like old chewing gum to him: the flavor has gone right out of them through overlong and overearnest mastication. Successive regimes and leaders on the make have used and abused Kongzi's authority too often for their own good.

But let us return to the basics first.

Ritual decorum and integrity are the two main threads of the teachings associated with Confucius down through the ages.[61] With-out a modicum of ritual decorum, integrity has no effective way to communicate itself, and with insufficient integrity, decorum becomes hollow display. One anecdote has Zigong, one of Kongzi's closest dis-ciples, saying,

> The Way of Kings Wen and Wu of Zhou has not collapsed; it lives in the people. Those of superior character have grasped the greater part of it, while those of lesser parts have grasped a bit of it. Every-one has something of the Way of Wen and Wu in them. Who, then, does the Master not learn from?[62]

What is most striking about American and Chinese perceptions during the last century or so is their equal obliviousness to the simple fact that "everyone has something of the Way" in them. If they would "Only Connect," Chinese and Americans could profit a great deal from listening to and learning from each other. Some attempt of this sort is long overdue, since John Dewey voiced the following senti-ments in 1926, which seem no less applicable today:

> China is rapidly growing up. . . . It will henceforth resent more and more any assumption of parental tutelage, even of a professedly benevolent kind. . . . Politically, the Chinese no longer wish for any foreign guardianship. . . . In the next ten years we shall have to . . . alter our traditional temper of patronage, conscious or uncon-scious, into one of respect and esteem for a cultural equal.

Still, "even the most intelligent thinker will, if he talks too long about cultures and civilizations, begin to spout nonsense."[63] Therefore, the authors of this book respectfully submit that, in the spirit of Kongzi, we should try talking less and attending more to social praxis, in the hope of wreaking as little destruction and restoring as much dignity to social life as humanly possible. If the chief feature of daily life in the twenty-first century is an inability to restrain ourselves for the benefit of others,[64] the Confucian exhortation to conquer selfish impulses and "return to the rites" may be just the antidote we need to make communities flourish. The lives we save may be our own.

SUGGESTED READINGS AND VIEWINGS

On twentieth-century research into the origin(s) of the *Ru*, see Zufferey in "Suggested Readings" for chapter 1.

John E. Young and Janice B. Corzine, "The Sage Entrepreneur: A Review of Traditional Confucian Practices Applied to Contemporary Entrepreneurship," *Journal of Enterprising Culture* 12, no. 1 (March 2004): 79–104. Like the Singaporean government, this article argues the competitive advantage to be gained from following the Sage Entrepreneur.

For an entrée into Kang's "One World" thought, see K'ang Yuwei [Kang Youwei], *Ta t'ung shu: The one-world philosophy of K'ang Yuwei*, translated and annotated by Laurence G. Thompson (London: Allen & Unwin, 1958).

On the creation of the academic discipline of "comparative religions," see Norman Girardot, *The Victorian Translation of China: James Legge's Oriental Pilgrimage* (Berkeley: University of California Press, 2002); Warren I. Cohen, *East Asian Art and American Culture: A Study in International Relations* (New York: Columbia University Press, 1992), argues that many of these attitudes were shaped by exhibitions of Chinese art in the United States.

On missionary work in China, see Jacques Gernet, *China and the Christian Impact: A Conflict of Cultures* (Cambridge, England: Cambridge University Press, 1985); and Kenneth Scott Latourette, *A History of Christian Missions in China* (New York: Macmillan, 1929).

On recent constructions of Ruxue, Rujia, and Confucius: John Makeham, *Lost Soul: "Confucianism" in Contemporary Chinese Academic Discourse* (Cambridge, England: Cambridge University Press, 2008); Vincent Goossaert, "1898: The Beginning of the End for Chinese Religion," *Journal of Asian Studies* 65, no. 2 (May 2006): 307–35.

On the use in wartime of neo-Confucian writings as a weapon in occupation politics, see John Hunter Boyle, *China and Japan at War, 1937–38* (Palo Alto, CA: Stanford University Press, 1972), esp. ch. 12.

On the politicized goals of the young discipline of archaeology in China, see James Leibold, "Competing Narratives of Racial Unity in Republican China: From the Yellow Emperor to Peking Man," *Modern China* 12, no. 2 (April 2006): 181–220; also Ian C. Glover, "Some National, Regional, and Political Uses of Archaeology in East and Southeast Asia," in *Archaeology of Asia*, edited by Miriam T. Stark (Oxford, England: Blackwell, 2006), 17–36.

For viewing: Judith and Bill Moyers, *A Confucian Life in America: Tu Wei-ming,* Films for the Humanities & Sciences, 1994.

On "discontinuous" writing systems in China, see Imre Galambos, *Orthography of Early Chinese Writing: Evidence from Early Chinese Manuscripts* (Budapest: Department of East Asian Studies, Eötvös Loránd University, 2006).

For contemporary dilemmas about China's place in the future, see Gloria Davies, *Worrying About China* (Cambridge: Harvard East Asian Monographs, 2007); Henry Rosemont Jr., "Whose Democracy? Which Rights? A Confucian Critique of Modern Western Liberalism," in *Confucian Ethics: A Comparative Study of Self, Autonomy, and Community* (Cambridge, England: Cambridge University Press, 2004), 49–71.

For the difference between early Greek "virtue" ethics and early Confucian "role" ethics, see Eric Hutton, "Character, Situationism, and Early Confucian Thought," *Philosophical Studies* 127, no. 1 (January 2006), 37–58; Mary Paterson Cheadle, *Ezra Pound's Confucian Translations* (Ann Arbor: University of Michigan, 1997).

Epilogue

The legendary rulers Fuxi and Shen Nong are far from us in time,
In this whole wide world, few return to the true.
Hurrying, the old man from Lu [Kongzi]
Would mend the tears to make it pure and new.

THE POET TAO YUANMING (365–427 CE) LOOKED TO "THE OLD man from Lu" to make sense of life in a chaotic era. As preceding chapters have shown, Tao was merely one of many eloquent voices trying to imagine what Confucius would do in his own age, as if an answer to that question would effectively repair not only their sense of the world, but also their displacement within it. The radical subjectivity that many have brought to the seemingly "historical" and "objective" figure of Confucius is equally obvious in assertions like that of Lu Jiuyuan (1139–93 CE), who said, "I do not annotate the Classics; the Classics annotate me." This book intends to help readers make their way through a dizzying array of practices and beliefs that have been attributed to Confucius over the centuries by adherents and critics alike. Its method is to follow the sage advice offered once by the historian Gu Jiegang (1893–1980) to "take one Confucius at a time." This method acknowledges that as humans our ways of thinking and talking are inevitably saturated with outdated metaphors, eroded figures of speech, and old ghosts that rattle around among our mental furniture. No old ghost—aside, perhaps, from Chairman Mao himself—appears quite as vividly to those of Chinese descent as Kongzi, the Master.

Chapter 1 opens with a comparison of the two earliest and most authoritative accounts of Confucius's life: the lengthy formal biography of Kongzi (aka Confucius) that appears in China's most famous work of history, Sima Qian's *Shiji* or *Historical Records* (compiled ca. 100 BCE); and the abbreviated portraits of the Master found in the *Analects*, a compilation that probably dates to ca. 100 BCE, even though some passages—especially those framed as Kongzi's dialogues with his disciples—may reflect older traditions. Sima Qian's biography appears in a section of the *Shiji* titled the "Hereditary Houses," whose entries typically trace the fortunes of the main families who ruled the Central Plain between the founding of the Zhou dynasty, ca. 1050 BCE, and the unification of the realm by Qin in 221 BCE.

Kongzi is one of only two *individuals* to appear in the "Hereditary Houses" section. The other is Chen She, the rebel leader who sparked the chain of events that toppled the short-lived Qin dynasty, which had unified six major rival kingdoms for a mere decade, from 221 to 210 BCE, forging the first empire in the area we know as "China." (Think terra-cotta warriors.) Readers of the *Shiji* have always assumed that Kongzi was included in the "Hereditary Houses" section because Han thinkers and statesmen saw him as an "uncrowned king," a person of enormous influence who, in some sense, "ruled" over the hearts and minds of all, even if he had no kingdom. By implicitly linking Kongzi and the rebel Chen She, it seems possible, however, that Sima Qian intended to highlight Kongzi's rebellious nature. After all, as readers will discover in chapter 3, Kongzi's compilation of the *Chunqiu* was meant to "criticize emperors, reprimand feudal lords, and condemn the high officials so that the business of a true ruler could be known," and criticizing high officials had always been the sole prerogative of rulers. Though Kongzi never attained such rank, he was emboldened by his sense of Heaven's ongoing favor when he blamed his political superiors, past and present, for the sorry state of the world he knew. Yet another curious link between Chen She and Kongzi has Kongzi's lineal descendant Kong Ziyu being one of the first to forsake the Qin house to join forces with Chen She.

While the *Analects* portrays Kongzi as a sage who manages, even in defeat, to accept his fate gracefully, the *Shiji* biography portrays Kongzi, from his youth through the middle years, as an ambitious adviser unwilling to take, or incapable of taking, the time to understand the complexities of local politics, let alone hold his tongue. In other words, Sima's Kongzi is impatient, headstrong, and outspoken to the point of indiscretion. By the *Shiji* account, only after Kongzi abandons his fruitless quest to achieve high position does he begin to understand and undertake his predestined task: to restore the powerful traditions of the rites and music of olden times to the cultivated men and women of his own benighted age. The pivotal scene in the *Shiji* biography in which Kongzi accomplishes this transition from brash know-it-all to thoughtful learner has Kongzi working hard at learning to play a musical composition. Finally, after fifty straight days of practicing, Kongzi completely internalizes the rhythm, lyrics, and intentions in the piece created by that paragon of virtue, King Wen of Zhou. By "channeling" King Wen, Kongzi then becomes a simulacrum of his exemplar, whose civilizing influence radiates throughout the entire Central States region. Following this dramatic transformation, Kongzi begins to order and edit the *Odes* and the *Documents*, to consult the *Yijing*, and to compile his famous *Annals* in the last years before his death. By chapter's end, Sima's Kongzi has become a "local hero" of sorts for the area near Queli, the capital of Lu. He has also begun to garner a reputation in kingdoms closely allied with Lu, especially Chu to the south. But it is by no means inevitable that he will go on one day to be hailed as the single most significant figure in all of imperial history in China. How he posthumously manages to become that singular figure is the story taken up in chapters 2 and 3 of this book.

Chapter 2 depicts the slow but steady growth of Kongzi's reputation over the course of two and a half centuries after his death. Initially Kongzi's reputation grew in part as a result of reflected glory, for several in the circle of disciples he had taught filled high-ranking posts with distinction. But in part it grew through the spirited defenses of his ethical Way by the thinkers Mencius and Xunzi, two of Kongzi's most famous ethical followers—neither of whom was a direct disciple, but both of whom hailed from the vicinity of Lu. If elegant defenses of the local hero had not been offered by Mencius (a century after Kongzi) and by Xunzi (a century after Mencius), the Master's name might have disappeared from sight. A Han tradition remarks that Mencius and Xunzi together "tarted up" Kongzi's teachings, making them more "glossy and appealing" by adapting their arguments to suit the tastes of influential contemporaries. Mencius accomplished this by forging a tight equation between the aristocrat's arduous training in preparation for battle and the disciplined commitment to cultivation of the gentle Confucian Way by the noble in spirit. Also in his defense of Kongzi, Mencius devoted much time to refuting several explicit charges to which Kongzi was particularly vulnerable: first, that Kongzi's love of lavish rituals was distinctly at odds with his purported concern for the common people, since expensive and time-consuming rituals and musical performances inevitably meant more exorbitant taxes and levies on the poor in states whose budgets were already busted, owing to military campaigns waged against rival powers; second, that Kongzi's talk of "graded love," which meant that greater favor was owed to one's kith and kin than to any extrafamilial relation, placed far too many unnatural restrictions on human feelings while threatening the supreme authority of the state; and, third, that Kongzi's preoccupation with securing office undermined a still more basic duty to preserve one's person from harm, since the body was received from one's parents and held in trust for the family. Mencius's spirited defense of the Sage was badly needed, since Kongzi's teachings in Mencius's time were not as popular as those of his rivals Mozi and Yang Zhu, whose well-reasoned arguments left the Master open to censure.

That left Xunzi, teaching shortly before unification in 221 BC, to confront the more subtle charges against Kongzi—the very sort of fault-finding that would have devastated Kongzi's long-term reputation had they gone unanswered. For example, Xunzi dedicated much time and effort to rebutting the most serious objection registered against Kongzi by Xunzi's famous peer, Zhuangzi: that Kongzi's beloved "ritual consists in being false to one another," since the language and gestures of ritual are inherently "unnatural" to humans and must be learned. Xunzi replied that humans could hardly jettison all instances of artificiality in their lives since (a) all of culture was artificial by Zhuangzi's measure, and (b) society and politics both demanded certain forms of social grease if they were to function well. Therefore, Kongzi, Xunzi argued, asks humans to carefully consider what *sorts* of refinement most conduce to a social order that assures all humans will "achieve their proper place," and so enjoy a sense of dignity and self-worth.

A final critic who appears in chapter 2 is Wang Chong (27–97? CE), an Eastern Han student of the Classics living some six centuries after Kongzi. A summary of Wang's arguments concludes chapter 2 because they show—contrary to the common wisdom—that long after Han Wudi's reign (r. 141–87 BCE) in Western Han, even among the classicists, Kongzi's reputation was still not entirely secure. Wang's criticism of Kongzi boils down to five points: (1) the Classics associated with Kongzi as author or editor are just as riddled with error as other books and therefore cannot be treated as infallible; (2) Kongzi failed to elucidate many of his ideas when he conversed with his own disciples; (3) Kongzi often contradicted himself, while good teachers convey a consistent message; (4) Kongzi's chosen disciples displayed no special aptitude for learning the Way, nor did they demonstrate any notable commitment to it, which suggests that Kongzi was hardly an inspiring teacher; and (5) Kongzi was no proper pedagogical model, as he failed to push his students to clarify their own thoughts about either ethical or practical dilemmas. Ironically, then, in Wang Chong's view, on teaching—the very aspect of Kongzi's reputation that historically faced the fewest detractors—the Master was unreliable and erratic.

Moving into the imperial era, chapter 3 lets us see the single most troubling question that preoccupied Han thinkers and statesmen: If Kongzi was indeed such a paragon of virtue and compassion, why did he never rise to high office in his own lifetime? After all, the legendary sages Shun and Yu had ascended from the ranks of commoners to become Sons of Heaven, and Heaven had sent sage-kings to the Central States every five hundred years or so. What had gone wrong, then? Han theorists were understandably obsessed with this single question, for they were hard-pressed to explain such historical anomalies, especially in view of the rise of the commoner Liu Bang to the position of Han dynastic founder, for Liu Bang was a boor and a coward, and remarkably un-sage-like. Those in the employ of the Han throne devised the most powerful response to these misgivings about Kongzi's lack of worldly achievement. They insisted that the landless Sage, in seeming desperation, had constructed in his writings a veritable realm of the imagination where he would reign supreme forever. Moreover, from that lofty, albeit imaginary vantage point, Kongzi offered his full patronage and godlike powers in support of the Han whose dynastic rise he had not only predicted but also planned for. By this logic, Kongzi had composed the *Annals* or *Chunqiu*, the single piece of writing most closely associated with Kongzi during Han, to provide the Han governing elite with a blueprint for how to consolidate the powers of a centralized state. Through the "subtle wording" of that text and the application of past examples to contemporary situations, the Han could, in effect, rule in the name of Kongzi, the semi-deified "uncrowned king" of remarkable prescience who, in death, sat at the right hand of the High Lord in Heaven. Accordingly, under Han, the *Annals* of Kongzi, thought to contain the most significant pronouncements of the Sage, became the primary classic consulted when ruler and ministers set their minds to interpreting the laws, building a more unified world through administrative reforms, or contemplating the sympathic relations between microcosm and macrocosm. Thus by the end of the Han period, Kongzi's signal lack of illustrious forebears and reputable descendants was posthumously remedied: Kongzi was duly awarded his own place in the ranks of the star gods; he was also appointed First Ancestor to a long line of Kong family members granted hereditary noble status.

This story of Kongzi's compilation of the *Annals* evidently drove all the other stories circulating about Kongzi during the four centuries of Han, inspiring the lesser-known but equally compelling portraits of Kongzi as seer-prophet, scholar-etymologist, and even as the astral Black Lord deity, informing the powerful images of Kongzi as teacher, editor, and compiler of canonical texts. By Han definition, a sage is one who manages handily to convert "disasters into blessings," thereby earning the admiration of succeeding generations. That the man Kongzi, whose political acumen was so derided by most of his contemporaries, somehow achieved a fame far greater than princes and kings constituted proof positive that Kongzi's Way merited investigation and implementation—or so many Han thinkers asserted.

Chapter 4 describes the fate of Confucius in the eight centuries after the collapse of Han power ca. 200 CE. It does so by shifting the focus away from the pre-Han and Han primary sources presenting authoritative portraits of Kongzi to yet another early text called the *Zhongyong* or *Constant Mean,* attributed to Confucius's grandson. (As both hereditary privilege and the Kong family power grew mightily in the immediate post-Han period, the link forged between Master and grandson became ever more important in thinkers' eyes. Furthermore, in the post-Han period, texts like the *Mean* proved instrumental in salvaging the reputation of Confucius once his erstwhile standing as patron for the Han ruling line became a liability rather than a sign of sagely prescience.) Two commentaries to the *Mean*—one by Zheng Xuan (127–200 CE), the greatest commentator living at the end of Eastern Han, and the second by Zhu Xi (1130–1200) in Southern Song—become the subject of chapter 4, first because they ably encapsulate nearly the entire range of thinking about the significance of the Master's teachings in middle-period and early modern China, and, second, because they reveal the huge gulf that separates late Han from late Song thinking about the Way, even among groups of Confucian adherents. Since Zhu's commentaries on the Four Books (the *Analects,* the *Mencius,* the *Great Learning,* and the *Mean,* the latter two being separate chapters in the original *Liji* or *Rites Record*) served as the basic curriculum for the civil service examinations during the six centuries from 1313 to 1905, familiarity with the main tenets of Zhu's readings represents, in turn, the first step to be taken when tracing the evolution of Confucian traditions in late imperial China.

According to legend, Kongzi supposedly transmitted his most mature formulation of his teachings shortly before his own death to his grandson. The commentator Zheng Xuan, believing this legend to be true, positioned the *Mean* squarely at the center of his coherent and orderly synthesis of the entire "Confucian" canonical corpus, intentionally replacing all the older commentaries—each devoted to a single one of the Classics and treating that canon in piecemeal fashion by chapter and verse—with a veritable textual monument that skillfully wove together references to all the Classics into a single, powerful whole. Like nearly all of his contemporaries in late Eastern Han, Zheng showed a historicizing bent. Zheng dedicated himself to tracing the "subtle wording" embedded in the Classics that purportedly predated Kongzi by many hundreds of years, seeking his ultimate inspiration in the figure that supposedly inspired Confucius himself: the Duke of Zhou, the legendary statesman credited not only with consolidating the Zhou dynastic fortunes, ca. 1050 BCE, but also with devising the systems for the rites and music. Again, in company with most of his contemporaries, Zheng wanted to read into the *Mean* a distinction entirely absent in the original: a distinction between "human nature" (the basic endowment of capacities and appetites given to all) and "talent" (imagined as a kind of energetic stuff apportioned differently to different people). Zheng also analogized the various modes and expressions of the sovereign's commitments and activities to the sequential operations of the Five Cosmic Phases, importing what was, for him, a current (and therefore highly anachronistic) terminology into his reading of the older *Mean* so as to provide a secure cosmological foundation for his portrait of the exalted ideal sovereign.

Most important, however, Zheng Xuan acquired his sense of Confucius the thinker from three sets of writings, which, like the *Analects*, by middle to late Western Han (206 BCE–8 CE) had been ascribed to Confucius himself or to members of his inner circle (for not very good reasons, in the eyes of some modern scholar-skeptics): (1) the *Chunqiu* or *Annals*, which describes the steady disintegration in the domestic and diplomatic spheres of moral authority in Confucius's home state of Lu during the years 722–479 BCE; (2) the *Xiaojing* or *Classic of Filial Duty*, which celebrates the virtues of loyalty and filial submission as the twin building blocks for the state and patriline; and (3) two treatises included in the *Record of Rites* (which Zheng himself raised to the status of Classic), the *Constant Mean* and the *Great Learning*, both of which sketch the potential for charismatic power invested in the reliably humane and measured conduct of the *junzi* (a term often applied to the ideal ruler as well as to the better men in his service).

While the majority of Western Han thinkers emphasized the importance of the *Annals* and their three main commentaries in their treatments of Kongzi, underscoring the message that the *Annals* political program represented the Master's central legacy to the legitimate rulers and ministers of the Han, resort to the *Constant Mean* was frequent during the two centuries of Eastern Han, a time of weak central power whose state-sponsored ideology tended to exalt the emperor, as if in compensation, endowing him with semi-divine powers on a par with those of Heaven and Earth. By Zheng's time, the *Mean* was thought to be one of the texts most in tune with current cosmological and social constructions, which located a mysterious, divine, and resonating charismatic power in both the public and domestic actions of the sovereign and, to a far lesser extent, his representatives. Zheng's insistence that the authoritative person never wavers from the Way, regardless of who is watching—in the words of the *Mean*, that he "protect his divine qualities even when alone" (*shen qi du*)—was expressly designed to inject a higher moral standard into the politics of the day when many leading figures boasted of moral "flexibility" and factions battled for favor at a corrupt court. Zheng's further insistence on the authoritative leader's reverence for the ancestors could plausibly be construed by contemporaries as a harsh rebuke of the leading contenders for power. Conflating secular and sacred, in a manner true to the teachings of Kongzi, Zheng wanted his commentary on the *Constant Mean* to convey a single lesson: that the awesome privilege of creating new rites and music must be reserved for sage-kings on the throne. Still, Zheng was hardly averse to prescribing new paradigms for the responsibilities of the sage-king, in action and at rest, and he thereby set the stage for a "new" and revised Confucius suitable to the post-Han realities.

Writing nearly a thousand years after Zheng Xuan, Zhu Xi had the temerity to posit his teachers and himself as among the only qualified interpreters of Confucius's "subtle wording," claiming for himself the mantle of Zisi, Kongzi's grandson, and of Mencius. Thus Zhu Xi claimed undisputed legitimacy for his own particular readings of the Classics even when they departed dramatically from readings offered by earlier authoritative traditions. Zhu focused much of his attention on the *Constant Mean*, treating it as the final word and summation of Confucius's teachings; conveniently for Zhu, the *Mean* provided the best available canonical justification for Zhu's own cosmological and social constructions crafted to defend his version of the Confucian Way against detractors well versed in Buddhist metaphysics and Buddhist views of human nature. Zhu's peers and followers were all conversant with the strict Buddhist division of the originally unified heart-mind (*xin*) into "selfish emotions" (the seat of destructive desires) at war with the "higher mind" open to the divine laws (i.e., Principle). Accordingly, Zhu Xi's commentary likewise posited the existence of two such minds within each human, with each mind in continual if somewhat one-sided conversation with the other, except for those sages able to transcend selfish desires and external deceptions to commune with the infallible Mind of Dao (also known by the synonyms of Mean, Integrity, and Principle). That infallible Mind, it need hardly be said, is the proper object of single-minded contemplation for all would-be seekers after Dao. Unfortunately, the infallible Mind is "barely perceptible." For all those who are less than sages, glimpses of it must be gleaned painstakingly from successive investigations of the patterns of society and cosmos. Book learning and ordinary erudition, by Zhu's theory, offered the single best hope for marshaling and correlating such gleanings. This emphasis on book learning was itself a reflection of the new pervasiveness of text culture in Zhu's era, reinforced by the more meritocratic civil service examinations. Zhu's reading of the *Mean* therefore stands in stark contrast to that of Zheng Xuan, who looked elsewhere for its core message, to the sublime power of the sovereign's active interventions within the communities of the living and the dead.

In his reinterpretation of the *Constant Mean*, Zhu found it useful to depart from tradition, assigning some parts of the Classic to Kongzi himself (thereby lending them much greater authority) and others to Kong Ji or Zisi, Kongzi's grandson. Of course, Zhu Xi and his readers reckoned that only those sections assigned to Kong Ji could contain errors, though, in the main, the grandson was a faithful transmitter of his grandfather's mature teachings. Generally speaking, the parts Zhu assigned to Kongzi tended to discuss Heavenly Principle, whereas the parts assigned to Kong Ji concerned the Way of Man. Zhu in this way shifted the main subject of the text from the exemplary sovereign ruler to gentlemen of great cultivation and learning, cast by Zhu as persons very much like himself, scholars and teachers in loyal opposition to the government. From this, other changes by Zhu followed. For instance, Zhu tended to gloss over some parts of the canonical *Constant Mean* text, specifically its opening section depicting the emotions as admirably balanced and centered prior to taking action. He also redefined some key terms and phrases in the text. "Protecting one's divine qualities when alone," to take but one example, no longer referred to the sovereign's conduct within a domestic setting, as in Zheng Xuan's reading, but rather to the gentleman's ceaseless vigilance about his own motives and inner qualities even when not engaged in the performance of his social and political duties. Ideally, this interior work of self-cultivation gradually culminated in Integrity, a wholly inner quality of perfect wholeness and power, and this became the main focus of Zhu's readings, supplanting the earlier commentaries' concern with powerholders' tangible deeds and public displays of authority. Key to Zhu's message was the notion that all men like himself, either by nature or by dint of hard work, could attain sagehood, and thereby harness all the powers of the universe to their own interior efforts.

Many different titles for chapter 5, "The Supreme Sage and the Imperial Cults," were possible, since this chapter explores the transmogrification of Kongzi from First Teacher and Supreme Sage to an explicitly divine figure who is the object of established cults with specialized rituals, especially during the last three dynasties of imperial China—Yuan, Ming, and Qing. Twice a year, in spring and fall, from the mid–eighth century until the fall of the Qing in 1911, officials in the capital and in the empire's main administrative centers had rendered cult offerings to Confucius as a very high-ranking god within the imperial pantheon, positioned just below Heaven itself but above the Sun, Moon, and Five Planets. While this cultic Confucius held a distinguished place in the cosmos, he evidently remained accessible to exemplary humans and amenable to their influence. During these biennial ritual events, Confucius Temples throughout the land bustled with activities in which Confucius figured as both symbol and ultimate source of inspiration for the empire-wide civil service examinations, the de-facto "ancestor" of classical learning.

Readers may glean several noteworthy (if all too often overlooked) principles from chapter 5's review of the history and doctrinal content of these sacrifices and the pantheon:

1. In the three-tiered hierarchy of gods corresponding to the three tiers of the earthly administration (imperial, ministerial, and lower-ranking officials), various gods held sway over particular albeit overlapping spheres, while ancestral spirits were believed to be able to move *between* the tiers with unusual freedom, reflecting the critical importance of filial piety to the state cult.

2. Typically the state-sponsored Confucius cult, in contrast to those of Daoism and Buddhism, did not promise personal salvation in this life or the next for those offering cult; instead, blessings would be conferred more broadly upon the communities and constituencies of those offering cult.

3. The efficacy of such sacrifices was believed to depend more upon the celebrant's inner purity than upon his punctilious performance of the cult's ritual procedures.

4. The imperial rites, which somewhat erratically until 739 had focused sometimes more on the Duke of Zhou and sometimes more on Kongzi, were split in 739 in such a way that Confucius thereafter served as primary exemplar of the gentleman steeped in classical learning, and the duke represented the paragon of the loyal public servant.

5. Over time, the doctrinal content of the state-sponsored curriculum was distilled—or watered down, if you will—to a core set of teachings well suited to bureaucrats in the imperial service.

6. The Confucius cult survives, in somewhat distorted form, in the cults offered today in East Asia (People's Republic, Taiwan, and South Korea) and in the Chinese diasporic communities (e.g., Indonesia).

Interestingly, a review of the history of the Confucius cults shows that it was during the decades following the collapse of Han, specifically in 241 CE—precisely the time when standard accounts allege the influence of Confucius to be waning and Daoism and Buddhism waxing—that the extant records detail the first attempts to fully integrate imperial sacrifices to Confucius within the rest of the state-sponsored cults. Meanwhile the later histories show, equally astonishingly, that neo-Confucians of the twelfth century unceremoniously hauled down from their honored places in the Confucius Temple two of the four masters considered as late as the eleventh century to be the best proponents of Confucius's Middle Way, Xunzi and Yang Xiong (53 BCE–18 CE). To retain the old symmetry of four masters supporting Confucius, the reputed authors of the *Great Learning* and *Constant Mean*, Zheng Shen and Kong Ji, were enlisted to join Yan Hui and Mencius in the Temple by Kongzi's side. This reconfiguration of the Four Masters is one tangible sign of the enormous gulf separating the classical-era faces of Confucius from those of late imperial China.

Nonetheless, even in Song, as chapter 5 notes, any impulse by the throne to promulgate a narrow or precise definition of Confucian teachings tended to meet with stiff resistance from cultivated men inside and outside officialdom. The Song state's efforts spearheaded by Wang Anshi (d. 1086) to increase centralization in many areas of cultural and political life had manifestly failed. The first unequivocal imposition of a state orthodoxy occurred later under the Yuan, Ming, and Qing dynasties, when candidates sitting the civil examinations were required to follow Zhu Xi's commentaries on the Four Books in their essays. (Even in late imperial China, however, teachers in private academies were free to proselytize divergent views, so long as they were not openly treasonous, in this enjoying far more freedom than "heretics" in medieval and early modern Europe. This explains why, centuries after Zhu Xi, it is accurate to speak of many thriving and evolving Confucian traditions—not just one unitary "Confucianism"—that generally traced their origins back to one of two main lines of transmission, that following Zhu Xi and the Cheng brothers and that espousing Wang Yangming [1472–1529]. It also explains why a few sturdy critics like Yuan Mei [1716–1797] continued to gently mock the Master.)

While it is hard to gauge the impact of the Cheng-Zhu orthodoxy on court and society under the relatively short-lived Mongol-Yuan dynasty, when the Mongols put a strict limit on the number of Chinese eligible to sit the civil service exams, there is no doubt that Zhu Xi's influence made itself felt in every aspect of the Confucius cult from early Ming through late Qing. Zhu's influence can be discerned in the decision in Ming to replace sculpted or painted images of the Sage and his disciples with wooden tablets in Confucius Temples throughout the realm. This decision overturned a centuries-old precedent, and it was no surprise when, in Qing, Zhu Xi was elevated to the rank commensurate with Kongzi's immediate circle of disciples. As we have seen, doctrinal and ritual shifts occurred fairly often within state-sponsored "Confucianism." Meanwhile, proponents of the late imperial orthodoxy sought to settle a number of centuries-old questions about the place of Confucius as uncrowned king, supreme sage, and first teacher.

Chapter 6 explores the role of Confucius as Founding Ancestor of the Kong family, the only noble line to have persisted through the rises and falls of successive dynasties from Eastern Han times until the collapse of the Qing dynasty in 1911. Based mainly on sources from the Ming and Qing periods, the chapter outlines the distinct but overlapping practices of the ancestral and imperial cults devoted to Confucius through a reconstruction of three recorded offerings made to Kongzi by his seventy-first-generation descendant, Kong Zhaohuan (1735–1782). After Zhu Xi (1130–1200), performing family rituals assumed ever greater significance, since Zhu made reverent performance of the various family rituals—especially those connected with marriages, mourning, and the auspicious ancestral cult—a key status marker for any families claiming an illustrious patrimony. As a result, Kong Zhaohuan, as young scion of the Kong family line, with the help of liturgical experts, tutors, and advisers, engaged in a variety of practices designed to impress all the powers of Heaven and Earth with his great filial devotion. These expressions took the form of daily offerings to the heads of the five most recent generations of his family (from deceased father to great-great-grandfather in the direct line) represented by portraits; veneration of Master Kong, the Founding Ancestor of all Kong family descendants in the Ancestral Temple; and the seasonal offerings presented to the Kong Temple (also dubbed the Culture Temple or *Wenmiao*). In the seasonal offerings, Kong Zhaohuan, at the behest of the Qing emperor, paid homage not only to Kongzi himself but to all the outstanding sages before and after who had contributed to the eventual triumph of the Middle Way.

Whether engaged in the daily prayers offered to his ancestors within the family or leading imperial envoys who traveled to Qufu to honor his Founding Ancestor, Kong Zhaohuan performed the complementary roles of officer of the state, humble supplicant before his ancestor Confucius, and official representative of the enormous Kong clan, with some twenty thousand members in the Qufu area alone. Thus Kong Zhaohuan's devotions were expected to confer benefits upon the dynasty, upon the Kong family, and ultimately upon the entire realm, as a result of exploiting the collective influence of all members in the distinguished Kong patriline. Each role had its own venue, taking Kong Zhaohuan from his in-house temple to the all-important Kong Temple in Qufu, the latter—replicated in every main administrative seat of the realm—being open to all males who aspired to become cultivated "gentlemen," with the former, the Ancestral Temple, closed to all but the male members of the Kong family.

Chapter 6 reminds readers of the single canonical principle that informed all ancestral sacrifices in imperial China: that pious descendants, after the requisite purification rites, recalled in detail their ancestors' daily activities, smiles, gestures, preoccupations, and predilections, composing a complete mental image of the ancestor from these discrete elements that would be powerful enough to conjure the dead. By such practices the ancestral dead were restored to life, if only for the duration of the sacrifices. These arduous exercises entailing memory, invocation, and a measure, perhaps, of selective amnesia became the principal means to convert personal knowledge of the worthy dead (firsthand or via texts) into practices capable of sustaining the auspicious influence of the ancestors over succeeding generations. The solemn fasts, the consecration and offering of dishes, and the reading of prayers all underscored the interdependence of the living and dead while establishing secure lines of communication between earthly and spirit realms. The efficacy of these repeated applications to the dead, as readers of Zhu Xi's injunctions will recall, supposedly depended on the degree of inner purity to be found in the most direct lineal descendant while offering ancestral sacrifice. The greater the purity of the supplicant, the more likely that the punctilious ancestors would overlook minor lapses of decorum.

The history of the Kong family patriline would hardly be complete without mention of the "villainous Kong Mo," a hereditary indentured tenant of the Kong family, who, in hopes of inheriting the entire Kong family estate in the turmoil following the collapse of the Tang dynasty in 905, falsely claimed to be the most direct lineal ancestor of the Sage. Kong Mo's treachery was nearly unparalleled in the long course of Chinese history: though a dependent of the Kong family, he nearly succeeded in executing his plan to murder not just his master, but all of his master's relatives. Still worse, Kong Mo purportedly intended to put an end to the entire ritual structure centered on efficacious cult offerings to Kong-fu-tzu (Great Master Kong, Confucius). As Kong Mo well knew, ancestors would receive cult only from their biological heirs, absent special ritual arrangements for the adoption of an unrelated person into the family line. Fortunately for the Kong family and for the realm, one genuine Kong family member, Kong Renyu, survived Kong Mo's plot and ultimately succeeded to the hereditary title of duke in the early tenth century.

Chapter 6 introduces readers to the sorts of theological concerns that tended to preoccupy ritual specialists of the Ming and Qing courts—for example, whether pious veneration of the worthy dead was better facilitated through prayers before plain wooden tablets of uniform size and quality or before painted and sculpted images. The ritual reforms of 1530 resulted in the removal of all painted and sculpted images from every state-sponsored temple in the empire. A notable exception was made for the Kong temples, which retained the lifelike images that had been the focus of cult offerings, in Qufu at least, from before 221 BCE. (Curiously, a similar theological problem divided Protestant and Catholic theologians at just about the same time, with Protestants condemning as idolatry the use of effigies and purging local churches of these offending images.) Theological compromises had to be forged whenever famous sons came to be exalted

over their fathers, as was the case with extraordinary teachers and dynastic founders. According to the Five Classics prescriptions, a son
could not take precedence over his father, but there was the belated
decision, in the fourteenth century, to institute the first cult offerings
for Confucius's own father, Shuliang He, in Qufu. Finally, chapter 6
offers intriguing glimpses into the complex gender relations believed
to pertain among the worthy dead in late imperial China: Kong Zhaohuan's great-grandfather received cult offerings, along with two of his
wives, only one of whom had produced a boy and heir, and Kongzi—
referred to as Founding Ancestor—and his wife, along with his son,
grandson, and their wives. The various rites controversies described
in chapter 6 attest to the unsuitability of applying to pre-modern
times the modern dichotomies pitting public against private, and state
against family.

The seventh and final chapter of this book opens with a description of the 1898 "Hundred Days Reform" project led by the radical
reformer Kang Yuwei. Whereas before Kang, Kongzi was credited
with founding the Ru 儒 ethic of public service and with serving as
chief moral exemplar for professional classicists holding office and
teaching (in which logically distinct roles Confucius made his appearance in the state, local, and Kong family pantheons), Kang Yuwei
would have made his highly selective reading of Confucian tradition
the basis for a new "state religion" (*guojiao* 國教) modeled more
closely on Christianity than on indigenous Chinese traditions. Kang
fully intended this new Chinese religion to (a) receive state sponsorship; (b) require absolute adherence by all Qing subjects; (c) suppress
rival religions, including Daoism, Buddhism, and Christianity; and
(d) successfully merge religion and politics. Recoiling from Kang's
proposals, traditionalists countered Kang's creation with an ahistorical invention of their own that was no less false: they spoke of "secular Ru" guided by Kongzi's vision of a just state that condemns or
renders innocuous all manifestations of "superstition" (i.e., religion).

Thus began the series of oscillating culture wars that have played
themselves out in the twentieth and twenty-first centuries. The keen
desire to fix a definitive narrative about Confucian traditions within
the larger context of Chinese history expressed itself in four major

culture wars during the twentieth century: the May Fourth Movement (1919–26); the New Life Movement under Chiang Kai-shek (1934–37); the "anti-feudal" mass movements directed by Mao Zedong, which culminated in the "Criticize Confucius" campaigns of the early 1970s; and the New Confucian Revival of the 1980s and 1990s. These culture wars cast Kongzi/Confucius by turns as "national savior" or as "proponent of a slave mentality" requiring strict submission to political and family hierarchies. In the twenty-first century, the Communist Party has belatedly embraced Kongzi in the hopes that greater deference to the Master may condition a restless population to conform to a more "aesthetic and harmonious" society, despite severe dislocations caused by a rapidly expanding economy and ethnic separatist movements. Hence the decision in late 2007 by the People's Republic's official Xinhua News Agency to unveil an "official" portrait of Confucius that recalls the laughing Buddha far more than it does the grave Master of legend.

Three snapshots of recent events occurring within the tightly connected circles in Asian media, politics, and academia capture a few of the dominant approaches to rethinking the role of institutional Confucianism (less so of Kongzi himself) within state and society. The snapshots chosen for analysis portray the so-called Third and Fourth Wave New Confucians based in the academic strongholds of Hong Kong, Taiwan, South Korea, and (increasingly) the People's Republic, all of whom seek, for good reasons and bad, to adapt Kongzi's message to the demands of today's world. Those featured in the snapshots include two ministers in the Singaporean government who routinely invoked the name of Confucius in order to sanction one-party rule over a multiethnic community. And there is, last but not least, the bizarre Yu Dan, a popular TV personality and self-styled self-help guru who cheerfully appropriates the *Analects* as grist for her media mill.

This chapter argues that most, if not all of the freakish twists taken by Kongzi's reputation in China before, during, and after Deng Xiaoping's (1904–1997) triumphant return to power in 1978–80 faithfully mirrored the highs and lows of China's self-confidence about its own place as "rising dragon" in a postmodern age, particularly in relation to the United States, the declining superpower. Therefore, the final sections of this last chapter consider (mis)perceptions of Confucius and China in the United States over the course of the last century or so, which have shaped (and sometimes twisted) American politics and policy. In this context, the chapter places the United States' reconstruction efforts in Asia after World War II; its struggle for dominance during the Cold War; its eagerness to fight proxy wars in Korea and Southeast Asia aimed at weakening communism in general and China in particular; and, more lately, the official encouragement of U.S. investment in China, the pegging of the Chinese RMB to the American dollar, American dependence on cheap Chinese imports, and the PRC's $288-billion investment in U.S. government bonds to subsidize America's exploding deficit.

Chapter 7 insists that it is worth taking the figure of Confucius seriously, if only because the twenty-first century will require ever greater cooperation between the two superpowers, and Confucius's role in Chinese history provides one of the very few possible meeting grounds for Chinese and American leaders confronting a host of seemingly intractable problems, including the environment and education. The chapter therefore concludes with three views of Kongzi articulated by Herbert Fingarette, Henry Rosemont Jr., and Roger Ames—scholars who, like it or not, have revolutionized the way Americans see and teach Confucius and China. Strong defenders of early Confucian traditions all (though for different reasons), Fingarette, Rosemont, and Ames together urge upon us (a) a stronger code of reciprocal relations between superior and subordinate (with both equally conscious of their mutual obligations) to function as a useful corrective for alienation and antisocial behavior; (b) a greater reliance upon extended families and communities designed to nurture the elderly, the infirm, and the young; (c) more holistic views of the cosmos, consonant with environmental stewardship; (d) a more sophisticated notion of human potential, fundamentally uncoupled from biological inheritance, national identity, or religious institutions and ideas, that might conceivably provide "common ground" for multiethnic communities seeking parity; (e) a revised notion of "human rights" that foregrounds economic justice as the key to citizen participation and responsibility, so as to give greater voice to the poor and disenfranchised currently ignored in the so-called democracies; and (f) a greater focus on academic achievement and hard work in conjunction with less preoccupation with personality, genius, and celebrity to ameliorate the *fin-de-siècle* impulses toward narcissism and solipsism.

One cannot expect to understand the role of "tradition" in China or the United States today without knowing what happened in those countries within the recent past. As Søren Kierkegaard remarked, "We live forward, but we understand backward." Nor do families, societies, or states typically exist for very long without feeling the need to invoke the ancestors in order to construct identities. Kongzi's call for past traditions (plural) to be "warmed up" or adapted to current exigencies, coupled with the increasing speed of the global circulation of ideas, compels us to ask if inevitable changes can ever be channeled toward proper ends. Possibly. We cannot know unless we try. That would be Kongzi's answer, at least. Kongzi himself deemed the effort to become a clear emblem of one's values and virtues to others an impressive way of being and acting in this world. And, it seems, Americans have remarkably little to lose if we choose to explore the implications of that practical answer. Now, Cassandra-like, Chalmers Johnson, the erstwhile conservative critic of Mao's exploits, catalogs instances of the disastrous "blowback" stemming from the recent foreign-policy initiatives of the United States. Both practical and ethical considerations, then, propel us to get better acquainted with our global neighbors' history, as well as our own. The very figure of Kongzi, that protean dragon riding the times, has always promised that triumph can be wrested from adversity by dint of hard work and humankindness. But if Americans continue to react as if "history is bunk," ever fewer options will remain.

Zhang Zai (1020–77), a Song dynasty thinker, wrote the following when he looked back at the sweep of the Confucian tradition:

The affairs of Heaven and Earth are nothing more than transformation. The intentions of Heaven and Earth are nothing more than divine. To understand transformation and plumb the depths of the divine is to be good at emulating and implementing the affairs and intentions of Heaven and Earth. . . . One who is not ashamed in the privacy of the house is not disgraced before Heaven and Earth. The heart and mind and inner nature are Heaven and Earth. To preserve the heart and mind and nourish the inner nature . . . is to serve Heaven and Earth.

Heaven and Earth have amply supplied our lives with wealth, high status, good fortune, and kindness. However, poverty, low status, worries, and sorrow are also expressions of the love of Heaven and Earth, there to help fulfill me. If in life I faithfully serve and obey the two powers and if in death I take my ease in their minds and do not create disorder, then I am . . . their perfectly filial child.

Soaring to mystical heights, Zhang Zai's account yet manages to convey what it means to practice the Middle Way in the journey of life. Contrast his elevated register with the cynical summary of Kongzi's life and reception proffered by Lu Xun, China's most famous writer of the twentieth century: "Confucius's establishment as a 'fashionable guru' was something that happened after his death. In his own lifetime, he had a pretty rough ride. . . . Confucius owes his exalted position in China to the powerful. It had nothing to do with the masses of the common people." Each of these opposing statements tells us something profoundly true. It is one of the challenges facing us that we now, as ever, ignore at our peril the host of contradictions dragged in the wake of the multiple lives of Confucius. But, "If it is really possible to govern countries by decorum and yielding, what more need be said?" Nothing but the Master's fervent wish, apparently: "In dealing with the aged, to be of comfort to them. In dealing with friends, to be faithful. And in dealing with the young, to cherish them."

AMERICAN PERCEPTIONS OF THE CHINESE[1]

| The Age of Contempt *1840–1905* "Yellow Peril" heathens[2] | The Age of Benevolence *1905–1937* "The Missionary's Golden Age" | The Age of Admiration *1937–1944* Allies "Forever" | The Age of Disenchantment *1944–1949* Civil War in China |

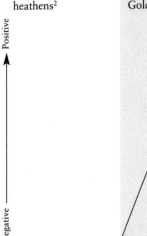

Positive

Negative

China as the "sick man" of Asia

1840–48 California Gold Rush; massive Chinese immigration

1882 Chinese Exclusion Act; Chinese immigration forbidden

1889 Short-lived Hundred Days Reforms

1900 Boxer Rebellion; defeat of China by allies, including U.S.

1905 Japan defeats China

1905 boycott in China against U.S. products

Influx of mission schools and hospitals

1911–25 Sun Yat-sen nominal head of KMT

1914–18 First World War; crisis of confidence in Western civilization

1925 Charlie Chan, the genial sleuth

1925 or 1926 Chiang Kai-shek becomes Christian

1931 Pearl Buck's *The Good Earth*

1931 Mukden Incident; Japan seizes Manchuria

1934 New Life Movement under Chiang Kai-shek

1935 Lin Yu-tang's *My Country and My People*

1937 Japan invades China

1937 *Good Earth* film seen by some 65 million people

1938 Edgar Snow's *Red Star over China*

1941 Japan attacks Pearl Harbor

1941 U.S. enters the war, with a united front in China

1944–49 Civil War in China

1945 Japan defeated

April 1949 Communists seize Nanjing, KMT capital

Oct. 1, 1949 Mao proclaims the People's Republic

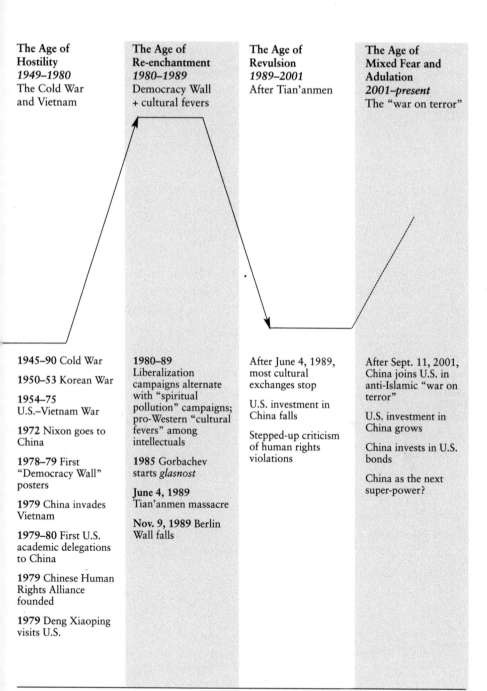

The Age of Hostility
1949–1980
The Cold War and Vietnam

The Age of Re-enchantment
1980–1989
Democracy Wall + cultural fevers

The Age of Revulsion
1989–2001
After Tian'anmen

The Age of Mixed Fear and Adulation
2001–present
The "war on terror"

Column 1 (Age of Hostility):

1945–90 Cold War

1950–53 Korean War

1954–75 U.S.–Vietnam War

1972 Nixon goes to China

1978–79 First "Democracy Wall" posters

1979 China invades Vietnam

1979–80 First U.S. academic delegations to China

1979 Chinese Human Rights Alliance founded

1979 Deng Xiaoping visits U.S.

Column 2 (Age of Re-enchantment):

1980–89 Liberalization campaigns alternate with "spiritual pollution" campaigns; pro-Western "cultural fevers" among intellectuals

1985 Gorbachev starts *glasnost*

June 4, 1989 Tian'anmen massacre

Nov. 9, 1989 Berlin Wall falls

Column 3 (Age of Revulsion):

After June 4, 1989, most cultural exchanges stop

U.S. investment in China falls

Stepped-up criticism of human rights violations

Column 4 (Age of Mixed Fear and Adulation):

After Sept. 11, 2001, China joins U.S. in anti-Islamic "war on terror"

U.S. investment in China grows

China invests in U.S. bonds

China as the next super-power?

---

1. This chart adopts Harold Isaacs's work, *Scratches on Our Minds: American Views of China and India* (Armonk, New York: M. E. Sharpe 1958, 1980) for its synopsis before 1980. As Isaacs's work was revised last in 1980, this chart seeks to extend its insights into the present era. NB: Isaacs cautioned against the idea that any one of these ages "stamps itself uniformly on its time."

2. Predating the Age of Contempt is Isaacs's Age of Respect (the eighteenth and early nineteenth centuries, when the French *philosophes*, Leibniz, and the American Founding Fathers celebrated the achievements of the Chinese, specifically their separation of church and state and their cultural attainments.

Notes

1 Kongzi ("Master Kong") is the Chinese name rendered in English as "Confucius." This chapter speaks of Kongzi or the Master for reasons that will become obvious with succeeding chapters of this book.
2 *Ru* is the term now conventionally rendered as "Confucian."
3 Something very like this verse is said of Kongzi by Yan Hui in *Analects* 9/10. In closing his biography with this paean of praise, Sima Qian announces his own allegiance to Kongzi as an exemplary historian.
4 The *Analects,* typically regarded now as the most valuable entrée into Confucius's teachings, was less esteemed in the early empires, as indicated by the following: While by mandate the Five Classics were to be transcribed on bamboo strips two Han feet, four inches long (the same size used for imperial edicts), and the *Xiaojing* on strips half that length, the *Analects* was to be transcribed on strips only eight Han inches in length, according to Zheng Xuan (127–200 CE), whose statement tallies with one by Wang Chong (27–97? CE). (One Han foot corresponds to 23.1 cm.) The *Zuo,* once confidently dated to ca. 400 BCE, is now believed to be a multilayered text that may have reached final form as late as Western Han, before the time of Liu Xin (d. 23 CE). Kongzi figures in some stories in the *Zuo* as a being with godlike prescience and vast erudition.
5 Kongzi is one of only two individuals to appear in the "Hereditary Houses" section, the other being Chen She, the rebel leader who put into motion the chain of events that eventually toppled Qin. Readers of the *Shiji* have always assumed that Kongzi was included in the "Hereditary Houses" section because he was regarded in Han times as "uncrowned king," a person of enormous influence and authority who, in some sense, "ruled" over the hearts and minds of all those who followed his example. It is worth considering, however, whether Sima Qian might not have meant the placement of this biography to convey a hint of Kongzi's rebellious nature. After all, the subtle wording of Kongzi's compilation of the *Chunqiu* was designed to "criticize emperors, reprimand feudal lords, and condemn the high officials so that the business of a

true ruler could be known." (See chapter 3.) An example of the storm of criticism that arose from Sima Qian's decision to place the biography of Kongzi in the "Hereditary Houses" section may be seen from Wang Anshi's (1021–1086 CE) "Criticism of the Hereditary House for Kongzi," translated by David Pollard, in *The Chinese Essay* (Hong Kong: Renditions Press, 1979), 350–52.

6   The *Annals* dates Meng Xizi's death to 518 BCE, not 535. In the *Zuo*, however, essentially the same anecdote occurs under the year 535, but it credits Meng Xizi's advice to seventeen years later. Meng's son, named Yizi, died in 481 BCE.

7   More often translated as "imaginatively (心) likening (如) oneself [to another]," so as to empathize with another's plight.

8   The comparison may hint at Kongzi's role in guarding the legacy of the Zhou house, since the dog guards the house.

9   *Analects* 6/18, which recalls 2/4, "At forty, I no longer suffered from perplexity; at fifty, I heard Heaven's dictates," etc.

10 See the next chapter for such characterizations of the Ru as experts in classical learning.

CHAPTER 2

1   The name of Mozi (tradit. 470–390 BCE) is often coupled with that of Kongzi in Qin and Han texts, and Yang Zhu (370–319 BCE) is portrayed as a major rival and critic of Kongzi by both Mencius (fourth century) and Xunzi (third century).

2   To be fair, Mozi doesn't seem to object to small-scale sacrifices in which family or community members gather to drink and eat or listen to musical performances.

3   There the retort is, "Master Yang is wise but he does not understand that some things are fated. Only somebody who truly understands fate is not deluded."

4   See the *Hanshi waizhuan* for this anecdote.

5   Under the broad rubric of "the laws," Han Fei includes not only the penal code and tax laws, but also administrative laws and job descriptions for the imperial bureaucracy, which are to have the force of law.

6   The focus here will be on the first seven chapters of the extant *Zhuangzi*, the so-called Inner Chapters, which most scholars agree are most likely to have been written by a single genius. The rest of the work (the Outer Chapters) is generally deemed to be by later, Han and even post-Han, hands. As will become clear, the tone of the Inner Chapters is far less sectarian.

CHAPTER 3

1   Modern historians believe, of course, that the Qufu Confucius, whose stories were compiled about four centuries after his death (see chapter 1), may be a combinatory figure like the Buddha, Laozi, Moses, David, Jesus, and

even the Evangelists. It was common, almost de rigueur, to attach a name and cycles of stories to great texts, oral or written, to ensure their survival through time.

2 The *Analects* ascribed to Kongzi and his circle never show the Master writing the *Annals*. The closest that Kongzi ever comes to being a historian is in *Analects* 15/25, in which he remarks (with asperity), "I can still remember the days when a scribe left a blank [rather than fill in the gaps with figments of his imagination]." Note that the *Analects* enjoyed a measure of influence during Han, but it was always regarded as "elementary education" (lower-level teaching) and not the masterwork of Kongzi himself.

3 The common wisdom has it that in the post-Han period of disunion, or "Six Dynasties," the reputation of Kongzi plummeted. Neither the extant historical records nor the philosophical literature supports this view, however.

4 One Han legend makes this metaphor literally true, saying that, during the "restoration of Eastern Han," in the years 23–25 CE, the thorn bushes that were growing in profusion in Queli [now called Qufu], the old home of Kongzi, all died in one day, leaving an unimpeded trail more than one thousand paces long from the site of the old lecture hall of Kongzi to the town gate. See the *Kong congzi* for further details.

5 Ban Gu (22–92 CE) probably initiated parts of this myth himself, as the work of a Japanese scholar, Fukui Shigemasa, has shown. Ban, a relative by marriage to the Han imperial house, was doubtless anxious to please his ruler, and what better way than to imply that the Han house was predestined to rule thanks to Kongzi's patronage? Ban's writings, however, show the Han rulers looking to many sources of legitimacy besides Kongzi. Huang Jinxing 黃進興 (Academia Sinica, Taiwan) correctly believes that it was nearly a century after Han Wudi, around the time of Wang Mang (r. 9–23 CE), that "Confucian" classicism became the fashion at court; he also shows that it was even later, during the Tang, that "temple schools" (*miaoxue*) became routine parts of the complexes of the Kongmiao (temples dedicated to Kongzi). According to Huang, it was these *miaoxue* that for the first time established in all the major cities throughout China a tight link between the cult to Confucius and activities at the local government schools.

6 A concern with widow chastity, for example, first appears in Legalist texts.

7 Not until the Song period were Kong descendants enfeoffed in perpetuity, though they were granted hereditary titles long before.

8 Julia Murray's work on the *Shengji tu* (see Suggested Readings) shows that visual as well as literary portraits of Kongzi remained popular down through the ages.

9 Not everyone agreed with this assessment, however. Wang Anshi, the great eleventh-century reformist, went so far as to criticize the *Annals* as "disjointed and fragmentary reportage."

10 Nearly sixty years ago the scholar Homer H. Dubs found that there was no *gengzi* day in the eleventh month, twenty-first year of the reign of Xiang

Gong, so the second eclipse recorded in the *Guliang* commentary to the *Annals* is the result of scribal error or deliberate interpolation. Note also that on the *gengzi* day, in each of the four seasons, couples are to mate, according to the *Chunqiu fan lu*, one commentary to the *Annals*.

11 First, it is not certain that Kongzi actually edited or authored the text (since many early sources, such as the *Analects*, do not mention it), and second, it is not certain what his motivation might have been.

12 For example, the *Annals* contained at least four mutually contradictory statements on the single subject of government service: one saying that an officer must not do as he pleases or instigate affairs on his own initiative; one saying that if an officer can find a way to enhance the security of his state's altars, and otherwise bring advantage to it, he may decide matters on his own; one saying that going forward or retreating is up to an officer; and another saying that when an officer receives word of a parent's death while on a mission, he may slow his advance so that he can more easily be recalled.

13 For the *Constant Mean*, see chapter 4. The propensity to insert Kongzi into the Rites canons, to which the *Zhongyong* belongs, falls short of fully endorsing an official orthodoxy, but it does show that Kongzi's followers in Han were in a position to try to canonize Kongzi the man.

14 One story compares his mouth pouring forth divine lessons to a deep and fertile marsh (*Yuan shenqi*, first cited in 25 CE). He also had joined teeth, in the form of the planet Mercury. For Xunzi, Kongzi's "hollowed out" forehead resembled the mask of an exorcist.

15 This connection may be yet another reason why Sima Qian puts Chen She and Kongzi in the "Hereditary Houses" section of his monumental *Shiji*.

16 Had the Kong family stories any foundation in truth, it is difficult to see why (a) Kongzi would not have known his father's identity, and (b) Kongzi was nearly barred admission to a minister's house on the grounds that his forebears were undistinguished.

CHAPTER 4

1 Sima Qian, Zheng Xuan, and Zhu Xi concur that Confucius's grandson, Kong Ji (aka Zisi), authored the *Zhongyong*. Zheng states that Kong Ji "compiled it to illuminate his ancestor's virtue." Most modern readers remain unconvinced of this attribution, but since this chapter aims to situate the text in ways that Chinese commentators historically understood it, we shall let pass the question of the text's actual author.

2 The Thirteen Classics comprise the *Changes, Documents,* and *Mao's Odes*; three ritual canons, i.e., the *Rites of Zhou, Ceremonial Rites,* and *Record of Rites*; three commentaries on the *Spring and Autumn Annals*, i.e., *Zuozhuan, Guliang zhuan,* and *Gongyang zhuan*; the *Analects; Filiality*; the *Erya* dictionary; and *Mencius*.

3 Zheng Xuan also interprets *zhongyong* in the text as the "constant mean."

4 Zheng Xuan says this line proclaims the *Mean* as sublime (*zhimei* 至美), whereas Zhu Xi says it is innate and possessed by everyone (*ren suo tong de* 人所同得).

5 Numbers in parentheses correspond to Zhu Xi's division of the *Constant Mean* used in most English translations of the text.

6 Shun was chosen to accede to the throne for his extraordinary filiality and exemplary matrimonial devotion shown to his two wives, both daughters of the king. Upon ascending the throne, Shun brought order to the cosmos by regulating the stars and performing proper rites to High God (Shangdi 上帝) and the other gods that inhabited the mountains and streams. As the true king, Shun performed his sacred duties of setting the calendar and standardizing rites and music, which established the foundation for peace throughout his domain.

7 Zheng Xuan glosses the transitive verb *ti*, which typically means "to give body to" or "to give substance to," as "to give birth to." Given that ancestors are the subject of *ti* and their descendants its object, *ti* should be construed as "procreation." The word *shi* often means to be dispatched by a superior, but the context leaves open a certain degree of volition on the part of those who fast and purify themselves, so it is translated as "to induce."

8 Compare this with a similar and parallel passage in the "Fundamentals of Sacrifice" in the *Record of Rites*: "The pious man's sacrifice certainly receives the blessing."

9 In classical Chinese, the word *cheng* (Integrity) also functions as a transitive verb, meaning to actively make something attain Integrity.

10 Zhu Xi reads this passage differently: "Anciently, there were good rulers, but no evidence of their rites remains today, so the people will not follow them. Presently, the good man is not revered as a king and so the people will not follow." Who might such a good man be? "*Anciently*," says Zhu Xi, "refers to the kings of the Xia and Shang dynasties whose rites were good but could no longer be followed. *Presently* refers to sages like Master Kong, who, though accomplished in the rites, was not revered as the sovereign."

11 This passage appears in the "Documents of Yu" of the Modern Script Text version of the *Book of Documents*. Xunzi uses this same formulation to explain how the mind becomes deluded in "Dispelling Delusions."

12 In living things, *qi* is a force that animates the body. The term defies easy translation because the sources use it differently. In early sources it is an essence that animates the body inherited from one's ancestors and is thus shared within a common descent line. Zheng Xuan said, "All things are born by the *qi* of the spirits." Zhu Xi further identifies *qi* as the fundamental character of the mind, which is individuated and thus not strictly familial.

13 In *Instructions for Practical Living* (New York: Columbia University Press, 1963), 16–17, Wang Yangming refutes Zhu Xi's reading as creating two minds.

14 Zheng Xuan mentions only five sages in his commentary: sage-kings Yao and Shun; the Zhou dynastic founders kings Wen and Wu; and Confucius.

CHAPTER 5

1 The word *sacrifice* means to consecrate or to render something sacred by offering it to god(s) and, as such, appropriately conveys the classical Chinese word *ji*, which graphically represents two hands held up before a spirit. In Confucian sacrifice, animals were prepared in a kitchen in advance of the ceremony and presented to the spirits as part of a larger feast. Confucian rites stressed presentation of a complete feast, not the ritual killing of animals.

2 The reigning Han emperor had granted Confucius the posthumous title of Exalted Ni, Duke of Consummate Perfection, in 1 CE, when sacrifices were only performed in Qufu. The sources do not make clear if the memorialist, Pei Songzhi (372–451), sought to extend the Han precedent to court regulations or if he was responding to a practice that contravened the Han precedent, either overtly or in ignorance of the precedent. The Wei capital was located in Pingcheng, roughly 200 kilometers west of modern-day Beijing, in 489.

3 The four disciplines include virtuous conduct, speech, government, and culture and learning, described in *Analects* 11.2.

4 This passage from the "When King Wen Was Heir Apparent" (*Wenwang shi zi*) chapter of the *Record of Rites* was first adduced to authorize the cult in 550 CE under the Northern Qi dynasty (550–577 CE).

5 Xuanzang founded the Consciousness-Only (*Weishi*; Sanskrit: *Vijnaptimatra*) school of Buddhism.

6 "When King Wen was Heir Apparent" (*Wenwang shi zi*), *Record of Rites*. See note 4 above.

7 Xunzi and Yang Xiong would be removed on grounds of heresy in the fifteenth century, when the court embraced a restrictive conception of Confucian truth.

8 Chapter 4 discusses an example of this criticism in Zhu Xi's critique of Han and Tang commentaries on the *Constant Mean*.

9 Zhu Xi promoted a narrow version of the Cheng brothers' Yi-Luo School called the Dao School, or Learning of the Dao. The court later canonized this school, which is referred to as Cheng-Zhu orthodoxy.

10 During the Ming, three celebrated events at court incited persecution of their critics, but none of the three was doctrine-related: the Yongle emperor's (r. 1402–1424) usurpation of the throne in 1402, the Jiajing emperor's (r. 1521–1566) posthumous enthronement of his father, and eunuch usurpation in the late Wanli reign (r. 1572–1620).

CHAPTER 6

1 *Analects* 3.12. Following the *Lunyu zhengyi* commentary (Liu Baonan, *Lunyu zhengyi*, 3: 53–54), the full passage may be rendered, "Sacrifice [in the ancestral temple] just as [one's kin] were alive. Sacrifice to spirits as living [i.e., serve the dead the same way that one serves the living]. The Master said, 'If I do not offer the sacrifice myself, it is like not sacrificing at all' [this means that if Kongzi leaves home or is sick and cannot offer sacrifices to his ancestors personally and sends a surrogate, then solemn reverence has not been realized in the heart]."

2 Fifteenth day of the eleventh lunar month of the Qianlong emperor's eleventh year.

3 He Qingxiao (1713–1779).

4 The sacrifice here includes a goat and a pig—prepared in advance of the ceremony—five baskets of grains, and five bowls of sauces and celeries on each of the five altar tables.

5 Always on the first *ding* day—the fourth day of the ten-day cycle—of the second month of each season.

6 The court attached the land and the peasant families that lived on it to the Kong estate on a hereditary basis.

7 Kong Sihui's record of this genealogy's compilation, dated August 25, 1329, is the earliest extant account of the Kong Mo episode. Sihui was himself embroiled in a dispute with a competing Kong line over ducal succession, during which the court transferred the title among three lines, culminating in Sihui's appointment in 1316.

8 The founding ancestor of the duke's lineage, Kong Sihui, occupies the primary position at the middle altar, followed by four generations of the living duke's ancestors, who are arrayed by twos on the founder's left and right. The tablets on the founder's left occupy the senior position (*zhao*), while those on the founder's right occupy the junior position (*mu*). Thus the tablets on Sihui's left belong to the living sacrificer's great-great-grandparents and grandparents; those on his right belong to the sacrificer's great-grandparents and parents. Just as "stage left" corresponds to the viewing audience's right, the founder's left corresponds to the sacrificer's right.

9 Kong Yuqi (1657–1723); first wife: whose natal surname was Zhang (1654–1679), first daughter of Zhang Xuanxi (governor of Zhili, Shandong, Henan); second wife: Ye Canying (1666–1692); third wife: surnamed Huang (1677–1764).

10 Kong Chuanduo (1674–1735); Portraits: *Da zai Kongzi*, p. 88, *Kongzi xiang Yanshenggong ji qi furen xiaoxiang*, p. 43. Second wife: Li Yu (1675–1714).

11 Jihuo (1697–1719).

12 Surname Wang (1692–1752).

13 Kong Zhen (d. 1296) was stripped of the title in 1259 on the grounds that he "did not serve with learning and refinement."

14 See note 8.

15 Kinship organizations did not conceal genealogical information, which, in the case of the Qufu Kongs, was published in book form. Rather, they protected the original, handwritten version used in ancestral rituals.

16 The commentary explains, "This passage means that the ancestors correlate with Heaven."

17 Kong Mo's descendants kept the Kong surname; thus not everyone surnamed Kong in Qufu was Kongzi's descendant. Genealogical sources refer to these families as Kongs of the outer court, or simply "outer Kongs" (*wai Kong*). I use "authentic Kong" to convey the distinction stressed in the Kong family sources, which refer to Kong Renyu's descendants as Kongs of the inner court, or "inner Kongs" (*nei Kong*). In conversations as recently as 1995, representatives of the Kong family said family genealogists still keep track of these differences.

18 The most vociferous advocates of removal gave as their main reason that the use of images betrayed Buddhist and Daoist influences; that they confused imperial and ancestral rites was a lesser consideration. The court declined to remove spirit images from the Kong Temple in Qufu when they were removed from other Kong temples in the capital and throughout the empire in the early Ming.

19 The five phases are cosmic operations that govern qualities of particular things. Each phase corresponds to a series of attributes. Wood: blue/green, East, sour, the *jue* pitch (E). Fire: red, South, bitter, the *zhi* pitch (G). Earth: yellow, Center, sweet, the *gong* pitch (C). Metal: white, West, spicy, the *shang* pitch (D). Water: black, North, salty, the *yu* pitch (A). Chen Yingshi, "Theory and Notation in China," in *The Garland Encyclopedia of World Music*, 7: 115–26.

20 In addition to the Kongs, the Four Surnames included descendants of Yan Hui, Zengzi, and Mengzi. The Yuan court established a school for educating sons of the Kong, Yan, and Meng families in 1261. The Ming court added the Zengs in 1587.

21 This rite used six rows of dancers when performed at local temples, and eight rows when performed in the capital to designate it as a court-patronized ceremony.

22 Although the insignia are mentioned in the *Rites of Zhou*, royal and imperial courts observed this tradition only inconsistently before the Qing.

23 Originating Sage, Duke Mu Jinfu; Abundant/Enriched Sage, Duke Qifu; Bequeathed Sage, Duke Fangshu; Prosperous Sage, Duke Boxia; Adoring Sage, Duke Shuliang He.

24 Compare this with the meat offerings to Kongzi of ox, goat, and pig, plus ten baskets and ten bowls of victuals.

CHAPTER 7

1 The first Asian rendering of "religion" was a Japanese neologism coined in 1869 (*zongjiao*; *shukyo*); it took off in the 1880s, perhaps under the impulse of the first academic treatments of "religion" (especially "world religions" and "comparative religion") as an academic discipline in the 1880s and 1890s. Before that time, Ru learning, like Buddhist and Daoist doctrines, was regarded as a "teaching" (*jiao*) or "technique" (*shu*) resulting in a "a skilled way of life." For Kang's more utopian strain, see his posthumously published *One World Writings* (under Suggested Readings). For a new study on Legge, see Girardot, also under Suggested Readings.

2 As the story goes, the Guangxu emperor was put under house arrest in the palace; and the Dowager Empress had him murdered when she lay on her deathbed, fearful lest he—restored to power after her demise—recall Kang from exile and persist in such follies.

3 In 1916, Cai (1867–1940) became president of Peking University. Then, in the early 1920s, the Kuomintang wreaked further destruction on many Buddhist and Daoist temples associated with "superstitions."

4 A wacky spoof of Wikipedia called "Wikiality" (www.wikiality.com) captures this confusion: "They even named a religion after him [Confucius], called 'Confusionism' [*sic*]. No one knows a lot about it, because it's not considered a Path to Accepting Jesus Christ as Your Personal Lord and Savior. At the same time, Confusionism isn't a One-Way Ticket Straight to Hell because they don't technically have a Church or anything. Confusionism just wants you think about stuff and stuff like that. So no Americans practice Confusionism. . . ."

5 Arguments that the CCP is not actively promoting the pro-Kongzi affair in China today are belied by several undeniable facts: (1) that Yu Dan's *The Analects: Insights* were given free to hundreds of thousands of the poorest peasants at the Chinese New Year, in the hope that this would reduce social friction; (2) the same book was forced upon prisoners in Chinese jails; (3) Confucius Temples (*kongmiao*) are now conducting classes for middle-school students in the rudiments of "Confucian" teaching; and (4) the establishment of Confucius Institutes is a major part of China's foreign-policy initiatives within the last few years.

6 From the conclusion to the movie *The River Elegy*, one of the most influential "documentaries" shown (twice) in the PRC in 1988. A complete English translation of the entire script of the three-part series can be found in the periodical *Chinese Sociology and Anthropology* 24, no. 2 (Winter 1991–92). Two subsequent issues (24, no. 4, and 25, no. 1) contain commentaries and reviews of the persuasion piece, which argued, in extreme form, the negativity and intellectual inertia of all tradition.

7 Nonetheless, large parts of the Chinese empire became "spheres of influence" under the Western powers for long decades before Japan invaded the north-

ern provinces in 1935. Thailand and Japan were never colonized outright, either, but neither was anywhere near as powerful as China at the dawn of the nineteenth century.

8 In 1071 the statesman Wang Anshi made three of the Five Classics, read through his own commentaries, the basis of the state-sponsored examination curriculum, in place of the poetic compositions that had been favored earlier. From 1313 to 1904, Zhu Xi's commentaries on the Four Books formed the core curriculum tested by the state qualifying examinations. See chapter 4.

9 Geremie Barmé, "History for the Masses," in *Using the Past to Serve the Present*, edited by Jonathan Unger (Armonk, NY: M. E. Sharpe, 1993), 260.

10 In the late nineteenth and early twentieth centuries, discussions routinely pitted China as "the sick man of Asia" against Japan, discounting crucial differences between the two states: China was five times larger than Japan; China's far greater racial, ethnic, and linguistic diversity posed serious obstacles to mobilizing the forces for change; and, perhaps most important, China's economic ideals (influenced by Mencius) limited the rate of taxation on farmland, and so precluded the sorts of massive state expenditure on infrastructure that occurred in Meiji Japan. In addition, by the mid–nineteenth century, the Tokugawa *bakufu*'s policies had forced lower- and middle-ranking samurai into such severe debt that they had little stake in supporting traditional political and cultural institutions.

11 In the United States, Deng Xiaoping is usually portrayed as Liu Shaoqi's protégé, though they were of the same political generation and sometime rivals. As targets in the Cultural Revolution, they were treated as equals, although leaders of different political factions (Liu as head of the workers in "white" areas, and Deng as leader of Sichuan and of the Hakka Red Army leaders).

12 Zheng Jiadong, *Dangdai xin ruxue lunheng* (Taipei: Guiguan tushu gonsi, 1995), 8.

13 John Hutchinson, "Re-Interpreting Cultural Nationalism," *Australian Journal of Politics and History* 45, no. 3 (September 1999), 394.

14 Two obvious exceptions to this characterization are (1) Jiang Qing 蔣庆, former academic and (after 2001) full-time social activist, who as a self-proclaimed follower of Wang Yangming (1472–1529) has been critical of Mou Zongsan and all proponents of "abstract postulates of a far-removed metaphysics" but equally opposed to Western-style democracy; and (2) Li Zehou 李澤厚, who insists that Confucianism is so central to Chinese culture that it needs no special efforts to revitalize it.

15 Yu Ying-shih wrote of "traditional" China, "Although Confucian (*rujia*) culture was in a degenerate state [during the Republican era, 1911–49], it nevertheless controlled the activities of daily life . . . from marriage and funeral customs to seasonal festivals." Lu Xun would have disputed Yu's assessment, for he wrote in his essay, "Confucius in Modern China," "Compared with the later imported Sakyamuni, he [Kongzi] cut a rather poor figure. True,

every county had a Confucian Temple, but this was always a lonely, neglected place where the common folk never worshipped. If they wanted to worship, they looked for a Buddhist temple or a shrine to some deity."

16 *Xue* means "learning" (not erudition, but learning how to operate in an exemplary fashion in the world); it is to be distinguished from *jiao* (doctrine, ideology, cult).

17 John Makeham, *Lost Soul: "Confucianism" in Contemporary Chinese Academic Discourse* (Cambridge, England: Cambridge University Press, 2008), p. 55.

18 The terminology used of successive generations is confusing and unstandardized. Some call three people—Mou Zongsan, Tang Junyi, and Xu Fuguan—the "second generation" after Xiong Shili, and others speak of Xu and his compatriots as the Third Wave, counting as the First Wave the Axial Age contributions of Kongzi, Mencius, and Xunzi, and counting the Song-Ming teachings (said to culminate in the teachings of Wang Yangming) as the Second Wave. To revive Karl Jaspers's idea of the Axial Age (ca. 800–200 BCE), in which many different cultures more or less simultaneously awakened to the need to rationalize religion through a "humanist turn," was the bright idea of Tu Wei-ming [Du Weiming, in Pinyin] of Harvard University, an idea designed to facilitate dialogue between civilizations. However, Tu's definition of Rujia-style thought is so vague as to be meaningless: (1) being politically concerned; (2) participating in society; and (3) attaching importance to culture.

19 Although the term "New Confucian" (*Xin Rujia*) was coined in 1963, it has never been well defined. In general, it refers to those who profess cultural and political conservatism (the Chinese version of "family values") and great nostalgia for the past; some see these as the primary methods by which to morally rearm the Chinese for a possible future Armageddon. Given the parallels between the American neoconservative movement and the Chinese neo-Confucianist movement, I have chosen to highlight the similarities through the use of the "neo-Con" moniker.

20 This unitary focus on the Doctrine of Mind and Nature means to co-opt the philosophical works of Hegel and Alfred North Whitehead, both of whom often used the same phrase.

21 From a talk by Liu Shuxian, as cited in Umberto Bresciani, *Reinventing Confucianism: The New Confucian Movement* (Taipei: Taipei Ricci Institute for Chinese Studies, 2001), 398.

22 For Mou, Heaven is not an anthropomorphic god, but the name for the moral order itself.

23 Yu, *The Power of Culture: Studies in Chinese Cultural History* (Hong Kong: 1994), p. 161.

24 At the 1988 "milestone" symposium at the Singapore Institute of East Asian Philosophies, the mainland scholar Fang Keli announced to the international community that he and the members of his research team had identified the

representative New Confucians; he also planned a book series to be titled "Key Selections from New Confucian Studies."

25 Yet a fourth *Daotong* proposal, floated in Taiwan, posits a straight-line, mind-to-mind transmission from the Sage to Chiang Kai-shek!

26 In 2004, one-party rule in Singapore by the PAP (People's Action Party) was "returned" to Lee Kuan Yew's own son. NB: Goh is a very common Hokkien name. The two Gohs are unrelated.

27 How little any of these five attitudes has to do with Confucianism is shown by the case of Singapore's closest neighbor, Malaysia. A Muslim country led by a Muslim leader, Mohammed Mahathir, Malaysia is run in very much the same way as Singapore, but justified by "Muslim values."

28 The cover of the "Con Ethics" textbook shows a phoenix rising from the ashes, symbolizing the immortal teachings of Confucius and his followers, rising from the ashes of the twentieth century to be reborn in the new global era.

29 *Straits Times*, February 4, 1982. In the same interview, Goh called the Confucian ethic the "direct parallel [*sic*]" (i.e., counterpart) to the Protestant ethic in EuroAmerica.

30 *Straits Times*, December 31, 1982. See also Beng-Huat Chua, *Communitarian Ideology and Democracy in Singapore* (London: Routledge, 1995), p. 67. Cf. Jason Tan, "The Rise and Fall of Religious Knowledge in Singapore," *Journal of Curriculum Studies* 29, no. 5 (September 1997): 603–24.

31 Gan Yang 甘陽 (Philosophy Institute, Chinese Academy of Social Sciences) in the 1980s criticized those "vulgar Confucianists" who insisted that the modern value of Confucianism should be gauged according to its alleged ability to promote industry, mercantile spirit, natural science, and democracy. See Du Weiming, et al, *Ruxue fazhan de hongguan toushi* (Tapei: Zhengzhong shuju, 1997), pp. 595, 596, 599.

32 This message certainly resonates. It is why, in April 2007, the Chinese government sponsored two forums, hosted simultaneously in Hong Kong and in Xi'an (at a reported cost of US $1 million), dedicated to the interpretation and promotion of the *Dao de jing* (Way and Its Power) associated with the legendary sage Laozi (whom Han legend makes the old teacher of Kongzi).

33 The seemingly innocuous term "blending together" (*ronghe*) in reality carries a strong ideological charge, since minority ethnic groups are asked to "blend together" with the manifestly superior majority or "Han" culture under the leadership of the CCP.

34 Colin MacKerras, *Western Images of China* (Oxford: Oxford University Press, 1989), p. 187.

35 A clear majority of Republican-era entrepreneurs and diplomats received their college education in institutions under the direction of American church organizations. This goes a long way to explain what Isaacs calls "the natural history of American images of the Chinese" as pagans with potential who qualify to be "wards" of American democracy, not to mention the Confucian-Christian "dialogue" promoted by the "Boston Confucians." After all, "Confucian religion"

(*Rujiao*), as conceived since the Jesuits in the early seventeenth century, is said to differ from most other world religions in its "this-worldly focus" that eases interfaith dialogues and ecumenical encounters. With Christian conversions on the rise in today's PRC, this dialogue may soon shift its home, however, with unpredictable consequences. However, collusion between missionaries and early Western imperialism, well documented since Kenneth Latourette's *A History of Christian Missions in China* (New York: Macmillan, 1929), never eased tensions between the two countries in the past.

36 Here, in all likelihood, we see the lingering effect of Pearl Buck's *The Good Earth* (both the novel and movie versions). Buck, daughter of Protestant missionaries in China, undoubtedly has had an enormous impact on American views of China.

37 See Carma Hinton, *Small Happiness* (1986).

38 The title of Christopher Lasch's book.

39 Herbert Fingarette and Henry Rosemont, especially, are interested in issues of everyday morality (not metaphysical reality), and so I have dubbed them "ethical realists." This term recalls Iris Murdoch's description of moral change as an "unselfing" process, by which she does not mean the replacement of selfish motives with altruistic or self-sacrificing ones, but an evolution toward a "selfless respect for reality" accompanied by a growing distaste for cheap consolations for the ego (self-pity, gluttony, fantasy, etc.).

40 Henry Rosemont, "Who Chooses?" in *Chinese Texts and Philosophical Contexts: Essays Dedicated to Angus C. Graham*, edited by Henry Rosemont Jr. (Chicago & La Salle, IL.: Open Court, 1991), p. 26.

41 As Roger T. Ames writes in *The Democracy of the Dead* (Chicago & La Salle, IL: Open Court, 1999), p. 7, "The irony of this situation is intense: Western ethnocentricity is expressed in a firm belief in the universality of our (provincial) ideals." The political scientist Arik Dirlik is convinced that any revival of Confucianism in modern Asia can be little more than Asian self-Orientalism fomented in a conspiracy between the authoritarian state and free-loading and/or vainglorious intellectuals. See Suggested Readings.

42 Many Americans see the unfavorable balance of trade with China as a major cause of American economic ills. As for energy, if China keeps increasing its consumption of energy at its present rate, the price of oil will soon double the current (January 2008) record price of $100 a barrel. As for military prowess, China's military buildup offers the best excuse that the Pentagon will ever have to keep asking for nuclear submarines, F-16s and the like, which offer no real defense against a young zealot with an IED strapped firmly to his chest.

43 The term "new pragmatism" has been used rather narrowly in philosophical circles to refer to the positions outlined by Richard Rorty (d. 2007), whose work drew heavily upon that of John Dewey. Only Roger Ames would call himself a new pragmatist. Both Fingarette and Rosemont eschew the moral relativism identified with the new pragmatists.

44 Cf. *New York Times*, "The Dance of Evolution: A Theory of How Art Got Its

Start" (Science section, F1, F3, November 27, 2007), notes that the "visual, gestural and vocal cues" that mothers and infants spontaneously develop to communicate with each other "abide by a formalized [i.e., ritual] code." In the views of some experts, "These affiliative signals between mother and infant are aesthetic operations," "formalizing, exaggerating, repeating" ways of manipulating expectations and responses. Evolutionary forces may employ ritual and aesthetic appreciation to insure that "the relative weakness of the individual can be traded up for the strength of the hive."

45 Herbert Fingarette, *Confucius: The Secular as Sacred* (San Francisco: Harper-SanFrancisco, 1972), p. vii. Fingarette was the first Western-trained philosopher to approach the *Analects* as a work of sophisticated philosophy. Fingarette gently pointed out that the early translators of Confucius into Western languages—learned Catholic and Protestant scholars, priests, and missionaries—treated Kongzi in much the same way that they treated Socrates, as a learned pagan of impeccable saintliness whose doctrines at many points approximated the Truths of Christian Revelation. (The so-called figurists of the French mission to China during the seventeenth and eighteenth centuries even posited the existence of a complete Ur-text underlying the Chinese Classics that would be in perfect accord with Christian dogma.) Later translators and interpreters of the *Analects* (including Yu Dan) have often imported Buddhist and Daoist ideas into the text.

46 Nylan has changed Fingarette's "man realizes himself" to "humans realize themselves." (Confucius: *The Secular as Sacred*, p. 16.)

47 Su Shi (1037–1101), in his examination essay on the *Constant Mean*.

48 Rosemont makes a similar point in his essay "Whose Democracy?"

49 See Rosemont's essay entitled, "On Knowing (*zhi*): Praxis-Guiding Discourse in the Confucian *Analects*."

50 Gayatri Spivak, *Outside in the Teaching Machine* (New York: Routledge, 1993), p. 171.

51 As *Analects* 4/10 puts it, the *junzi* aligns himself with what is best and right, wherever that may be. *Analects* 18/8 had Confucius saying of himself that he is different from others in that he has no "thou shalts" or "thou shalt nots." *Analects* 19/3 enjoins us to "go with those with whom it is proper to go." Cf. 17/13; 17/24.

52 Rosemont, "Human Rights: A Bill of Worries," in Wm. Theodore de Bary, *Confucianism and Human Rights* (New York: Columbia University Press, 1998), p. 64.

53 This list comes from Rosemont's writings.

54 Ames, *The Democracy of the Dead*, 125.

55 Ibid., 9.

56 Ibid., 162.

57 Jean Pfaelzer, *Driven Out: The Forgotten War against the Chinese Americans* (New York: Random House, 2007).

58 This is Geremie Barmé's term.

59 Ostensibly modeled upon the German Goethe Institutes, the Confucius Institutes advocate authoritarian and paternalistic sentiments in their Chinese-language textbooks. Many readers will be familiar with the ongoing textbook controversies in Japan and in the United States; for China's own recent banning of the books, see listserve.asia@gmail.com ("Shanghai: new history, old politics" by Li Datong). See also Jocelyn Chey, "Confucius Redux: Chinese 'Soft Power' Cultural Diplomacy and the Confucius Institutes," unpublished paper. Waseda University opened the first research-based Confucius Institute in April 2007.

60 Henry Maspero, *Taoism and Chinese Religion,* translated by Frank Kierman (Amherst: University of Massachusetts Press, 1981), 136. The plan is to have five hundred Confucius Institutes operating by 2010. The irony is that where CIs have taken root, the government has cut back on support for university teaching of Chinese languages.

61 *Cheng* 誠 (here translated as "integrity") implies "wholeness" and "oneness" (see above); it encompasses a sense of humaneness and of duty; *cheng* also describes the central good said to result from reliably humane conduct (*ren* 仁). The *Constant Mean* therefore describes *cheng* as a way of acting and a reward for good action. Traditionalists sometimes name the two main threads of Kongzi's teachings as *ren* 仁 and *li* 禮 (ritual decorum), or *li* and *shu* ("consideration"), synonyms for this same deliberate way of acting.

62 *Analects* 19/22.

63 Orhan Pamuk, cited in Pico Iyer, "A View of the Bosporus," *New York Times*, September 30, 2007 (book review). Pamuk was the 2006 Nobel Prize winner for literature.

64 James Katz, Director, Center for Mobile Communications Studies, Rutgers University, quoted in the *New York Times*, November 6, 2007 (letters to the editor).

Index